ABBA UNABASHED

Fifty Years of Fandom

Very Unofficial...Very Unauthoritative

Freddie Holmen & Garry Holland

© Freddie Holmen & Garry Holland 2023

All rights reserved

No part of this publication may be reproduced, stored in a retrieval system or transmitted in any form or by any means, electronic, mechanical, photocopying, recording or otherwise, without prior permission.

To ABBA, their fans and our families

Also by Garry Holland:

Eurovision: A Funny Kind of Euphoria

Big Dreams, Bum Notes: How Music Led Me to Eurovision Oblivion

A Man Called Eurovision

Contents

	Introduction: Two for the Price of Two	1
1.	That's Us: A Pair of Personal Voyages	5
2.	Letting the Music Speak: A Review of the Albums	43
	- The Studio Albums	43
	- 'Live' Albums	73
	- Compilation Albums	76
3.	The Songs They're Singing: Part 1	81
4.	Masters of These Scenes: Part 1	116
	- Eight Key TV Appearances	116
	- Three Key Movies	125
5.	The Songs They're Singing: Part 2	132
6.	I Do Wanna Talk: ABBA Jabber	164
7.	The Songs They're Singing: Part 3	186
8.	Masters of These Scenes: Part 2	219
	- Original Official Song Videos	219
9.	Our Winners Take It All: Roll of Honour	245
	Epilogue: Only One of Us	262
	About the Authors	273
	Acknowledgements	275

Introduction: Two for the Price of Two

It's Sunday the fourth of September 2022 and we're standing less than ten metres away from ABBA. Or it feels like we are. Sort of. We've successfully suspended disbelief and now a rollicking, extended, satisfyingly indulgent version of 'Gimme! Gimme! Gimme! (A Man After Midnight)' is thundering out of the PA. It seems to be passing straight through our diaphragms (causing our internal organs to resonate at a frequency well beyond their design specification) and then out into the packed family crowd. Not sure exactly how many festival-goers are crammed into this end of the Kinecroft – a lovely green space surrounded by ancient earthworks in the Thames-side town of Wallingford – but it's a hell of a lot. Impressively, regardless of age, they all seem to know most, if not all, of the words.

Because that's what ABBA do, isn't it? It's what they've always done – reach into the hearts of every kind of people and set up permanent home there. Lastingly, immovably. And it's what they and their music still have the power to achieve, over fifty years on from the band's birth. Even though, on this occasion, it's not actually the sainted quartet of Agnetha, Björn, Benny and Anni-Frid providing the delivery mechanism but 21st Century ABBA – a supercharged, truly excellent act booked for the traditional Sunday afternoon tribute slot at the superb annual Bunkfest.

And what a brilliant booking 21st Century ABBA are proving to be, wowing the crowd from up there on the main stage and whipping them up into a giddy old state with a relentless cavalcade of can't-go-wrong, nailed-on classics. Soundtrack to all our lives and that sort of thing. It's a setlist showcasing every song you'd reasonably expect, except that 'Knowing Me, Knowing You' is missing. But there's only so much magic you can cram into an hour that simply flies by on a pulsating sonic wave of heady euphoria and high-octane nostalgia.

Amid a blizzard of rushing adrenalin and surging emotion, this is proving a perfect appetiser for what's slowly, steadily and surely approaching us down the tracks: the year 2024. Exactly half a century since ABBA first blipped onto our individual radars with that seismic Eurovision win in Brighton. An anniversary set to be marked in the most obscenely perfect manner conceivable as the contest decamps to Sweden once again. Evidence of a higher power looking over us, you'd like to think. If only we were religious, we could get slightly religious about it.

But for now that's all very much in the medium-distant future. Leaning on this barrier on this particular September Sunday afternoon, in the very front row, really is the only place to be. What's more, for this particular pair of dyed-in-the-wool ABBA fans, it represents a bit of a first. A collector's item. An ABBA-related excursion involving the two of us and requiring a reasonable level of calendar/diary coordination that was actually executed successfully. As envisaged. As planned. Not derailed by chance or our own incompetence. Not shot down by global events beyond our control. Not thrown into disarray by a combination of circumstances that probably should have been foreseen but foolishly weren't.

With few exceptions, down the decades, they've all gone the same way: our feeble attempts to emulate ABBA by entering a song for the Eurovision Song Contest, first for Austria and then for the UK; our desire to simply go to the contest together and savour its unique blend of occasion, entertainment and trademark WTF-ery; our plan to go on a joint pilgrimage to the ABBA Museum in Stockholm, where we could at least pay homage to their inimitable genius and moan about the price of Swedish beer; our resolve to obtain tickets for two adjoining seats at the ground-breaking *ABBA Voyage* show in London. None of it coming to pass – for reasons that were, on some occasions, exceptionally good and, on others, not remotely good enough.

Full disclosure and all that. We both count ourselves as big ABBA fans. But that's a broad church and, for these two members of the congregation at least, it definitely stops short of fanatical or slightly scary. We'd argue that we're probably pretty typical, as decent-sized fans of the band (indeed, any band) go – following their career resolutely and weaving them into our lives for half a century but without getting too weird about it. Certainly big enough fans, though, for their music to qualify as very important and very, very special to us.

This book is an opportunity to share some of that with you – wherever you are on the scale of ABBA fandom between the casual and the obsessive. Our experiences, our views, our thoughts, our beliefs – none of it authoritative, none of it based on any special insight or inside track, and much of it no doubt a bit odd and inexplicable to your eyes and ears. But that's the brilliant thing about music – and being a fan of anything. In the final analysis, it's all very personal and highly subjective and nothing else really matters. So in this book you'll find two people's views, two people's stories. No more, no less than that. Two for the price of one, if you will. Or two, depending what price point we end up going in at. But for us it offers a kind of redemption – an opportunity to see a joint ABBA-related project through to completion for once, as well as a chance to go on the record with our enduring love for this extraordinary band.

You see, ABBA's music really is all about the mark it leaves behind – in your heart, your soul, your brain, your day-to-day existence. Just lying there, ever-present, even when temporarily dormant, awaiting the moment to spark wildly into life. And that's just what 21st Century ABBA are managing to achieve right now up there on that stage. This might sound peculiar but it's actually turning into a really emotional afternoon. It's something to do with hearing this music performed 'live': from opening number 'Waterloo', neatly prefaced by the recorded voice of David Vine and the sound of the crowd in the Brighton Dome on the sixth of April 1974, right through to the inevitable, exuberant encore of 'Dancing Queen'. ABBA's music in the flesh – a small reminder, perhaps, of what a genuinely compelling 'live' act the band would surely have become had circumstances been different and they'd devoted more time to touring. But might that have come at a price? Might it somehow – through fatigue or, dare we say it, disillusion – have eroded the quality of the truly magical material they produced in the studio? We'll never know.

Maybe some things are best left where they are. Maybe it's best not to fail prey to the temptation to indulge in too much what-iffery. They say the past is a foreign country where things are done differently. But, where each of our fifty years of fandom are concerned, we're not sure we'd want ABBA to have done anything differently at all. Except perhaps relocate 'King Kong Song' to a quiet animal enclosure somewhere.

Moved to mark the fifty years since Brighton by compiling this book – one tiny contribution to keeping the band's massive legacy alive, kicking and singing from the rooftops – we set out for your consideration this very personal, very heady cocktail of thoughts, opinions and memories. Ah yes... That's the knub of it right there.

Because, when it comes right down to it, it's all about the memories that ABBA have kindled in us and the joy they've been bringing for all these decades – even down to unexpectedly gate-crashing our lives once again, so late in the day, with the brand-new *Voyage* album that generated so much pleasure, provoked so much discussion and debate, and created so many new memories to go with all the old ones. The way old friends do.

So settle down, get those albums on in the background and immerse yourself in the world of ABBA and ABBA fandom. Join us as we celebrate the glorious, undiminished ability of ABBA and their music to leave you feeling that you're first in line and, naturally, having the time of your life.

How can we resist them?

Freddie H. & Garry H.

October 2023

That's Us: A Pair of Personal Voyages

One of the fantastic things about the ABBA faithful is that we're such a diverse bunch. More than that, each and every one of us has experienced the band in a distinctive, ultimately unique way, depending on how the music first infiltrated our lives and burrowed into its fabric. Here, we explain when, where and why we each got into ABBA – and how their music has stayed with us ever since.

To make it easier for you to keep track of whose words you're reading at any point, we've used different typefaces for Garry and Freddie. You may not feel you need this subliminal nudge right now, but later chapters see us changing writer frequently, and with reckless abandon…

Garry's voyage:

Sunday the twenty-eighth of February 1978.[1] The day before ABBA came. Not sure exactly what I was doing. Probably a bit of history homework. Most likely an essay on Henry VII's fiscal policy or something equally mesmerising. I probably wanted to clear the decks a bit and get the essay out of the way because, possibly unprecedentedly, I'd agreed to go to the cinema on the Monday evening. It wasn't my idea. My schoolmate Jase had come to the view that he wanted to go and see *ABBA: The Movie*, which had opened the previous week at the ABC a couple of miles down the road in our forgotten corner of London. Not that he was an ABBA fan. Not that I was either. Nor indeed was Si, destined to be the Third Man in this unlikely triumvirate of 16-year-old ABBA-goers who, for the price of a bus ticket and a cinema ticket, were on the brink of nakedly betraying their deepest-held musical principles for no musically defensible reason whatsoever.

---

[1] I finally managed to calculate the precise date only comparatively recently thanks to what's widely known as 'new information' becoming available, having previously and erroneously placed my fateful trip to see *ABBA: The Movie* two days too early.

If I was listening to a bit of music whilst dissecting Henry VII's long-overdue reforms of the Exchequer, what might have been on the turntable of my trusty, dusty, slightly temperamental Sharp stereo player?[2] Maybe Jethro Tull's seminal *Aqualung* album or their even more audacious *Thick as a Brick*. Or possibly something by a newer band ploughing a well-worn rock furrow: perhaps Lone Star's intermittently impressive *Firing on All Six*. On the other hand, it might easily have been Kraftwerk. I'd asked for the *Trans-Europe Express* album for Christmas and duly got it. I think it was what you might call a punt. I'd never heard a single note of it but (armed with positive memories of *Autobahn*) I'd been sufficiently intrigued by the LP sleeve when perusing it in my local record shop to add it to my Christmas wish-list of albums, where it slotted in just after Camel's prog-lite classic *Rain Dances*. Nor had I been disappointed when I'd shoved it on the turntable bright and early on Christmas morning, as 'Europe Endless' melted luxuriantly from the tinny old speakers (wires re-re-re-re-soldered to keep the musical show on the road) in all its neo-baroque splendour.

All I can say for sure is that, whatever provided the soundtrack to my incisive but doubtless largely plagiarised analysis of Tudor financial policy, it certainly wasn't ABBA. YUK! ABBA was 'pop' music! And 'pop' music wasn't 'proper' music! For starters, 'proper' music didn't put in much of an appearance on *Top of the Pops*, where Radio 1's crack squad of irritating DJs provided the irritatingly 'wacky' links linking the irritatingly superficial three-minute hits. Which was why I hadn't watched the BBC's flagship pop music show for a good two years or maybe three. No. 'Proper' music fans would shun such frothy flim-flam in favour of *Sight and Sound in Concert* or *The Old Grey Whistle Test*, even though the latter regularly tested your credentials with some super-noodly, less than accessible obscurity and now also featured the odd tick-box inclusion of something from the iconoclastic world of punk and New Wave. And while their precise rollcalls of favourite bands varied a little, Jase and Si were broadly singing from the same hymn sheet. Mind you, it would have been a pretty odd hymn sheet that featured the Sex Pistols' 'Anarchy in the UK', a perennial favourite with both of them if I remember correctly.

---

[2] This had been bought via my mum's Burlington mail order catalogue a couple of years earlier, probably involving fifty weekly payments of 80p or something like that.

So how in the name of all that's holy did even the vaguest outline of a profane trip to see something as obviously lightweight as *ABBA: The Movie* start blipping on our social radar?

When ABBA did their massive floor-wiping job on the opposition at the 1974 Eurovision Song Contest in the Brighton Dome, I'd been twelve years old. I'd been allowed to stay up to watch the whole show (on a similar basis to the way I used to be allowed to stay up to watch the whole of Eurovision's pseudo-sporting counterpart, *It's a Knockout/Jeux sans Frontières*). And I well remember being fleetingly excited by the memorable blast of crisp, fresh Nordic air that the Swedish entry had sent rifling through the hallowed but tired old halls of this now venerable competition. Indeed, "the ABBA group", as BBC 1's David Vine so memorably described them during the preceding postcard, had beautifully crystallised the dying embers of the glam rock revolution in their three-minute glitter-fuelled barnstormer 'Waterloo'. Unusually for Eurovision, music was the winner that night (as well as Sweden, obviously).

My mild allegiance to these surprising Swedes actually proved reasonably enduring for a boy of my age, as I also vividly recall rooting for ABBA (mildly) as they climbed steadily towards the number-one spot in the UK singles chart. Like much of Britain, I was only too delighted that they'd knocked the mawkish 'Seasons in the Sun' off the top spot. I probably counted as a fan on some level, then, albeit an extremely pallid, watery and ephemeral one. That allegiance, however, didn't actually extend as far as parting with any pocket money to add 'Waterloo' to my small but steadily expanding record collection. In my defence, I'd only recently invested in the rumbustious Mott the Hoople single 'The Golden Age of Rock 'n' Roll' and pocket money didn't grow on trees or indeed anywhere else back then. I also remember being pretty impressed by 'Ring Ring', which later got the odd run-out on Radio 1 in its role as the almost successful follow-up to 'Waterloo'. Subsequently, though, my path and ABBA's forked off into some fundamentally different regions of the musical landscape. To cut to the chase, in my eyes ABBA became the sort of group[3] that your auntie would profess to "quite like" (not least because they were "so well turned-out"). This was in stark contrast to songs dismissed as "all that noise" – the go-to, catch-all middle-aged/elderly person's critique of any piece of music featuring a reasonably prominent lead guitar part or hairy drummer.

Yet even the most ardent anti-pop zealots would have had to concede that Agnetha and Frida had something really rather remarkable about them. Especially when it was straight teenage boys who were doing the remarking. So this was the decisive factor, I'm sure, which enticed our treacherous triumvirate to shelve our musical credibility for one night only and add *ABBA: The Movie* to our list of must-see films for February. But I'm sure we'd have dismissed our invidious plan, should we have cared to share it with any of our contemporaries or (absolutely unthinkable) our families, as something we were doing, in the highly tiresome lads' parlance of the time, just for a *LARF*!

But what looks like a doable plan in theory can look a whole lot less sensible when you actually get round to doing it. In this particular case, the prospect of getting caught out queuing for ABBA by any of our schoolmates (or indeed teachers, dinner ladies, representatives of the Board of Governors etc.) was so terrifying and indeed unthinkable, such a potential hammer blow to our all-important yet paper-thin 'street cred', that it surely accounted for our peculiar decision to hit the flicks on a Monday. And when we arrived at the cinema, it was pretty much as we feared. In the queue for the box office we'd be rubbing shoulders almost exclusively with six-to-fourteen-year-olds, plus in most cases their mums, which was something I most definitely hadn't had to do when, just over a week earlier, I'd gone to my first-ever 'proper' gig: Canadian prog-metal icons Rush at the Hammersmith Odeon on the UK leg of their *A Farewell to Kings* tour, an experience which had left my ears ringing for a good twenty-four hours or so.

From Rush to ABBA in eight days. A vertiginous descent, by any 'proper' music fan's standards. No wonder I felt slightly queasy as

---

[3] NB They clearly didn't count as a 'band' – a pivotal distinction in the mind of any teenage lover of proper, as opposed to pop, music.

we super-self-consciously shuffled towards the box office to sell our souls not for rock 'n' roll but for a reasonably priced ticket to see ABBA: The Movie. What to do? Brazen it out and go in all guns blazing? Go for broke and boom out our requirement in the best declamatory fashion?

"One for ABBA: The Movie, please..." I mumbled, so inaudibly that the woman behind the glass had to crane her neck right forward. I think I read many emotions in her face, ranging from contempt to pity by way of puzzlement and profound amusement. Probably just my paranoia, of course. She was probably just considering how best to snaffle a free choc-ice at the end of the evening.

Tickets bought, we managed to make it all the way into the gloom of the cinema itself with only one major security scare, courtesy of a case of mistaken identity. Si thought he saw 'Knobby' Norman from school in the other queue for some inferior feast of cinematic entertainment, prompting him to bundle Jase and me unceremoniously behind an ageing pillar of suitable width. Alarm over and safely in our seats, we nevertheless maintained our vigilance in exemplary fashion, adopting a safety first, second and third policy by hunkering down uncomfortably low in our seats just in case anyone in there might be able to positively ID us, possibly using some state-of-the-art thermal imaging equipment.

The supporting feature turned out to be ABBA's 'Take a Chance on Me' video, as the song was currently in residence at number one on the Hit Parade, as 'Fluff' Freeman might have put it. I think I'd already seen a bit of the video on the telly, but the enormity of the screen in front of us maximised its impact a hundred-fold – at least in terms of its effect on three semi-drooling adolescent boys. (In that more innocent age, a fearsome combination of bare shoulders, thigh-high boots, seductive winking and lip gloss was almost guaranteed to wreak savage hormonal damage.) Nor, when it hit the screen, did the main feature do much to restore calm on the hormone front. But this masked a much deeper truth.

Around a quarter of the way into the film, the unthinkable happened. I REALISED I WAS REALLY ENJOYING THE MUSIC... Many of the songs I'd never, ever heard before – or even heard of. But here these obscurities came, cascading over me – 'Tiger', 'He

Is Your Brother', 'Rock Me', 'Why Did It Have to Me?', 'Intermezzo No.1', 'I've Been Waiting for You' – and, in powerful combination with the better-known stuff, metaphorically grabbed me by the throat, daring me to deny the shocking, disorientating truth: ABBA WERE BLOODY GOOD! On and on and on it went. The melodies, the voices, the energy, the charisma, the *variety*: ABBA were clearly neither a one-trick pony nor just a singles band. In a word, from both a creative and a performance perspective, they had serious *talent*.

And after I'd been pummelled by the non-stop barrage of brilliance for over an hour, the scene with 'Eagle' in the lift capped everything off in stunning fashion. Am I allowed to use the word 'ethereal'? Blimey. What a *song*. Was it my ears or was this number actually a bit prog rocky? What's happening to me? Is this what Saul felt like on the road to Damascus? Well, only if he'd just witnessed a supercharged performance of the joyous 'So Long'. The scales had fallen from my ears, if such a thing is even possible. When I finally walked out of the cinema just under two hours after I'd walked in, some very strange, confessional words were rebounding around my head at deafening volume: "I'm Garry and I think I may be an ABBA fan..."

Suddenly I had a very, very dark secret.

But I wasn't alone. Si had experienced a similar epiphany on that cold Monday evening. Indeed, Si and I (but not Jase) went back to the ABC the following Saturday evening to see *ABBA: The Movie* all over again, dragging another schoolmate with us and clearly exhibiting the tell-tale symptoms of addictive behaviour. SATURDAY EVENING! I KNOW!! MADNESS!!! Maybe, deep down, we somehow *wanted* to get caught.

But a real fan, of course, buys records. And a real ABBA fan couldn't indefinitely rely on catching 'Dancing Queen' or 'Happy Hawaii' on Junior Choice (what depths I stooped to...) on Saturday and Sunday mornings, surreptitiously tuning in on a tinny transistor radio under the bedclothes like some sort of resistance fighter in Occupied Europe. *ABBA: The Album* was out and doing very good business. I needed to own a copy. But how to procure one? Fortunately, Si had been going through the self-same agonies and had cracked first. He'd bought the LP. He hadn't actually played it yet because his parents rarely went out. And headphones weren't really a 'thing' yet for your average cash-strapped teenage music fan. Nevertheless, the least I could do was step out over the parapet, join him in the line of fire and await the withering hail of scorn that, when my cover had finally been compromised, would inevitably be sprayed in my direction by friends, family and possibly random members of the public. Nor was the internet a 'thing' either, of course, so a discreet online purchase simply wasn't an option. And mail order would have been *way* too complicated. Yes, the realisation hit me like a freight train – a freight train carrying a full cargo of whatever the opposite of musical credibility is. I'd have to walk brazenly into a record shop in broad daylight and even more brazenly buy an ABBA record.

I couldn't pull off this nefarious deed in my regular record shop. Obviously. I'd only recently bought a Paul Kossoff double album in there. I had a reputation to protect. They'd probably refuse to sell *ABBA: The Album* to me anyway. Any other album they'd be fine with. But not *ABBA: The Album*. They'd see my act of purchase as a form of self-harm and feel duty-bound to save me from myself, from my transient lapse of reason. Or worse still, they'd just take the piss a bit and I'd never be able to darken their doors again. They had experience. My see-through soul would ensure that they'd be able to spot instantly any unconvincing fib that I was buying the LP for an ageing family member.

Having agonised over the problem, I came up with a solution frankly brilliant in its simplicity. I'd go to a different record shop. I'd have to go by bus, but that would put an attractive amount of distance between the dark deed and my real life. Psychotherapists today would probably talk in terms of compartmentalisation. They'd also, no doubt, have predicted correctly that, once I'd got off the bus, it would take me a good twenty minutes to summon up the courage to physically enter the shop. Even then, I gave the rack marked 'A' a very wide berth while I confronted my ethical dilemma. Dare I make a quick grab for the empty sleeve of *ABBA: The Album* which, surely, would be nestling at the front of the rack?

There was no-one else in the shop, except the girl doing her nails behind the counter. OK. It was just me, her and the *The Album* album. This was it. But now I could see that the *The Album* album wasn't where I expected the *The Album* album to be. Dare I spend time rummaging for it in the 'A' rack? Obviously not. I might accidentally pick up an Allman Brothers album and spend the next three weeks pretending I'd been bitten by the US Country Rock bug. But the alternative was less than appealing too. I'd have to go and ask the assistant. And minimising the need to say anything at all had been one of the keystones of my so-called strategy.

Past the point of rational thought, an adrenalin surge helpfully made up my mind for me. More specifically, it decided my best bet would be to rush the counter. Forward I lurched, slightly unsteady on my feet, the very epitome of teenage self-consciousness, at unnaturally high velocity. Once my legs stopped I checked my position. I was (somehow) exactly where I needed to be! But the main hurdle was still to be negotiated. Would I now be able to frame a meaningful, comprehensible sentence? Would my words be drowned out completely by the siege-gun-like hammering of heart against ribcage?

"Excuse me – have you got the *The Album* album?" I babbled semi-coherently. "ABBA's *ABBA: The Album* album?"

To say I was red as a beetroot, and almost certainly perspiring visibly, would be the most masterly of understatements. The assistant probably thought I'd contracted some kind of tropical disease. One that precluded me from making any kind of eye contact. Perhaps I'd drunk some infected water. Whatever the case, she clearly felt nothing but abject pity for me and the evil transaction was completed in a matter of seconds that felt to me like a good four and a half hours. Fortunately, she didn't dispatch me towards the racks with clear instructions not to come back unless I had the empty sleeve of the *The Album* album in my hand – which would mean I could be exposed in open country, so to speak, and would be vulnerable to getting caught with Exhibit A in my hands by any potential witness entering the shop. No. In the case of very popular albums, the shop kept multiple copies on the shelf right behind the till, so – in a triumph of ergonomics – the assistant expertly swivelled on her chair, plucked out a copy of the contraband and slid it into a plastic record-shop bag in a single, sleek, seamless movement drawing heavily on muscle memory. It all happened in the blinking of an eye. Then she took the four pound-notes offered by my trembling hand and returned to me eleven pence (or thereabouts) in change.

How mundane, how unremarkable my act of arch-betrayal must have seemed from her perspective. What little inkling she had that she was an accessory during the fact, complicit in my crime against cred. Maybe she had a long rap sheet in this kind of case, promoting such rite-of-passage musical treachery ten or twenty times a day. Whatever the case, I grabbed the bag from her without ceremony, half-expecting her to bid me "Get well soon!" as I spun on my heels and almost bounded for the door, high on a heady cocktail of guilt and filthy elation.

Yes, I'd done it! I'd crossed the heavily fortified frontier and made it into ABBAland!

Fortunately, my luck was in and no-one in an official or any other capacity asked to see the contents of my plastic record-shop bag on the way home. Once back in my bedroom, my trembling hands extracted the precious black vinyl disc from the sleeve, somehow managed to jab it onto the centre spindle of the turntable and turned the volume down to '2'. But as soon as the imperious 'Eagle' swooped into aural view, there was simply no viable alternative to cranking it up to '8' so I could wallow in its velvet-like caress. Loud and proud, the whole album was so magnificent, so irrefutably regal that I cared not a jot who else could witness my treasonous act against the Royal House of Rock. My newly forged ABBA fandom could simply no longer be constrained by the conventionally hyper-powerful forces of potential teenage embarrassment.

The only minor setback concerned the album cover. It wasn't the majestic blue gatefold (with the great picture of Agnetha and Frida in the centre spread) that had featured in almost every record shop's enormous window display for *ABBA: The Album*. No. Mine was a pretty underwhelming, white, flimsy, non-foldout version. Here, by a helpful quirk of Fate, my rash decision to go public paid handsome dividends when my Dad said he'd have a word with the owner of the record shop near his office and see if he still had one of the gatefold sleeves from his window display. Which he did. Downside? You could still see the little holes where the staples had been holding the sleeve in position. Upside? I didn't pay a penny for it. Even though I'd happily have shelled out anywhere up to three quid!

Before I forget, I ought to note, just for the record, that Si's dalliance with Team ABBA had regrettably proved fleeting. He soon-ish switched loyalties to the emergent Kate Bush, resulting in the equally sublime *The Kick Inside* album elbowing *ABBA: The Album* off the turntable of his vastly superior Technics hi-fi.

ABBA and I, on the other hand, had forged an unbreakable bond. The dam had burst and the flood gates had opened. From that point, posters and fan mags (especially the dreamlike *ABBA SPECIAL* and only slightly less special *ABBA SPECIAL 2*), plus slightly tacky annuals and even homemade badges of questionable taste, were very much the order of the day. Plus I even managed to recruit the occasional fifth columnist to abet my progress through ABBAland. One schoolmate, clearly with a golden career in international espionage in the offing, even went to the lengths of waiting until his family had gone out, then sneaking into his sister's room, pinching her copies of *Arrival* and *ABBA's Greatest Hits*, stealthily copying them onto two sides of a C90 Memorex cassette and then slipping it to me surreptitiously in the lunch queue. Shows just how easily people can get sucked into the world of crime.

But this home-taping outrage proved to be a one-off aberration (so to speak). I needed the albums and I needed the album covers. So, as 1978 wound on, I started backfilling my proper collection as and when pocket money permitted. By the summer, my own legitimate copy of *Arrival* and then its predecessor, the *ABBA* album, had both joined *ABBA: The Album* in my cheap Woolworth's metal record rack (LPs on the bottom, singles on the top) as ABBA jostled for priority with Jethro Tull and Kraftwerk, both of whom had somewhat inconveniently released very nifty new must-have albums in the spring of '78.

But what, you may well enquire, had been the general reaction of family and peers to my crossing of the pop Rubicon? (By peers I mean schoolmates, of course, not members of the House of Lords, who probably would have lengthily debated my act of treason had they been informed of it.) Well, it can probably be best described as a heady mix of mild astonishment, moderate amusement and, after the initial revelation, much apathy. They probably thought I was just going through a funny 'phase'. And I was. Just a bloody long one. Far from burning itself out in a fortnight, or until I was sufficiently distracted by the new Be Bop Deluxe album, this particular funny 'phase' (unlike dalliances in younger days with Subbuteo, Airfix kits, chess and Top Trumps, for example) would prove phenomenally durable. Destined to last longer than many a royal dynasty or regional war, it has yet to burn itself out forty-five years on.

A key rite of passage for me, of course, would arrive when ABBA actually released a new record with me firmly on the bandwagon. And let me tell you, there's barely a bandwagon I've ever leapt on that hasn't had a wheel fall off almost immediately. So it proved with ABBA. It turned out I wasn't so much a fan, more a jinx. Before I'd climbed on board, five of the previous six singles had been UK number ones. But now that torrent of success dried up with inexplicable suddenness. In fact, *none* of the next six singles would hit the top spot. The first of these relative failures was 'Summer Night City', which I first heard on the Peter Powell show while sitting in the back of my Dad's car as the family holidayed in Norfolk.

In his trademark boyish enthusiasm, Peter P also played the B-side – possibly a slightly surprising decision bearing in mind it was the 'Pick a Bale of Cotton/Old Smokey/Midnight Special' medley. I wasn't immediately blown away by 'Summer Night City', to be honest, and much less by the medley. But I knew the record would nevertheless soon soar to the peak of the charts, because that's what ABBA records did. Except this one didn't. It would end up stalling at a relatively lowly (and, for me, slightly embarrassing) number 6. Worst of all, it was clearly my fault. I'd put the mockers on ABBA. The copy I'd bought manifestly hadn't offset the droves of people who'd declined to buy it presumably as some kind of personal slight to me. It was, I concluded, the dictionary definition of natural musical justice – cosmic payback for my act of profound musical treachery.

Evidently, signing up as an ABBA fan wasn't going to be the plain sailing I'd confidently expected. Not that my own faith in them and their music was remotely shaken. Not in the least. But further tests of loyalty were soon to come. First, there was the much-anticipated appearance on *The Mike Yarwood Christmas Show* on the evening of Christmas Day. I was a quivering wreck of anticipation, for once that all too familiar bilious sensation late on Christmas afternoon having little to do with the prodigious volume of Quality Street I'd consumed (a kind of legal requirement at Christmas, of course).

But what an appearance ABBA's turned out to be! Our glorious Nordic foursome absolutely sparkled, literally and metaphorically, with Agnetha and Frida's semi-divine radiance completely stealing the show. Troupers that they were, they even survived the ordeal of a scripted 'interview' with mighty Mike impersonating Larry Grayson hosting *The Generation Game*. Memorable indeed. Except... The new song they chose to perform alongside 'Thank You for the Music' – and thus, I assumed, earmarked as the next single – was 'If It Wasn't for the Nights'. Now it was good. But to my ears, just like 'Summer Night City', it wasn't on the stellar level of 'Knowing Me, Knowing You' or 'Money, Money, Money', for instance. A terrible dread gripped me in bed that night, as well as the Quality Street-induced dyspepsia. Had ABBA already peaked? Had I trekked off in their wake simply to accompany them back down the mountain on my metaphorical toboggan?

Speaking of toboggans... My feeling of unease was further reinforced in January 1979 when, as the new single and taster for the upcoming new album, ABBA released not 'If It Wasn't for the Nights' but 'Chiquitita' (complete with snowman video). Again, a decent song but not necessarily one for the ages, in my book at least. (On the other hand, the riff-driven B-side 'Lovelight' was an absolute revelation and, to this day, remains one of my very favourite ABBA tracks.) And a couple of months later the equally snow-packed *ABBA in Switzerland* TV special did little to remedy this feeling of apprehension.

Great show, with Roxy Music and Kate Bush adding their considerable powers to it, but collectively the additional new ABBA songs showcased ('The King Has Lost His Crown', 'Kisses of Fire', 'Lovers (Live a Little Longer)' and 'Does Your Mother Know') again left me less than completely satisfied. Actually, that's an understatement. I got myself in a bit of a two-and-eight about it all – a sense of proportion characteristically proving elusive at this stage in my life. In fact, I got to the point where I was almost *dreading* the new album coming out. This would be the very first ABBA album to be released with me as a fan. What if it was rubbish? Had I truly put a hoodoo on their entire creative process and whatever Benny and Björn were getting up to in that shed on that Swedish island of theirs?

A few days later – and about three days before I got hold of a copy of the *Voulez-Vous* album on its day of release at the end of April 1979 – trusty old Radio 1 played the title track. As soon as the riff kicked in, I breathed a MAMMOTH sigh of relief. This was CLASS! This was EPIC! Everything was going to be JUST FINE after all! ABBA had gone a bit disco but without sacrificing their distinctive hallmark. They'd absorbed the zeitgeist but not been consumed by it. In the next moment, of course, I felt guilty for doubting them, in the way fans do. But faith can be a fragile commodity in the world of pop fandom. I'm not sure whether the vindication applied more to ABBA or to me. The basic fact, however, was this: ABBA hadn't lost it! 'Voulez-Vous' was a top-drawer ABBA track!

I especially loved the "masters of the sea" line, which I thought was very clever and gave me a mild flashback to the etherealness of 'Eagle' – my admiration only partially being lessened when I finally got the album and discovered the line was actually "masters of the scene". Whatever. To this day, I still sing my own version in my head (and sometimes out loud) whenever I hear this fabulous song. And it still stubbornly bubbles just outside my all-time ABBA top ten, although I'm well aware that most hardcore fans don't rate it as highly as I do. I am, therefore, contractually obliged to state that (like every song I happen to love quite a bit more than most people) 'Voulez-Vous' is…UNDERRATED!

As for the *Voulez-Vous* album, well – no sooner had the string quartet intro to 'As Good as New' started to assail my ears than I just knew we were indeed firmly back on solid ground. Front to back, the LP was a great listen and even a little magic dust seemed to have been sprinkled over the songs that had sounded somewhat pedestrian on *ABBA in Switzerland*, especially the epic album-closer 'Kisses of Fire'. For whatever reason, they sounded miles better in their primary habitat. Faith further restored, well and truly. And so it would remain, basically forever. I missed out on seeing them on the 1979 UK tour for what then seemed a very good reason but which now looks anything but – basically the fact that I'd have had to go by myself. The Billy No-Mates option was never popular with teenage boys. But this unforgivable non-attendance (which left a hole in my soul that's arguably never been adequately filled) was merely a blip.

Even my residual discomfort (and sense of personal responsibility) regarding the long drought in terms of chart-topping singles was to dissipate in the summer of 1980 when 'The Winner Takes It All' so deservedly reached the pinnacle of the UK Top 40. And when that was followed up just before Christmas with 'Super Trouper', well…the cosmos had clicked back into its rightful Newtonian equilibrium. The big poster of the *Voulez-Vous* album cover that I'd Blu-tacked to the wall of my first-year's room at university as soon as I arrived there in autumn 1980 eloquently affirmed, to anyone who dared visit me, my unshakeable and enduring commitment to the cause.

So it was, then, that I entered 1981 FINALLY knowing what it was like to be a fan of an ABBA that was surfing the very crest of the wave. With those two number ones tucked safely in the locker, plus of course the outstanding (and UNDERRATED!) *Super Trouper* album, my confidence for the future was sky high. What's more, the release of a credible dance hit in the shape of the 12-inch single of the excellent 'Lay All Your Love on Me' only bolstered it even further. Which almost inevitably meant the rollercoaster was about to take another unexpected dip…

When 'One of Us' was released as a single in December 1981, just a few weeks after my twentieth birthday, I'll admit I was massively taken aback. By this stage, I felt like I'd been an ABBA fan for a very long time indeed. I suppose a little complacency – perhaps even a touch of hubris – had set in. I was expecting the new record to be something amazing. So I was truly shocked to realise, the first time I heard it on the radio, that it just didn't grab me one little bit. More than that, it sounded a bit tired, a bit jaded and pretty uninspired to my ears. Worse even than *that*, it felt like ABBA were going back over old ground – or (surely I must be wrong?) going through the motions just a tad. Plus the song title's echoes of the somewhat cruel *Not the Nine O'Clock News* ABBA pastiche didn't help one jot.

So although the *The Visitors* album had come out at almost exactly the same time – and here's a really terrible admission – I held back from buying it. I was even put off by some of the song titles that met my eyes as I glanced down the back of the album sleeve in whatever record shop I happened to have been passing just after its release: 'Head Over Heels', 'When All Is Said and Done', 'Two for the Price of One', 'Slipping Through My Fingers'... The reliance on well-known proverbs didn't really sound too promising or too creative. I therefore continued to avoid committing to the purchase. BIG BLUNDER! When I finally took the plunge, in the wake of the single release of 'Head Over Heels', which was much more up my musical alley than 'One of Us', I found that I'd stumbled on my favourite ABBA album of all – a lofty status that *The Visitors* has yet to relinquish and is never likely to.

But with a kind of elder statesmen/women feel now pervading both their work and the public perception of the band, ABBA were about to peter out and fade away in somewhat unsatisfactory fashion. Neither of late 1982's very minor non-album hits, 'The Day Before You Came' and 'Under Attack', really wormed their way into my heart. Frida's solo tour de force 'I Know There's Something Going On', on the other hand... Well! That absolute gem of a song ticked absolutely every box for me. Just loved it. That vocal delivery. That drumming. That everything. A perfect pop single. But the breathtaking impact that this classic record (criminally UNDERRATED! by the great British record-buying public) had on me also had an obvious sting in its tail. If Frida was releasing solo records and they were BRILLIANT (if

UNDERRATED!), surely this was a clear omen that ABBA's days were well and truly numbered. Which of course they were. Sort of.

At this point I need to re-underline the fact that, much like 'I Know There's Something Going On', my ABBA fandom had been very much a solo project. With the exception of my schoolmate Si's all too brief tour of duty back in early 1978, not a single friend or family member was a true blood-and-guts comrade in the ABBA battalion. The downsides of this were substantial – not least the fact that I hadn't been able to find anyone to go with me to see ABBA on their 1979 tour. And amongst my peers at university, the only responses to my ABBA fandom can be broadly categorised as falling somewhere in the bleak no-man's land between disinterest and derision. To add insult to spiritual injury, a girlfriend or two even unleashed a poison-tipped ABBA-inspired verbal barb in my direction when they made the strategic and tactical mistake of going through my LP collection and judging me accordingly.

But as I made the seamless transition from undergraduate not working particularly hard to postgraduate not working particularly hard, I finally pinpointed someone who quite liked ABBA! Breakthrough! Maybe I wasn't that odd after all. This someone's name was (and you're probably way ahead of me here) Freddie. We'd hit it off immediately, for all sorts of reasons. And soon a musical collaboration was to be on the cards. I'd dabbled in quite a bit of music-making since my early teens and, when Freddie demonstrated that he was blessed with a very decent set of pipes as he walked into my room one day and locked note-perfectly onto the melody of the thunderous 12-inch-single mix of the Simple Minds classic 'Up On the Catwalk', it was abundantly clear that I needed to sign him up for the next in my long succession of ill-judged musical projects. Very much inspired by ABBA's example a decade earlier, this was to involve attempting to enter a song for the 1985 Eurovision Song Contest, to be held, appropriately enough, in Sweden.

I've already written about this fiasco-heavy operation in eye-wateringly pointless detail in another book,[4] so I'll not revisit old ground extensively here because I'm not sure I can cope with

---

[4] *Big Dreams, Bum Notes: How Music Led Me to Eurovision Oblivion*

reliving the trauma yet again. Once was therapy. Twice would be self-flagellation. Suffice to say, we tried and failed to enter a song for Austria. (They'd finished bottom of the Eurovision pile in 1984 and, after I'd carefully triangulated the possibilities, I'd concluded that they might just be desperate enough to hang their collective Tyrolean hat on one of my songs.) Being nothing if not deeply delusional, I was consistently upbeat about our chances throughout the course of the project. Indeed, I considered it a kind of divine sign-in-the-sky moment when, just before we were to venture into a proper, actual, real, authentic, professional recording studio, in the autumn of 1984, to record our demo tape, 'One Night in Bangkok' appeared almost out of nowhere (in those pre-internet days) and the Benny-Björn-Tim Rice musical *Chess* started chugging down the pipeline. Clearly, Benny and Björn's emergence from a long, long hibernation was just a way of Providence telling me to seize the Eurovision success dangling tantalisingly in front of me.

Well, I suppose Providence may have been telling me something, but it certainly wasn't that I was about to win the 1985 Eurovision Song Contest. Austrian TV did put our song on some kind of shortlist (which was probably, in reality, pretty long) but I couldn't really blame them when they ultimately placed their stake money on another song, coincidentally also written by British songwriters. The reasonable potential of our song had been steadily chipped away by cumulative musical missteps and, above all, the classic 'musical differences' within the band. And these differences became very, very obvious almost as soon as we turned up at the studio for our (relatively) cheapo eight-hour through-the-wee-small-hours recording stint. Once we were in the door, we met the Duty Engineer who'd steer us through the process and hopefully press all the right buttons at the right time and in the right order. But just when my credibility looked as if it might be about to sustain a lethal hit before we'd even recorded a note, ABBA (no less) came to my rescue. Let me explain.

To beef up our numbers, we'd made the schoolboy error of bringing on board a competent musician. But this competence came at a hefty price: this particular musician's utter disdain for Eurovision, Europop and, in fact, almost anything with a fighting chance of cracking even the lower reaches of the Top 40 singles chart, in the UK, in Austria and indeed in any other populated territory you could care to name.

"So what are you going to do with the song once it's recorded?" the Duty Engineer asked, as we sat in the control room equally mesmerised and intimidated by the galaxy of buttons, knobs, faders, switches and flashing lights surrounding us like an Andromedan star cluster.

"We're going to enter it into the Eurovision Song Contest," I replied, aware that our competent muso recruit had already folded his arms to signal his superiority to the proceedings and was clearly limbering up for a massive, disdainful eye roll and a really big tut.

"OK…" said the Duty Engineer. "Any outfits in that field you particularly like?"

"Yeah", I said, not daring to namecheck ABBA quite yet. "I'm quite big on Golden Earring…"

Roll of the eyes from our competent musician.

"Oh and Nena…"

Another roll of the eyes. But I had to go for broke, despite getting an unwelcome flashback to that record shop in 1978.

"And, of course, there's ABBA…"

HUGE roll of the eyes from our muso compadre, plus the definite beginnings of a superior smirk to accompany the tut, as he confidently waited for the Duty Engineer to launch into a withering verbal assault (which he could also energetically join in with) on the topic of throwaway pop music in general, European pop music in particular and the place among the inner rings of Dante's Inferno that had been assigned to this abomination as typified by Sweden's biggest and most successful musical export. I held my breath, waited for the backlash and prepared to take my punishment like a (super) trouper. And then the Duty Engineer did indeed give vent to his feelings:

"ABBA? I really LOVE that stuff! State of the art! If anyone ever asks me how to produce a great commercial record with superb production values, I just tell them to go and listen to ABBA! That *Voulez-Vous* album! Should be compulsory listening for any music producer..."

Perfect! Thank you, ABBA. Thank you so very much! Our enemies are vanquished and I can set about recording a low-quality Eurovision entry with a definite spring in my step. It's turned out that I owe you one, rather than the other way round.

Back to *Chess*. The musical proved to be everything I'd dared hope it would be. And a lot more than that, in point of fact. I was totally smitten and got to see it four (or was it five?) times during its West End run in 1986 and 1987. I couldn't get enough of the soundtrack double disc or the highlights cassette *Chess Pieces* and at one point I thought I might actually be morphing into Murray Head. I could even hit some of the notes he reached in his "What a scene..." party piece when he first strode on stage. Not all of the notes. Not by a long shot. That's why I'd recruited Freddie to provide the lead vocals for our failed Eurovision venture. But *Chess* was then, and still is now, my all-time favourite musical and if ever the opportunity has arisen to go and see even an am-dram version, I've grabbed it with both hands and tried to go along on multiple nights. Plus, of course, it delivered an ersatz ABBA chart-topper in the shape of 'I Know Him So Well' early in 1985. So yes, you've guessed it, I consider *Chess* a criminally UNDERRATED! piece of work that's utterly worthy of a place alongside ABBA's very best outputs. There. I've said it.

The following decades were to see no erosion whatsoever of my love for ABBA. The red hot lava of those six or seven initial years of following the band were to set solid into an immovable, unerodable and indeed core element in the musical baggage that I'd carry into the life ahead of me and would help sustain me through it. I never submitted to the wiles of *ABBA Gold*, admittedly.[5] But there again, compilation albums have never been

---

[5] At least not until September 2022 and I naively found myself visiting the Amazon website when I was still floating on air after seeing 21st Century ABBA.

my thing, although my wife and I did invest in the *Gold* and *More Gold* video compilations which became firm favourites with our children. Always nice to pass on the torch to the next generation.

And, over the years, giving the *Super Trouper* album a spin established itself as a family tradition on New Year's Day. In fact, almost without fail, the first week of January is a big ABBA week for me, with all the CD albums played multiple times, reliably leaving me with bitter regret that, in some misguided fit of decluttering, I got rid of my vinyl versions (even the blue gatefold sleeve of *The Album* with its staple stigmata, and the picture-disc version of the *The Singles: The First Ten Years* compilation) somewhere along life's bobbly old highway. But (ironically) it's a great way of decluttering the Christmas mindset, setting myself up for the year to come and launching myself into the next twelve months in an unremittingly fresh and positive frame of mind. Nor, over the years, did ABBA ever seem that far away as their work remained pretty consistently in the public eye, what with Erasure's cover versions, endless TV documentaries and of course the whole explosive, never-ending *Mamma Mia!* phenomenon.

Then, totally unexpectedly, after much time had passed, I kind-of got to sort-of plug 50% of that hole in my soul I mentioned a little earlier. In 2014, I managed to procure a couple of tickets for a very special evening. To celebrate forty years since the floor-wiping success of 'Waterloo' and to tie in with the publication of a lavish limited-edition book about the band that I couldn't justify buying, a one-off event had been arranged at London's Tate Modern, featuring (drum roll) personal appearances by Björn and Frida, no less. Among other things, this provided the perfect opportunity to cement the whole torch-passing thing, so I took my daughter along and we had a rattling good time fuelled by Swedish beer and the chance to rub shoulders (at a respectable distance) with luminaries like Mark Gatiss, who clearly has a love of ABBA on his impeccable CV. A great and memorable evening, for which I proudly sported my 'Andersson, Fältskog, Lyngstad, Ulvaeus' t-shirt purchased specially for the occasion. I don't suppose Björn and Frida would have spotted it from the stage, though, as we were standing about fifteen rows back. But they probably knew their own surnames anyway.

And what a surreal moment it was when they walked out in front of us to say a few choice words, none of which I can remember because I was too focused on ensuring that I didn't pass out or just start crying. Indeed, the subsequent medley by a young person's choir passed by in a bit of a blur of warm emotion and cold Swedish lager. Finally clapping eyes on 50% of ABBA really did seem to provide the icing on the cake of my (by that point) near-four decades of consistent and persistent ABBA fandom. What more could I possibly ask for?

Well, a new album, obviously. Except that it was never, ever going to happen, was it? Except then it did...

When it comes right down to it, I'm a soppy old git. So when, on Thursday the second of September 2021, in that extraordinary globe-spanning YouTube transmission which formally confirmed ABBA's comeback almost forty years after their unsatisfactory slow-motion dissolution, Benny uttered the magic words "...new album..." my eyes turned instantly to pools of water. We'd all foolishly dared to dream, of course, hadn't we? We'd all told ourselves that even two new songs – the ones already confirmed, thrillingly, to exist back in 2018, to tie in with the planned ABBAtars shows – were more than we'd any right to expect at this late stage in our ABBA-enriched lives. But we hadn't really meant it. WE WANTED A WHOLE ALBUM. And we actually got it. Forty long years had passed – an unfathomably long time in all our lives, including the members of ABBA themselves – when it finally transpired that the ABBA story hadn't petered out in 1982 after all with some less-than-stellar late material and the odd awkward TV appearance. There was still one glorious, age- and time-defying epilogue to be written. (Although, naturally, we'd STILL end up hoping for yet another sequel after that...)

As for the two new songs premiered on that incredible, emotional early autumn evening, I'll admit it took me a few listens to wrap my head around them. That's what shock can do to a man. But once I'd got myself together....WOW! WOW, WOW, WOW, WOW, WOW!!! 'I Still Have Faith in You' and 'Don't Shut Me Down' were right up there with the ABBA pantheon. Amazing days. For a full week, I gorged on those songs – and also on those odd 'reaction videos' so beloved of YouTube. I haven't had tears in my eyes on such a permanent basis since I accidentally stubbed my foot and broke a toe. On this occasion, the downside was that the two sneak-preview tracks probably fuelled unreasonable expectations for the *Voyage* album. They'd ignited the tantalising possibility that it might even prove to be their very best album of all.

When the stout cardboard envelope finally dropped onto my doormat late on the evening of Friday the fifth of November 2021, courtesy of the man in the Amazon Prime van, it was almost as if I was floating in a time tunnel, tumbling backwards down the decades to a period in my life when the ritual of obtaining and hungrily devouring a brand-new ABBA album had, for just a glorious couple of years, become an electrifying feature of the seasons' cycle for me. I almost felt moved to punch some staple holes round the edge of the CD's booklet inlay, just to roll back the years and afford myself a genuine sense of closure plus a proper perspective on the circle of life.

And with *Voyage* ABBA definitely fulfilled their side of the bargain. No doubt about it, so to speak. This was a good album. This was, beyond any question, a worthy addition to their mighty back catalogue. Here was a record replete with meaning and feeling. OK, maybe overall it wasn't quite as sublime as the almost faultless 'I Still Have Faith in You' and 'Don't Shut Me Down' had lured me into hoping for. But a new ABBA album! A proper, hugely enjoyable piece of work! Much to admire, reflect on, dissect and evaluate. Where would this album sit in the league table of ABBA's oeuvre? Would any of the individual songs break into my all-time ABBA top ten? These are key questions for any committed (and possibly committable) fan, of course. An awful lot of agonising – in car parks, at traffic lights, during sleepless nights and all the rest of it – lay ahead.

But the big picture was a great deal simpler to calibrate. What mattered above all was that *Voyage* represented a fitting end (perhaps...) to the phenomenal ABBA story. With its remarkable and courageous smorgasbord of styles, it certainly couldn't be accused of being a safe album. And although (at the time of writing) I haven't been to see the *ABBA Voyage* show (for Covid and flimsier reasons) and have instead started to gorge on ABBA tribute acts as a kind of substitution activity, to my mind my enjoyment of the *Voyage* album has more than reasserted the fact that I'm still right on board the ABBA train as it zips eternally on towards another town.

But above all *Voyage* simply reaffirmed what I first discovered forty-five years ago: in the right, skilled, inspired hands, pop music _can_ be 'proper' music too and _can_ more than warrant a lifetime's allegiance. And for me, that allegiance has simply never waned. For example, it still warranted my daughter giving me a pristine copy of the *ABBA Annual 1979* (replacing my long-lost copy that inexplicably went astray somewhere down the line in that decluttering frenzy I mentioned earlier) as a lovely surprise present to mark a 'big' birthday just ten days before *Voyage* was released. A proper gift, that one.

After grabbing a few superficial listens on the Friday, I must have played *Voyage* twenty-five times or more on Saturday the sixth of November 2021 – the day after it came. And 15,952 days after ABBA had.

Freddie's voyage:

For most straight boys, the earliest exposures to female heroes are always going to be memorable, seismic events. Especially for me, whose memory is not that great, I'll be honest. My earliest 'did I imagine that? No it was definitely real' recollection is being woken up for *The Nine O'Clock News* to see highlights of Mr Neil Armstrong doing his thing on the Moon in glorious monochrome in July 1969. A pretty good first memory, I think you'll agree.

But I was talking about the ladies. A few years on and it was the Munich Olympics of 1972. They belonged to Olga Korbut, the elfin-like creature who did battle with nightmare drill instructor and fellow Soviet Ludmilla Tourischeva in the gymnastics. At the tender age of eight, I was aware of the horrors of the terrorism that accompanied the Games, but I don't think it really registered. Olga – in my mind we were on first name terms, though it would be another eight years before I knew any Russian, so the conversation might have been a touch lacking – was twice my age, but I was captivated, besotted even. This was an awakening like no other. She was a girl, and girls were all right!

Hang on, I hear you say: what does a bit of lunar love and Olga ogling have to do with the most famous fab four since the original Fab Four? It's now 1974 and the Eurovision Song Contest is firmly ensconced in the year's Important List of Things to Watch, along with the FA Cup, Rugby's Five Nations and the Christmas Day *Top of the Pops*. The Brighton contest is often seen as a watershed in Eurovision, the day that one song altered the event's course towards global hugeness and consigned everything before it to the box marked 'a bit twee, odd or generally shite'. There's the impression that watching a good Eurovision song before 'Waterloo' was about as common as seeing a Hutu tribesman at the South Pole.

Not so, of course, but for me that was the moment that Eurovision got sexy. I wasn't massively into music; I'd never bought a record and the folks always had Radio 4 playing, so my weekly look at ladies was *Top of the Pops* and my annual treat was, you've guessed it, Eurovision. I remember older Eurovisions, but 1974 has become so large that it's blocked out everything else. I can't even remember where 'Waterloo' came in the running order – in the middle I think – but when it did come, boy did somebody light a fuse. Two beautiful angels with amazing voices and two energetic blokes who clearly knew their way around their instruments.

And the song! My, what a belter. Within the first few bars it had blown away the cobwebs from this slightly august and stilted institution. This was proper, powerful pop. The verse grabbed you by the scruff of the neck and the chorus flung you around, breathless and giddy. Packed with catchy riffs, a delicious melody and lyrics that were mind-bogglingly clever and succinct for someone composing in their second language – well, let's just say the word 'revelation' is very over-used but deserves its intended meaning on this occasion.

Looking back, over my shoulder – sorry, that's Mike & the Mechanics; stay on track, Freddie – and with a critical eye, it all looks a bit dated. You can't fault the song itself, it's as close to perfect as any song can be. Visually, though, it's very much mid-1970s fare. Frida's curly locks are not her best look, though she may have been the inspiration for a similar look among both men and women in England about this time. Agnetha's trousers haven't aged well, and for me it's impossible to look at her now and not see that this was before she had dental work, a move which elevated her to the Most Beautiful Woman on Planet Earth that Freddie Had Ever Seen.

It's all about context, though, and I need to remind myself that we were almost starved of glamour and mythic beauty in this fairly staid decade (staid in terms of female stars at least, televisually speaking). There were only three television channels, with no breakfast TV or Channel 4 in sight. The movies were a bit out of range for me at my age, unless I wanted to watch animation. We had no way of recording and endlessly playing back glimpses of goddesses. We'd not long emerged from the energy crisis and three-day working week, with both power and TV broadcasting time effectively being rationed. It was grim enough, though we didn't know it at the time. It's hardly surprising, then, that this particular musical event made such an impression.

This, like for 99.99% of other British people (who hadn't heard the albums *Ring Ring* or *Waterloo*, which had come out the month before), was my first exposure to ABBA, but it was this TV appearance that provided the platform for them to fine-tune their peerless pop songwriting, recording and performing capabilities and stay on our screens regularly for the next few years. I still hadn't bought any music at this stage and television was still a key medium for getting your work out there, so for me there was always the promise of seeing them in summer specials and Christmas specials as well as the regular interview or guest slot. There was so much incredible material for them to draw on year after year. I never heard the whole of the earlier albums, but the singles they released were über-catchy, brilliantly crafted and achingly beautiful.

Speaking of beautiful, I'm not going to lie to you: the ABBA attraction was mainly sexual for me. As I've mentioned already, so stop me if this is a bit tiresome, for a young teenager in the second half of the '70s there was heavy reliance on ABBA, Baccara, *The Kenny Everett Video Show* and Benny Hill for glimpses of faces and sometimes flesh belonging to women you simply didn't see on the High Street or in Woolies (google Woolworths if you don't know what the face of the UK High Street looked like in the latter part of the twentieth century). It was always visual for me, rarely aural, but the fact that they made such listenable music made for a big bonus.

Those TV appearances, though, sheesh! I realise the lads don't figure too much in this appreciation of ABBA, but the Bs were romantically intertwined with the As, so don't feel too sorry for them. Agnetha and Frida seemed to complement each other so well. Their voices sat together so perfectly: Agnetha's was slightly higher and had a purity to it that's hard to match, whereas Frida's was a little deeper, a little more husky, and for that, yes, a little sexier. Put them together and, well, I'm starting to sound like F Murray Abraham's Salieri in the film *Amadeus*. I could go on, but I don't want to put you off your snack.

Ah yes, back to the TV appearances and the ladies complementing each other. Both beautiful, one blonde and the other brunette, sitting on top of figures that when the clothes hugged them caused the blood pressure in most heterosexual males between thirteen and one hundred and thirteen to reach dangerously high levels. And don't get me started on that shiny lipstick stuff that Agnetha used to wear, framing the whitest teeth you ever saw in your life... I can't think of a more mesmerising close-up; you'd have to go back to an Elizabeth Taylor or Natalie Wood movie, I reckon.

Speaking of movies, in December 1977 *ABBA: The Movie* came out, capitalising on their immense popularity in Australia and filmed during the tour down under earlier that year. My memory is hazy but I'm pretty sure I was late to the party on this and didn't see it until early 1978. Prior to researching this book, I'd only seen the film once, forty-five-plus years ago. Why? Well, there are some films you should only see once. Take *The Silence of the Lambs*, for instance, or *The Sixth Sense*. Those were so damn scary and stay with you to this day, so why see them again? Same with 'ATM', though for totally different reasons. I wanted to be that nobody radio DJ, but I wasn't, so why relive the film? It left me with the thought 'why can't I be friends with ABBA? I'm sure we'd get on great!'.

Life is full of missed opportunities. As a kid I was into sport and went to sporting events. Because I wasn't really into music I never really went to gigs. Sure, there was the odd school performance and a bit of singing in the choir, but not a proper gig. It wasn't my thing. ABBA embarked on a major tour in 1979, playing the usual big venues like Wembley Arena. Then, after a number of nights at Wembley, for two nights after that, in mid-November, they played Bingley Hall, Stafford, before going on to Glasgow. Stafford was my local town, a small town in the Midlands. "Not a place that should delay you long", according to a well-known tourist guide, which was a touch harsh methinks. It was nevertheless a small town with a good venue that at the time secured gigs by The Who, Rush and so on. I guess it was kind of on the way for ABBA as they journeyed from London to Glasgow.

It was a big deal for Bingley Hall to get ABBA. They were huge. And I didn't go. I probably wouldn't have got tickets, since it was a 7500-capacity venue and they sold like the proverbial hot cakes. I was probably just a little bit young to go, a fairly immature, play-it-safe fifteen-year-old and £7.50 for a ticket back then was the price of a really good tennis racquet. So I didn't go.

A missed opportunity. A you-shoulda-been-there moment. A chance to see two of the world's most famous and most beautiful women, at the peak of the powers, in the flesh. A devastatingly good first-ever gig watching a global pop phenomenon at their absolute zenith. I'm not one to be bitter... By all accounts it was an amazing night, helped no doubt by the band's megastar quality and also the fact that at one point Agnetha wore the number nine centre-forward jersey from Wolverhampton Wanderers, the nearest top-flight football team, my football team. The team that would go on to win the League Cup that season, probably because of Agnetha. No, I'm not one to be bitter.

By 1980 I'd started to listen to a bit more music and had actually bought some records! The first record I ever bought was ELO's double album *Out of the Blue*. The list price of the album was an eye-wateringly expensive eight quid. Trawling through the shelves of the local record shop for the first time, I came across the album, with a couple of half-inch cut marks in the thick cover and marked down to half price. What's more, the vinyl was fine, as was the fold-out poster of the seven members of the band. This was too good to be true. I parted with my £3.99 and adorned the wall of my room with the poster. I can still name all the members of the band from that poster, which is a bit odd, if I'm honest. My first single? A while later, it was Daryl Hall and John Oates' 'I Can't Go for That (No Can Do)'. It took me a while to start parting with money for only two records. I know. A real muso.

My apologies, friends, I've digressed once more from my ABBA-laden legacy remit. The second album I bought? *Supapa Troupapa*! Riddled with magnificence it was: 'The Winner Takes It All', 'Happy New Year', 'Lay All Your Love on Me' and of course the title track with its circus theme. (I love a bit of circus, don't you? Not the animals of course, and the clowns leave me a bit lukewarm to be honest, but the skills, athleticism and acrobatism are hard to beat for excitement.) When all is said and done (so to speak), it's fabulous stuff. Then there's 'On and On and On' and 'Andante, Andante'... I might just need to pause for lunch and put it on again, bear with me.

I'm not one for nostalgia, but playing back the album now transports me to a time when life did seem simpler and the possibilities – and summers – endless. An ABBA album has the ability to make you feel a million dollars one minute and melancholic the next, in the mood to take on the world, and then feeling a touch wistful for a time that didn't really exist except through rose-tinted glasses. Take the segue from 'Super Trouper' to 'The Winner Takes It All', for instance. What a rollercoaster of emotions the band builds, no doubt drawing on the challenges in their own personal lives and the hideous dynamic of working and performing so closely together while their off-stage relationships were crumbling.

As I write my part of this particular chapter, I'm at the beginning of this journey to document fifty years of fandom. I'm only now realising how much fun it's going to be to do this, since I get to listen to the music all over again, and some of it for the very first time, especially if you count the early pre-ABBA stuff. I can listen to ABBA not just as I work, but *for* work as well. Happy days! I believe salespeople call that double bubble.

Fast forward to Christmas 1981. This magical period was the calm before the storm, in that it was my last Christmas before getting the head down study-wise and the culmination of seven years of secondary school with A Levels. I think we all knew life would never be like this again; you tend to know when something's ephemeral. I'd got particularly close to a friend of mine who'd recently joined the school in the sixth form and he had a pen pal over from Paris for the holidays. They were massive ABBA fans, far bigger than I was, and *The Visitors* had just come out. As a consequence it was on the turntable constantly. I was like a leech in their house over the festive period, and when we weren't at their house we were at the youth club playing ABBA.

This took my appreciation for ABBA to another level above *Super Trouper*. People talk about the soundtrack to their lives, but the Christmas of 1981 belonged to *The Visitors*. The music was the glue of our friendship which took us to Paris for a return visit to his pen pal (a girl, I didn't mention that), through A Levels, beyond ABBA's productive life span, and into the overlapping era of pop's heir apparent, Wham!.

And then ABBA were no more. They were done, in their early-to-mid-thirties, leaving us nothing but their music to listen to and their images imprinted on our minds, since we'd never again be able to see them 'live'. That's pretty much how it was for the next decade or so, as vinyl and cassette gave way to the CD and we had to upgrade our music collections into the new format, surviving on songs from a band that belonged to the past.

But then came *ABBA Gold*, towards the end of 1992. Once more, ABBA were at the front of our minds and the hits that were scattered over eight albums were now sandwiched together for us to gorge ourselves on non-stop. For me, it was only then that I realised how prolific they'd been. Except 'prolific' paints the wrong picture, because it suggests a volume of output, with quantity stressed over quality. ABBA had produced about an album a year, but it was the quality of the hits, together with the album tracks from the albums I knew, that hit home. The stuff was so damn catchy, all of it, and there was a lot of it. What chance did the younger generation have, hearing ABBA for the first time?

I was living in Scotland during this time, and the *Gold* album was never far from my car's tape deck. One weekend I was driving a bunch of mates down to a table tennis tournament a couple of hours away. They were a good bit younger than me, and one of them was very hung over. I insisted on playing *Gold*. At first, they raised their eyebrows at it, and you could tell they weren't looking forward to the lengthy journey if this was the musical fare on offer.

After a while they got into it and surprised themselves with how many of the songs were second nature to them. Gone but not forgotten were ABBA, living on through the legacy of the music. I said to them by about track three or four, and for almost every song thereafter, "Guys, it's just hit after hit after hit". The mood improved and even the woman with the hangover perked up. We arrived at the tournament in tip top shape and she went on to win the ladies' singles, getting better with every round as the dehydration effect subsided. Never mind *The X Factor*, it was the A Factor that won her the title, I'm convinced of it (A for ABBA, not alcohol...).

Then we come to the *Mamma Mia!* era. I've never seen the musical. I've seen a video recording of a school production, however, and both films. It's a cute storyline, well told, and nicely knits together the selected songs. The musical was superb, apparently, and still is for all I know. The first film was OK, the acting decent and the singing ranged from suspect to suspect. I'm not going to dwell on the films too much here, because for me they illustrate one key point: when the raw material is so, *so* good, you can do almost anything with it. It's the gift that keeps on giving, the richest trove of work to rival that of any other artist. The fact that other people, some of them amateurs, can try to recreate the originals, without even doing their own slant on the song in a cover version style, and the end product is worth paying to go and see is testament to how good that stuff is. For that reason, is there any other band with more tribute acts plying their trade across the globe?

I'm getting ahead of myself slightly here because I've failed to address the intervening periods between these memory milestones. One thread runs pretty much through the last four decades, well two threads actually: a thing and a person. The thing is Eurovision, natch, and the person is me ol' mate Garry, co-conspirator in this tome what you is reading.

ABBA were no more, but the annual Eurovision event was there to give our lives purpose. Broadcast every May (usually) to kick-start the northern hemisphere into summer, it's grown to become the single greatest reminder of the wide, wild, weird and wonderful world of music and culture. I say reminder because with our increased connectedness and the shrinking planet you tend to forget that, actually, we have very little in common with each other, certainly if our taste in music is anything to go by.

The early-to-mid-'90s was a bit of a Eurovision wilderness for me, but otherwise I've seen pretty much every Eurovision since '74. This is ABBA's fault, without doubt. When the world's predominant music genre – pop – takes entering and winning an event seriously, you know how important a vehicle it's become, and we can thank Sweden's most famous export for that. I adopt what I like to think of as a professional approach to the event, scoring each song apolitically and coming up with a top five that never meshes with the winning top five, but then there are many,

many books that have attempted to say why that sort of thing happens.

When I buy something that's about a fiver, I give it the Guinness value test. Let's assume that a pint of Guinness is about €5 or £5. Think about what went into producing that pint and getting it into my glass on my beer mat, in my local hostelry (my last one was called Glynn's, for what it's worth; other pubs are available). Think also about how long and how enjoyable the consumption of that pint is. Set against the Guinness example, then, how valuable is this thing I'm buying? Now this rule works for things costing multiples of a fiver, but not too big a multiple, you understand, especially if you have my tolerance for alcohol. Isn't it funny how we can spend £15 and have a great night, and £30 and have a lousy day?

What on earth is he banging on about now, I hear you mutter to yourself in your language of choice? Well, for every Eurovision entry, of which there have been over fifteen hundred in the last sixty-seven years, I perform the 'Waterloo' test. Where does this song stand against the greatest Eurovision song of all time? Does it have Napoleon conducting (actually that's an unfair question, more's the pity)? What's it like on the first listen, does it blow you away? Is it pretty good? Is it decent, likely to be a 'grower'? Is it utter pants? It is utter underpants? For the more discerning out there, is it a 'good' song but one which you don't particularly like? Or a bad one that you love, or one of the other two permutations? 'Waterloo' is the benchmark, the gold standard if you will, and when you stack each song against 'Waterloo' the latter is still pretty much at the very top, five decades on.

'Waterloo' was a fabulous song, expertly staged and exquisitely performed by four musicians who were easy on the eye (OK, I mentioned the conductor earlier and there were a couple of other lads on guitar and drums, and an orchestra, but you get the point), two men and two women, singing in English. It ticked all the boxes and then promptly ripped up the paper with a dynamism that took your breath away. That's how I felt at the time. And, incidentally, that was how I felt when I first heard 'Heroes' in

2015's version of the contest, performed by the impossibly handsome Måns Zelmerlöw. Sweden had done it again with a great song and superb staging (remember all those nifty graphics?).

I've just had a shufty at the ol' Wikipedia and the Swedes won the whole flippin' thing four times between 'Waterloo' and 'Heroes', and then again this year with Loreen's 'Tattoo', of course – 'Waterloo' being the first in the septet of victories. Bearing in mind Sweden's population and its geopolitical position on the, well, fringes of Europe, this is a phenomenal effort. You gotta put this down to two things: the 'ABBAffect' and the country's heritage of writing catchy-as-you-like popular music.

Back to my story... Towards the end of '83 I was coming to the end of my first term at college. I'd met a few folk whose company I'd liked, but you know what they say, you spend the second term breaking the friendships you made in the first term. I knew this going in, so was a touch circumspect those first few months. This wasn't helped by the fact that I was studying two dead languages, Latin and ancient Greek to be specific. These Classics students tend to be nerds par excellence, with an ability to bore you senseless, literally in the drilling sense of the word – you felt your life force slipping away through the hole they'd created. That said, there were a handful of unattainable beauties in the faculty, unattainable also in its literal sense given that these women were a good five or six inches taller than yours truly.

Anyway, I digress once more. The Classics department used to throw these occasional snack-based get-to-know-your-fellow-faculty-members afternoons. I usually tried to make these since as an impoverished student I could horse into the hors d'oeuvres and not have to get dinner (or tea, if you lived in the Midlands, like I used to). Also, there was a chance that one of the previous paragraph's unattainable beauties might be in evidence. As long as you didn't get cornered by an earnest bearded lecturer with a penchant for reducing lush poetry to highfalutin tosh, you were golden. These afternoons were my first introduction to foods I'd not experienced before, or since in some cases. Hummus, hmm, interesting one. And taramasalata, better known as 'bright pink hummus', what on earth was that about?

Instead, on this occasion, I found myself chatting to this bloke doing a PhD in late Roman history, or something of that ilk. Do you know what though? He was all right! Similar background to me, similar sense of humour, not a boring nerd, and not a knob. And, as we subsequently discovered as we knocked around over the coming weeks and months, a shared fondness for Eurovision. Now I say fondness, but Garry Holland, or me ol' mate Gaz as I generally refer to him, was very musical, wrote songs, was in a band, played instruments, could sing a bit too, and had something deeper than a fondness for Eurovision. As a committed Europhile, he had a *fascination* for it.

I should say at this point that I don't know quite when or how Eurovision became this iconic, glitzy and dare I say fashionable event on the entertainment calendar. Perhaps it was that the dials for pageantry, glamour and extravagance got turned up to eleven the last couple of decades. In the UK and Ireland, when I tell a friend or acquaintance that I'm really into Eurovision, they'll often look at me in an odd way. In my view, and Garry's too of course, I've always found Eurovision hugely accessible and hugely enjoyable. Funny too, at times, and cringeworthy also, and for all that still hugely enjoyable.

And so it was, namely through Eurovision, that we had another conversational string to our collective bow. This bow was then strengthened by accident when Gaz discovered that I could just about hold a note and my pathetically small vocal range was not only suited to the Simple Minds track I was singing along to but also to a project Gaz had his eye on. I knew that year or two in the school choir would pay off. And when Gaz 'haz' a plan, you tag along for the ride. You see, Garry H had his sights set on entering a song for Europe, aka Eurovision.

In terms of telling that story, he does a comprehensive and entertaining job of it in his book referenced earlier in this chapter. Suffice to say he'd met his match with my abilities. I was only providing my vocal cords. Gaz had written the song and he and his mates had provided the musical accompaniment. And when I say vocal cords, I'm perhaps being generous there. Let's just say we aren't talking Frida Lyngstad here, we're talking Freddie Holmen, with the singing ability of a pork pie. (It's not my real name, obviously, more a stage name, which is ironic since I've spent probably two minutes on the singing stage as FH, and it was utter carnage, but we gotta keep a bit of mystery, right?) I remember one of the rehearsals where I was trying to get to grips with the melody and meandering along the required tune, frequently getting lost on the way. It was at this point that Gaz delivered one of the most withering and memorable put downs I've ever had the misfortune to receive: "For f*ck's sake, Freddie, have you found a note you like yet?"

Over the following years Gaz and I have dabbled with music – again, he does everything, I show up and try and master the melody – and compared song reviews as each Eurovision comes and goes. An appreciation for ABBA and eulogising Eurovision have bound us together and bridged the waters that have separated, on and off, the countries we live in. ABBA may have gone the way of all natural things – or so we thought – but their music always lived on and Eurovision has always been a living, breathing organism.

Fast forward to 2020. It's the Coronavirus pandemic, and we both have a lot more time in the house, along with six billion other souls. Gaz has always delved deep and wide into the enormous fund of music the world has produced, whereas I've always been Mainstream Mike, skating along the surface. If it's in the Top 40 I'll probably listen to it. Generous soul that he is, Gaz takes it upon himself, for my edification, to rank his top ten tracks from some of his favourite artists. I simply listen to them and feed back my first impressions (in most cases) or considered views (stuff I know, much less common) of his selections. This takes on a life of its own and over the following weeks and months we span the genres and end up covering over a hundred artists, so over a thousand songs.

During this time, rumours start re-surfacing that the holy quadrinity that dares not be named is working on more new material (following the 2018 announcement that they'd recorded two new songs). Impossible. They haven't been together for over forty years. They were once married to each other, so how's that going to work out? The Bs have been doing *Chess* and their own projects and the writing credits for their catalogue of work which keeps getting reused is keeping them in the manner to which they've become accustomed. Besides, they're in their seventies for crying out loud, to borrow from Mr Meatloaf. Who produces new pop music that's good at that age? Plus, why would they bother? They've nothing left to prove and they're certainly not going to support the new music with a tour, which everyone does these days and which is where the money is, along with merchandise.

Well, blow me down. It's late 2021 and, like a phoenix risen to rid us of this viral malaise, the boys and girls from Stockholm have only gone and come back with a new album! After doing nothing for four decades, the band is back, re-formed – not reformed, thankfully – and ready to give us *Voyage*. Can you think of another band who have come back with the original members after such a long hiatus and given us new material? Can you imagine the first few phone calls? It must have been like something from *The Blues Brothers*. "We're putting the band back together." "Forget it, no way." "We're on a mission from God." Well, two out of three ain't bad – sorry, Meatloaf is back!

By the time I'd had *Voyage* for a shade under two months, I worked out that I'd listened to the album about a hundred times, and I'm not exaggerating. I do this a lot, playing an album over and over and over again. For me, it's always been about the album. I know this is going to sound like a contradiction, since I'm Mr Top 40, but even if it's a compilation I still want the full album experience. I still believe that anyone who produces an album has agonised over the track order so the least I can do is listen to it properly from start to finish. And I couldn't stop playing *Voyage*. I think it's something to do with deferred pleasure, and forty years is an ocean-going container-sized amount of deferred pleasure. I was addicted to *Voyage*, then I was simply obsessed, then it just about came under control. There's no cure, other than time. We're saving the *Voyage* analysis for another chapter, but let's just say that the weekly Gaz-Fred catch-up call was a bit one-dimensional for a while.

And that's just the music. You already know how important the visual side of entertainment is to me. And yet again ABBA have broken the mould, destroyed the machines, closed the factory and started again. They'll appear in concert! They'll party like it's 1979! They'll be seen by hundreds of thousands. They'll avoid the monstrous carbon footprint that comes with doing a stadium tour. And they'll do it in their prime without having to leave their house for a single show. The *ABBA Voyage* show – if that's not pure invention, magic even, I don't know what is. What's more, they've created a template for every successful band to go on forever, to live on as a 'live' act, or 'simulact', digitally cloning their perfect selves for every performance at a fraction of the traditional cost.

I'll be talking more about my trip to see the show at the ABBA Arena later in the book, and I'm trying really hard not to gush a spoiler or two, but it's worth saying right now that you know you're witnessing something truly special when the reality lives up to the hype. It's an absolute tour de force and every ABBA fan who can afford the trip should go at least once, especially if they're not lucky enough to have seen them in the flesh. This is in the 3D semiconductor-driven flesh, accompanied by special effects, animation and a 'live' band that will leave you open-mouthed. For this fan, it's hard to understate what this will do for their legacy and how it'll change 'live' performance for bands that are past their physical peak or will to tour.

My on-on love affair with ABBA has spanned almost the entirety of their existence. While I didn't know the *Ring Ring* album and the early days, I watched history unfold on our newish colour telly back in April 1974 and we've all seen what the future looks like after their 2022 fifty-year golden anniversary. Throughout that time the one thing that ABBA's music has done is what other great artists have done, in different amounts. They've made a connection with me and sustained that connection over time, throughout the journey. To have been able to do that over a span of time where, like everyone, I've been increasingly swamped with choices and claims for my attention is down to the fact that they got me early, got me totally and were able to keep me wanting more until they were ready to deliver their septuagenarian masterstroke.

I can't begin to imagine what the buzz will be like at Eurovision 2024 for the fiftieth anniversary of the Brighton victory. With Sweden winning in 2023 for a record-equalling seventh time – Loreen's second triumph after the 'Euphoria' of 2012 – the country has completed the circle in the most perfect way possible and will bring Eurovision home to the place that bore the band that enabled it to come of age. I might have to get to that show, I think; can't imagine the tickets will be that hard to come by...

So that's Freddie's tale. A case of hormones, hits and, perhaps, hagiography too. But this is a book about ABBA, so that's all right with me.

Letting the Music Speak: A Review of the Albums

ABBA have often been burdened with that slightly pejorative descriptor 'singles band'. But you and we know better than that. Because, in reality, they were anything but one of those ten-a-penny 'chart acts' for whom putting out an occasional long-player was a bit of a tiresome but unavoidable inconvenience. It's in those nine studio albums that the heart of the ABBA story lies. It's there that we see them in full flight, in all their diversity and complexity, and in relentlessly determined pursuit of musical perfection. The compilations and the 'live' albums have a role to play too, naturally, but it really is in that career arc stretching from Ring Ring all the way to Voyage nearly half a century later that the brilliance of ABBA finds its most startling, fascinating expression.[6]

The Studio Albums:

RING RING (1973)

Track listing: Ring Ring/Another Town, Another Train/Disillusion/People Need Love/I Saw It in the Mirror/Nina, Pretty Ballerina/Love Isn't Easy (but It Sure Is Hard Enough)/Me and Bobby and Bobby's Brother/He Is Your Brother/She's My Kind of Girl/I Am Just a Girl/Rock 'n' Roll Band

F:[7] Aren't there a bunch of phrases to describe something that's a mélange of styles? Some of them are complimentary, others less so: potpourri, a curate's egg, a mixed bag, 'something for everyone'. So it is with *Ring Ring*, as the formative ABBA are clearly

---

[6] We're using the original UK releases as the basis of our scribblings here.
[7] In contrast to Mr Holland, when writing the individual song reviews, I was hearing most of the pre-*Super Trouper* albums in full for the first time. I came back six months later to do these overviews, having heard the albums many more times. They may not yet be well-worn armchairs, but they've certainly taken on the cosiness of a comfy settee.

experimenting with a range of styles, not sure at this stage which way they'll go. Some of them are bang on the zeitgeist of the early '70s, others less so, but you can't deny the breadth of their attempts, nor can you question the influence of their songwriting expertise dating from their pre-ABBA lives. Uncharitably you might say they're throwing a bunch of sh*t at us – and I'm using sh*t in its American sense of 'stuff', more than making a qualitative judgement – to see what sticks, or at least stays around long enough to give them a whiff of where future success may lie.

For me, you can split the songs on *Ring Ring* into four groups: foot-tappers (I include 'Nina' in this group, which is reaching a bit, I know); early-'70s vibe; 'woe is me' ballads; and old-time dance hall-type stuff (I'm thinking of 'She's My Kind of Girl' and 'I Am Just a Girl', although the former was first used in a film genre about as far away from the dance hall as you can get...). The order of the tracks isn't as obliging, though, which in my view is undoubtedly a good thing.

We open with the title track, which as a single does just about enough to make the vast majority of us want to experience the rest of this first album. 'Another Town, Another Train' is a pleasant enough homage to the 'travelling tunesmith' topic, and then we get a deeper, darker turn with Ms Fältskog's depressing 'Disillusion'. 'People Need Love' rescues the mood well enough, before 'I Saw It in the Mirror' sends us back down and in fact plumbs the depths of the album. 'Nina, Pretty Ballerina' closes the original side one, providing a welcome uplifting number to give us the energy and optimism to turn the record over and get side two going. It's also a hint at the jauntiness that was to characterise some of ABBA's most successful work.

Side two opens with three songs that should belong in the dictionary definition of 1972/73: 'Love Isn't Easy (but It Sure Is Hard Enough)', 'Me and Bobby and Bobby's Brother' and 'He Is Your Brother'. There then follow two lovely 'sleepers' which are classic examples of the lads' easy control over swishy ballads, namely 'She's My Kind of Girl' and 'I Am Just a Girl'. Having treated us to a whole game of whack-a-genre the band then demonstrates its steely grasp of r 'n' r with the closing 'Rock 'n' Roll Band', which is just about strong enough to close out ABBA's inaugural album.

The Spotify Effect: Outside of the core original album, on Spotify you get some bonus insights into the world early ABBA occupied. Pre-ABBA songs get an airing which to me says a lot about their musical heritage but not necessarily that much about what they would graduate to after the first two or three ABBA albums. There are the charming-ish 'Merry-Go-Round' and 'Santa Rosa' which live firmly in the 'early-'70s vibe' camp, plus some delightful versions of 'Ring Ring' in other languages, no doubt currying favour with the large European music markets.

One-line summary: a curate's egg which merits digesting

Rating:[8] 3 stars

Favourite track: 'I Am Just a Girl'

I might hit 'skip' for:[9] 'Disillusion' – sorry, Agnetha!

Hidden gem: 'She's My Kind of Girl'

G: Formative, flawed and somewhat unfocused, *Ring Ring* is nevertheless (and slightly surprisingly) a pretty entertaining listen. In terms of sounds and styles, there's plenty of experimentation and exploration on show – not all of it entirely successful – but the net result is an intriguing panorama of paths that ABBA could have taken but didn't, and of paths that they most definitely did.

With all this in mind, this is an album best approached with fairly low expectations. That was certainly the case for me. Apart from *Voyage*, ABBA's first album was – perversely – the very last of their catalogue that I ever heard. In fact, I somewhat shamefully held out until the 21st century before finally summoning up sufficient courage to take the plunge and part with money for

---

[8] Maximum: 5 stars; minimum: 1 star.
[9] NB: I *NEVER* hit 'skip' so for me this category is very, VERY hypothetical.

it. I'd always struggled with the *Waterloo* album, so never felt remotely brave enough to grapple with its predecessor which, I assumed, would probably serve up more of the same, at best – and might even be a little bit worse. The unthinkable thought was that ABBA might have not just one but two iffy albums on their CV and I simply wasn't strong enough even to begin to process that terrifying possibility.

As it turned out, my fears were largely groundless. OK, my quality of life wouldn't noticeably deteriorate if I never heard 'I Am Just a Girl' or 'Nina, Pretty Ballerina' ever again. But there's more than enough here to float my boat, or at least nudge it down the slipway towards the water's edge. Even the high incidence of Björn lead vocals doesn't particularly trouble me. Ultimately, the low-cal cocktail of simple ditties plus the odd proto-classic (not least the title track), supplemented by spritely mixers in the shape of the occasional semi-guilty pleasure (notably 'Rock 'n' Roll Band'), plus scattershot forays into random subgenres (such as 'I Saw It in the Mirror', routinely rubbished by ABBA fandom), makes this a curious lucky dip of an album I'm happy to return to regularly. File this one under 'A' for 'A Certain Charm'.

One-line summary: a decent first step and an intriguing selection box of styles

Rating: 2.5 stars

Favourite track: 'He Is Your Brother'

I might hit 'skip' for: 'I Am Just a Girl'

Hidden gem: 'Disillusion'

WATERLOO (1974)

Track listing: Waterloo/Sitting in the Palmtree/King Kong Song/Hasta Mañana/My Mama Said/Dance (While the Music Still Goes On)/Honey, Honey/Watch Out/What About Livingstone/Gonna Sing You My Lovesong/Suzy-Hang-Around

F: The single 'Waterloo' is gigantic of course, but when you take the album as a whole you can see that the group are still experimenting with a range of different musical styles and haven't settled on the formula that's going to propel them to pop megastardom. Winning Eurovision wasn't a guarantee of international success, and you could argue it hasn't been since, but with the *Waterloo* album ABBA do just about enough to keep the momentum going. I've always felt you need at least two big singles to sustain an album, maybe one for each traditional side, and for me 'Honey, Honey' is the only other recognisable and 'acknowledged' success on the album. There's some ropiness and corniness here, and I feel that overall, in what was an important album when it came to consolidating the Eurovision win, there's a slight stumble but no fall, and then a slight recovery. But ABBA's longevity is still in the balance at this point.

Bang! *Waterloo* opens with the title track. It's a sonic boom, and possibly the most arresting start to any pop song. You're flung into the stratosphere for the giddiest of three minutes and it's inevitable you're going to come back down to earth. Indeed, you're down with the other kind of bang: the back-to-back pedestrianism of 'Sitting in the Palmtree' and 'King Kong Song'. 'Hasta Mañana' is a slight bounce back, a throw-back to the early '70s sound of *Ring Ring*, and the temperature rises some more with the solid enough 'My Mama Said' and 'Dance (While the Music Still Goes On)'.

Side two kicks off with, as you might expect, 'Honey, Honey' anchoring the second half of the album. 'Watch Out' is a surprisingly good notch or two up, reminding us that 'rocky' is a very strong second suit for ABBA, before we sag slightly in the midriff with 'What About Livingstone' and 'Gonna Sing You My Lovesong'. You're looking then for a strong finish and you're served up 'Suzy-Hang-Around' which is sweet but in my amateur opinion should be second on the side and not your closer. I would have closed with 'Watch Out', myself...

The Spotify Effect: the Deluxe Edition treats us to eight internationally derivative versions of 'Ring Ring', 'Waterloo', 'Hasta Mañana' and 'Honey, Honey'.

One-line summary: a slightly better curate's egg than *Ring Ring*

Rating: 3 stars

Favourite track: 'Waterloo'

I might hit 'skip' for: 'Sitting in the Palmtree'

Hidden gem: 'Watch Out'

G: *Waterloo* bursts straight out of the gate with the legendary title track – one of those songs whose relentlessly high profile over the last half-century makes it all too easy to clean forget what a brilliant, blistering, rollicking ball of life-affirming fun it is. As for its parent album, the ultimate Eurovision winner also brings a big downside to the party, setting into shockingly stark relief just how inconsequential and, at times, downright odd and inadequate much of the other material is.

For me, the album quickly falls off a cliff into some very unappealing crevasses – and way too much near-novelty-song nonsense – as ABBA continue to search for the path to the summit of Mount Pop but in completely the wrong direction. As bad luck and song sequencing would have it, the trio of tracks following in the title track's prodigious wake all nestle beyond redemption in the very deepest reaches of my less-than-authoritative personal pecking order of ABBA tracks. And that's before we factor-in the ultra-treacly 'Honey, Honey' and one or two other musical cul-de-sacs.

But it's not all bad news. Well, not quite. 'My Mama Said' and 'Dance (While the Music Still Goes On)' deliver a decent enough one-two, while a spark of life is briefly evident (though not really capitalised on) in 'Watch Out'. In its highly formative and derivative way, meanwhile, 'Gonna Sing You My Lovesong' gives just a whisper of a hint of a suggestion of a whiff of the trademark ABBA master-balladry that would soon deliver a welcome dent to all our psyches. But despite such intermittent flashes, I find *Waterloo* a pretty incoherent potpourri of a collection.

I suppose you could make a reasonable case that ABBA needed to explore a few no-through-roads before they pulled out into the traffic and found the fast lane to lasting fame and eternal greatness. But it's definitely the album I'd leave at home if I only had room for eight ABBA albums on any hypothetical trip anywhere – including the proverbial desert island where I'd doubtless end up listening to my ABBA collection sitting in a blinkin' palm tree, as a not-so poignant reminder of what I wasn't missing.

One-line summary: cul-de-sacs aplenty and even the title track can't save the day

Rating: 1.5 stars

Favourite track: 'Waterloo'

I might hit 'skip' for: 'Hasta Mañana' (just for starters)

Hidden gem: 'My Mama Said'

ABBA (1975)

Track listing: Mamma Mia/Hey, Hey Helen/Tropical Loveland/SOS/ Man in the Middle/ Bang-a-Boomerang/I Do, I Do, I Do, I Do/Rock Me/Intermezzo No.1/I've Been Waiting for You/So Long

F: ABBA *ABBA*, the double naming in case we needed reminding who they were, firmly puts the band in the popular music firmament. That's largely down to 'Mamma Mia' and 'SOS', which are all-time classics, ably assisted by 'I Do, I Do, I Do, I Do, I Do', 'Rock Me' and 'So Long'. The album as a whole is an improvement on *Ring Ring* and *Waterloo* but is still a bit uneven, at least taken alongside the albums that were to follow. With the two standout singles we're left wondering where on earth they came from, whereas the lads at this point are probably realising that they've officially made it: they've the critical mass of belters under their belt. They're classics with decades-long longevity.

The supporting act is strong too, but there's still room for a bit of padding in the form of 'Tropical Loveland', 'Man in the Middle' and the circus sideshow track that is 'Intermezzo No.1'. A lot of this album features in *ABBA: The Movie*, so we're afforded a rare glimpse into how they sound 'live',[10] as opposed to on this studio album. Garry will tell you that this album is often a go-to for him and I would tend to agree, to a degree.

What about the all-important flow of the album as a whole? 'Mamma Mia' is a lift-off like 'Waterloo' is to *Waterloo*, and the song is so good that the lads can afford to have two giant unmistakeable riffs, keyboard and guitar, running over each other rather than spaced out. 'Hey, Hey Helen' is a different feel altogether and for Gaz is the template for rock-pop perfection. 'Tropical Loveland' is a definite dip, but you know you're onto a great album when they can afford to wheel out 'SOS' on the same side as the title track. There follows a little flab in the form of 'Man in the Middle', and the old side one closes with 'Bang-A-Boomerang', which harks back to an earlier time in their career and wouldn't be out of place on the first two albums.

Side two offers a saccharine but steady start with the slushy 'I Do, I Do, I Do, I Do, I Do', before we're abruptly kicked up the backsides with 'Rock Me', a bit of a deep cut but a bloody good one at that. 'Intermezzo No.1' then gives us four minutes' vocal rest, an over-crammed dog's breakfast of an instrumental which served as a bathroom break for the ladies in the 'live' show, and would have provided a break for me if I was there too, I can't stand it! 'I've

---

[10] Notwithstanding a little 'cheating' here and there.

Been Waiting for You' – well, I've not been waiting for it, I'll tell you. These last two form back-to-back entries in Freddie's five least-fave ABBA tracks, as you'll see. It's a good job 'So Long' comes along to close the album, since it's a barnstormer of a number which leaves you wanting more, a lot more.

The Spotify Effect: no Deluxe Version of *ABBA*, but there are two extra tracks to beef up the original – the somewhat 'meh' 'Crazy World' and the toe-tappingly decent 'Medley: Pick a Bale of Cotton/On Top of Old Smokey/Midnight Special'.

One-line summary: establishes ABBA as serious pop players

Rating: 3.5 stars

Favourite track: 'Mamma Mia'

I might hit 'skip' for: 'Intermezzo No. 1' (my least-fave ABBA track, bar none)

Hidden gem: 'So Long'

G: Now we're talking! I've always thought that we're looking at quite the quantum leap here. Where on earth did 'SOS' and 'Mamma Mia' spring from? Pretty much out of the blue, I'd conclude, as there's very little on the first two albums to suggest that, just a year after *Waterloo*, such sure-footed, impeccably crafted, multi-dimensional slabs of pop perfection would sound the reveille and give the world the wake-up call that these former Eurovision winners were worth taking very seriously indeed.

Superficially, the *ABBA* album shares some similarities with its predecessors, especially the way it scoops droplets of inspiration from a bewildering variety of musical pools: a little doo-wop here, a bit of Motown-lite funk there, a touch of calypso somewhere else and a bit of glam rock in a different place altogether. What's new is that everything gels vastly better and benefits from a coherence in sound and feel simply not in evidence on *Ring Ring* or *Waterloo*. What's more, the underpinning quality of the songwriting is on a soaring up-escalator. This was the third ABBA album I added to my collection, in the summer of '78, and from the very first listen it had me utterly hooked.

I was already familiar with a lot of the material, of course, and not just the singles: numbers like 'Rock Me' and 'Intermezzo No.1' had helped rip up my preconceptions about the band when I'd crept into the cinema to gawp at *ABBA: The Movie* (twice) several months earlier. But there was still the odd gob-smacker in store – above all, the very much below-the-radar 'Hey, Hey Helen', which from that heady day to this has been an unshiftable fixture in my personal ABBA top ten, and very close to the top of it to boot. I don't care unduly for 'I Do, I Do, I Do, I Do, I Do' and never have, but with that sole exception I've always found this album a rattling good listen from front to back.

And that judgement fully factors-in even the 'problem' tracks which fans generally batter a bit ('Man in the Middle', especially), while 'So Long' remains one of my favourite album-closers by anyone, anywhere, ever. All in all, this album really was ABBA's key game-changer, managing to retain a welcome lightness of touch that dovetails with their fast-emerging, all-consuming musical brilliance to make this my go-to album if I just want to stick a bit of ABBA on. I love the cover shot too. Capturing ABBA on the cusp of breaking into the international bigtime, it invites us to share the thought with them that the fantasy might very well be about to get very real indeed.

One-line summary: ABBA finally arrive, one album early

Rating: 4.25 stars

Favourite track: 'Hey, Hey Helen'

I might hit 'skip' for: 'I Do, I Do, I Do, I Do, I Do'

Hidden gem: 'I've Been Waiting for You'

ARRIVAL (1976)

Track listing: When I Kissed the Teacher/Dancing Queen/My Love, My Life/Dum Dum Diddle/Knowing Me, Knowing You/Money, Money, Money/That's Me/Why Did It Have to Be Me?/Tiger/Arrival

F: *Arrival* is for me the first album where the band 'arrive', if you pardon the corny phrasing, at a more established signature sound that would characterise their continued greatness on the pop stage and their underestimated brilliance in the rock genre too. The album is propped up by another three humungous singles – 'Dancing Queen' (which cemented their 'we're here to stay' status), 'Knowing Me, Knowing You' and 'Money, Money, Money' (otherwise known as M3) – and is simply a better album by virtue of containing fewer fillers or turkeys. One word that sums up this album is 'maturity', it's writing at its mature best. The songs are taking on a more sweeping, orchestral and anthemic nature with the guys in full command of their medium. With *Arrival* comes the feeling that there'll be no more unevenness. This and subsequent albums will be rock solid and holistically intact.

After a somewhat throwaway and lightweight 'When I Kissed the Teacher', which suffers these days from being used in the most cringeworthy part of the fairly awful *Mamma Mia!* film sequel, we experience pop perfection in the form of 'Dancing Queen' which is perhaps ABBA's most popular song and probably the single biggest contributor to the band's bank balance (if you exclude the *Mamma Mia!* spin-offs). 'My Love, My Life' follows and is at the other end of the *Arrival* spectrum, for me probably the weakest track on the album. It's bettered slightly by the sweet and slightly cloying 'Dum Dum Diddle', though I do like the metaphor. 'Knowing Me, Knowing You', arguably the shining example of their melancholic musical maturity, closes side one. Having DQ and KMKY on the same side of an album is a gift almost beyond measure.

'Money, Money, Money', thematically and conceptually clever as heck, is one of the strongest openings to a side two you could wish for. It's so, well, tight and together. With KMKY and M3, on the CD and later versions you're hearing one of the great back-to-back duos of songs in the entire ABBA corpus. 'That's Me' follows, nice and dainty, leading into 'Why Did It Have to Be Me?', another clever and quirky number that oozes irony and charm. It's in stark contrast to 'Tiger' which gets the pulse racing and reminds us how well the band do 'upbeat' and how great it would have been if they'd done more 'live' concerts. 'Arrival' the song closes *Arrival* the album, a genuine near-instrumental 'album track' if ever there was one.

The Spotify Effect: similar to *ABBA*, there's no Deluxe Version but two extra tracks find their way onto the later incarnations of *Arrival*. The first is 'Fernando', a karaoke monster jam and probably very dear to the band's wallet. The second is 'Happy Hawaii', a remixed, reworded and 'Pacific-ed' rendition of 'Why Did It Have to Be Me?', which shouldn't delay you long.

One-line summary: continuing their stellar trajectory

Rating: 4 stars

Favourite track: 'Dancing Queen'

I might hit 'skip' for: 'My Love, My Life'

Hidden gem: 'Tiger'

G: By the time this album was released, of course, ABBA really had arrived. That's reflected, above all, in the clarity of what they deliver here, working for the first time within a pretty well-defined spectrum of intentions and ambitions – although, ABBA being ABBA, there's still scope to head off on the occasional semi-tangent and pull the occasional startled rabbit out of a hat. In many ways, *Arrival* has a decent claim to being the *definitive* ABBA album, in the sense that it's probably the closest one to what most non-hardcore fans think of as ABBA's sound.

That's not to say it's their <u>best</u> album; for any band which evolved as much as ABBA did over the course of those 'first ten years', it's something of a fool's errand to think of any single album or any single song as genuinely definitive. What you *can* say here, however, is that ABBA have unquestionably emerged from their sometimes difficult musical adolescence. And part of the deal is that you're clobbered mercilessly by a clutch of absolute drop-dead mega-classics. Both 'Dancing Queen' and 'Knowing Me, Knowing You' are top-drawer titans, with 'Money, Money, Money' trailing along not too far behind, while the supporting cast of extras ensures that *Arrival* pretty effectively sidesteps the 'three killers, rest fillers' trap.

Confidence and panache ripple through the proceedings, to such an extent that the band aren't afraid to cast the odd half-look back over their shoulders with 'Dum Dum Diddle' and the son-of-'He Is Your Brother' swagger of 'Why Did It Have to Be Me?'. And what better illustration of that confidence than the decision to hold back 'Dancing Queen' until the second track? Or the decision not just to make the underrated title track an instrumental (or as near to an instrumental as makes no difference) but also to defer its stately 'arrival' until the very end of the album?

It's almost as if, only after we've heard the album, do ABBA invite us to agree that they have indeed arrived. This is clearly a band that now knows exactly what it wants to do and how to do it. Even if there are still one or two less than stellar moments ('That's Me' has never completely convinced me, for instance, while 'Tiger' is just screaming for the handbrake to be fully released), the net result is a record loudly proclaiming that ABBA are locked on course to wherever the hell they want to steer their helicopter to next. This album is a powerful statement – make no mistake about it. And both its iconic cover and iconic title beautifully reflect that simple fact.

One-line summary: not perfect, but absolutely oozing with clarity and confidence

Rating: 4.25 stars

Favourite track: 'Knowing Me, Knowing You'

I might hit 'skip' for: 'That's Me'

Hidden gem: 'Arrival'

THE ALBUM (1977)

Track listing: Eagle/Take a Chance on Me/One Man, One Woman/The Name of the Game/Move On/Hole in Your Soul/Thank You for the Music/I Wonder (Departure)/I'm a Marionette

F: Where to start with *The Album*? Perhaps with the name of the album itself, which seems a touch maverick for a band releasing its fifth studio effort. But a genuinely high-class and coherent album it definitely is, hence the four and a half stars I give it. Why? Well, it's not like some of the other albums which have two or three sensational singles and a lot of other stuff that's not in the same league. 'Eagle', is course, splendiferous, and 'Take a Chance on Me' is an all-time top ten track in most people's ABBA lists, but there are no other crackerjacks in there. It's simply a whole bunch of very, very good songs setting and maintaining a very, very high bar. *The Album* is a peak for ABBA. It's the chronological peak, the middle of nine studio albums. It was also, you could argue, the peak of ABBA Mania, with *The Album* coming out at the same time as *The Movie*, and demand for the record outstripping the capacity of the pressing factories.

We're left reeling after the first ten minutes of *The Album*. It's a monster one-two opening punch, with the classic 'Eagle' kicking things off and taking us to places we can only imagine. On its heels is 'Take a Chance on Me', which is as close to perfect pop as you're ever likely to hear. So much going on in these songs, yet they work so well together. 'One Man, One Woman' has the tough act of following those two, and it's different again, a sweeping ballad that reminds us that this band has mastered yet another genre. Closing out a truly seismic side one is 'The Name of the Game', probably in many folks' top ten, but for me not one of their greatest efforts. Still flippin' good, though.

Side two opens with 'Move On', which, when I first heard it, was slightly unmemorable. With more plays though, it's a definite grower, strangely reminiscent of 'Another Town, Another Train' in the country-ish travelling musician style. 'Hole in Your Soul' pulls you out of your reverie with some driving, deep cut rock 'n' roll that would get the dead dancing. The rest of the side is devoted to three tracks taken from the touring *The Girl with the Golden Hair* mini-musical. 'Thank You for the Music' is of course hugely popular, though not a big favourite of mine, and for 'I Wonder' I would have exactly the same comment. *The Album* closes with 'I'm a Marionette', which is epic, edge-of-the-seat stuff that must have been as amazing to watch 'live' as it was to listen to, with the ladies strutting their 'look at me, I'm on strings!' stuff.

The Spotify Effect: while the oracle that is Wikipedia lists all the various CD and DVD versions of *The Album*, with lots of different language versions and mixes, Spotify goes with the 2001 edition, which boasts only one additional track. This is the Doris Day Mix of 'Thank You for the Music'. It's worth a listen and gives an insight into what ABBA unplugged might have been like if they'd been performing around twenty years later.

One-line summary: silly name, but serious pedigree on this album, blimey...

Rating: 4.5 stars

Favourite track: 'Eagle'

I might hit 'skip' for: 'Move On'

Hidden gem: 'Hole in Your Soul'

G: What do we get here? Simple! The classic sound of a now mega-successful band very definitely NOT resting on their laurels. I just love the fact that there's not the vaguest hint of ABBA knocking out a quick *Arrival 2* or churning out a couple of lazy 'Dancing Queen' re-treads. Far, far from it. Here, their music takes another huge step forward, wiping away almost every last vestige of their embryonic sound. Yet they're still eagerly sending out the scouting parties to explore new ground and plant ABBA flags there, not least in the three closing, high-class tracks from the mini-musical *The Girl with the Golden Hair*.

One thing that definitely doesn't change, though, is the positioning of an absolutely ginormous humdinger of a single not first but second on the track listing. In contrast to *Arrival*, however, we don't just get a good, solid foot-tapper to kick off proceedings before we get to the deceptive brilliance of 'Take a Chance on Me'. No – we get an absolute epic. Straying towards the frontiers of prog rock, 'Eagle' isn't just a masterpiece – it's a *long* masterpiece (especially by ABBA's standards), spreading its imperious wings over nearly six minutes of groove time. That's not just remarkable confidence for a chart-friendly 'pop band' – it also demonstrates an iron-clad commitment not to sell out on their creative vision.

And to say that the songwriting on *The Album* has grown and matured would be to damn it with the faintest of praise. But while almost everything feels a lot more 'adult', this in no way means the ability to deliver an endless river of memorable melodies has been clogged up with pack ice. For me, the only place where the risk-taking doesn't quite pay off is at the start of 'Move On': incorporating the spoken word into pop songs is always a highwire act and it doesn't really work here, sounding just a tad facile.

Apart from that, everywhere you look (and listen), you're met with unimpeachable evidence that Benny and Björn (and Stig Anderson, where relevant) are continuing to build on the solid foundations laboured over during the previous five years and constructing something deliberately designed to be super-resilient to the fads and foibles of passing fashion. As a result, we find jewels like 'The Name of the Game', an object exercise in how to fuse sparkling tunes with emotional maturity and genuine insight. Yet the greatest strength of *The Album* – certainly compared with the previous four albums – is perhaps its capacity to span styles and tempos while retaining its creative coherence. This is the record that leaves you in absolutely no doubt at all that ABBA are in it for the long haul.

One-line summary: bold, ambitious and another significant step forward

Rating: 4.5 stars

Favourite track: 'Eagle'

I might hit 'skip' for: 'Move On'

Hidden gem: 'I'm a Marionette'

VOULEZ-VOUS (1979)

Track listing: As Good as New/Voulez-Vous/I Have a Dream/Angeleyes/The King Has Lost His Crown/Does Your Mother Know/If It Wasn't for the Nights/Chiquitita/Lovers (Live a Little Longer)/Kisses of Fire

F: *Voulez-Vous* is an odd album to review, for a number of reasons. A long time in gestation, during the famous *Voulez-Vous* sessions it had a bunch of false starts and not much to show for six months' work in the studio before finding its feet. As an original album it's in the middle of the pack, but when you factor in the three additional, 'bonus' tracks, mentioned in the Spotify section below, this takes it up to truly stellar status. It's also thought of as primarily a disco album, since it came out at the time when disco was near its zenith, but again that does an injustice to the stomping 'Does Your Mother Know', the schlager-influenced, commercially enormous and deeply personal 'Chiquitita', the dreamy 'I Have a Dream' and the anti-dreamy 'Angeleyes'. It's yet another album showcasing the band's very high comfort levels with a variety of genres, though you could argue that the later albums do narrow their focus somewhat.

On the original release, side one stumbles out of the blocks slightly with 'As Good as New', showing early disco pretensions before sliding into pure pop. The album's title track firmly hoicks us back into the domain of darn-good-disco, and was the result of the lads heading to the Caribbean for a bit of musical inspiration – perhaps not as incongruous as it sounds – and to be closer to the US, the ancestral home of disco. Track three slows things down with their banker of a ballad – 'I Have a Dream' – which was to become synonymous with optimism and kids' choirs. There follows the other half of the 'Voulez-Vous' double A-side single, namely the solid-enough 'Angeleyes'. The end of the side features 'The King Has Lost His Crown' and these two back-to-back 'love gone wrong' songs are a bit of a Debbie Downer on what for me is a somewhat iffy side one.

Fear not, though, because 'Does Your Mother Know' storms out of the side two gate with a spare pair of bopping shoes in the best Ulvaeus-led vocal track in the ABBA repertoire. 'If It Wasn't for the Nights' then stakes its claim as the most disco-ish track on the album and is surely a love child of the lads and The Bee Gees, though how that works biologically is beyond me. 'Chiquitita' lowers the pace but raises the bar with a truly beautiful ballad that rightly claims its place at the ABBA top table (it's a very large top table by necessity, probably more of a banqueting table, if I'm honest). 'Lovers (Live a Little Longer)' then bangs its head on that same bar in an effort to jump up and match 'Chiquitita' but ends up falling way short. 'Kisses of Fire' brings up the rear of the original album, rather timidly methinks.

The Spotify Effect: the Spotify version of the album is the 2001 release, which extends the number of tracks from ten to thirteen. And, well, what an addition it is. 'Lovelight' is the sandwich, a luscious, schmaltzy and clever pop-rocker. The slices of bread are two absolute behemoths, the sensationally seasonal 'Summer Night City' and the pop perfection that is 'Gimme! Gimme! Gimme! (A Man after Midnight)'.

One-line summary: Oui, je voudrais bien, merci...

Rating: 3.5 stars

Favourite track: Does Your Mother Know

I might hit 'skip' for: I've been known to put the kettle on during 'Lovers (Live a Little Longer)'

Hidden gem: 'If It Wasn't for the Nights'

G: On the surface, this might be celebrated (or possibly dismissed) as ABBA's party album. In some ways, it might even be seen as something of a backward step. Lighter, brighter and superficially less serious than its predecessor, it actually disguises its diversity pretty well and, while it absorbs some of the spirit of disco, it's never completely submerged by the waves that had been inundating dancefloors worldwide. No – happily, it's got 'ABBA' written through it like a stick of pop-rock, with the baneful exception of the annoying disco strings on 'Lovers (Live a Little Longer)'.

One of this album's most obvious features is the absence of stellar singles. For the first time since *Ring Ring*, an ABBA album doesn't deliver one of those songs that a vast majority of (normal) people would namecheck if you asked them to list five ABBA songs off the top of their head. But in a strange way the result is a more even album. It operates at a satisfyingly high level right from the get-go with the irresistible 'As Good as New', doesn't yield too much ground at any point in the proceedings and finally parts company with you with the glorious fadeout of 'Kisses of Fire' evaporating into the ether while simultaneously burrowing its way deep into your heart.

With consummate skill, it takes some marked changes of pace in its stride and even manages to absorb tracks like 'I Have a Dream' and 'Does Your Mother Know' which might, in lesser hands, stand out as sore-thumb oddities. Even the less-than-essential offerings – notably 'Lovers (Live a Little Longer)' – don't really force the album to break step. This, then, may be the ABBA album that best delivers a good deal more than the sum of its parts. I particularly love the way it dupes you into thinking you've just been listening to a happy album, even though, emotionally speaking, there's a full house spectrum of joy, love, loss, melancholy and yearning in the shop window here. Plus ABBA once again opt for the trick of warming you up with a classy opener before unleashing a mega-single – even though the title track ended up under-performing in the singles charts and never truly secured the unconditional adulation of the ABBA faithful in the same way that some of their other anthemic rabble-rousers achieved.

Interestingly, this is arguably the first ABBA album where the choices for release as singles were far from obvious. It's not just that you could make a decent case for at least eight of the songs; there's also not that much to choose between them in terms of singles potential. And maybe, in the final analysis, that's what *Voulez-Vous* comes across as sounding like – a high-class jigsaw of decent-to-very-good singles or potential singles that somehow just lacks a hard-to-define missing centrepiece.

One-line summary: just a really good, cohesive listen from start to finish

Rating: 4.25 stars

Favourite track: 'Voulez-Vous'

I might hit 'skip' for: 'Lovers (Live a Little Longer)'

Hidden gem: 'Kisses of Fire'

SUPER TROUPER (1980)

Track listing: Super Trouper/The Winner Takes It All/On and On and On/Andante, Andante/Me and I/Happy New Year/Our Last Summer/The Piper/Lay All Your Love on Me/The Way Old Friends Do

F: *Super Trouper* was the first ABBA album I ever bought. It's also the best, in my humble opinion. It came out in November 1980 and still managed to be that year's best-selling album in the UK. After the disco vibe of *Voulez-Vous*, and the dip in disco's fortunes, the band returned to their pop métier and delivered their first effort without a single rocky number. ('Our Last Summer' has just a sniff in that direction but doesn't cross the line.) It's a consistently brilliant album of brilliantly crafted songs, drawing on more than a hint of personal experience. For example, 'The Winner Takes It All' refers to separation where ironically there's almost never a winner, 'Super Trouper' is about being on tour when you'd rather be cuddled up on the sofa with your kids, and 'On and On and On' is about Stockholm high life. And while best doesn't always mean favourite, in this case this is my favourite ABBA album too. There are so many great songs packed into this and I love a bit of circus, me, so the visual feast provided by the record cover and title track video is the icing on the cake. Great fun this album, with a large dollop of reflection and melancholy too. It's got everything.

When an album starts with the title track, either there's not too much else to the album so you'd better go hard early, or there's so much in the rest of it that you can confidently start as you mean to go on. Put *Super Trouper* in the second category. And the track 'Super Trouper' is the perfect exposition of the yin-yang effect of being away on tour. 'The Winner Takes It All' follows up to provide another of those ABBA album one-two punches that leave you gasping at the quality on display. 'On and On and On' picks up the pace expertly and boisterously, almost a sister song to 'Summer Night City'. 'Andante, Andante' comes next and, as the name suggests, is a slow and luxurious ballad. Closing side one is 'Me and I', which is excellent and could just as easily be called 'Synth City'.

Side two opens with 'Happy New Year' and, considering the album came out in November, was pretty well-placed for a good few spins on the first of January. If there's a dip in this album, there's a tiny one in the form of 'Our Last Summer' and 'The Piper'. Two perfectly decent songs in their own right, but when you're surrounded by giants the comparison is inevitably unflattering. That's OK though, because hot on their heels is 'Lay All Your Love on Me', an absolute screamer of a toon with just a hint of disco heritage and overflowing portions of delicious melody. It's all-time top five ABBA stuff for me. Closing the original album is something different, a (slightly enhanced) 1979 tour recording of 'The Way Old Friends Do'. It's an encore-leading, 'Auld Lang Syne'-like celebration of an almost perfect album. Bravo!

The Spotify Effect: all of the first eight albums on Spotify (with the exception of the Deluxe Versions of *Ring Ring*, *Waterloo* and *The Visitors*) are the 2001 editions. The 2001 *Super Trouper* contains the original ten tracks plus two extras. You're left wondering why they added these two, since 'Elaine' is very much in the 'meh' category and 'Put on Your White Sombrero' has a nice Latin feel but is only marginally better than 'Mexican meh'.

One-line summary: spectacular (a one-word one-liner…)

Rating: 5 stars

Favourite track: 'Lay All Your Love on Me'

I might hit 'skip' for: Are you mad? OK, 'The Piper'

Hidden gem: 'Me and I' (not very hidden, actually)

G: This is one of those albums that simply doesn't generally get the love it deserves. To my ears, *Super Trouper* delivers ABBA's most consistently high-quality set of songs to date. Highly polished yet never cold or clinical, it takes all the ingredients that make ABBA great and ratchets them up one more notch. Timeless singles? You've got them: not only does 'The Winner Takes It All' still generate feverish admiration more than four decades later, it was also pursued into the upper reaches of the charts by the iconic title track and the effortlessly masterful 'Lay All Your Love on Me'. Classic non-singles? Take 'Happy New Year' and 'Our Last Summer', both of which have broken the shackles to reach a wider audience in more recent years. Overlooked deep cuts? Give 'Me and I' a proper (and I mean proper) listen and revel in this exceptional display of songwriting, arrangement, performance and production. Or maybe you just want songs that SAY something? Look anywhere and everywhere on this top-notch album. Diverse themes, styles, tempos and moods are expertly corralled and channelled into a coherent direction. All things considered – and I know this is something of a contrarian view – you can make a strong case for this being the sound of ABBA hitting their peak.

But that's not to say new territory isn't still being staked out and new possibilities tested. 'The Winner Takes It All' is evidence of that. But so too, in its small way, is closing out the album with a (sort of) 'live' track – though 'The Way Old Friends Do' also cleverly echoes, just a little, the way 'Arrival' rounded off that earlier album. Plus, in 'On and On and On', we find arguably ABBA's most vampish track, with the prospect of one-night nooky shamelessly rearing its head.

But some things you can still rely on: a potential album-defining track rocks up second on the track list, after another fantastic track has been sent out ahead as an advance party; your emotions are given the usual gut-wrenching rollercoaster ride; plus, naturally, beneath the glossy veneer lurk industrial amounts of doubt, darkness and despair. Like its immediate predecessor, this album really gels. The difference is that it does so at a significantly higher level.

Ultimately, faced with the impossible question 'what ABBA album would you take to a desert (or a deserted Baltic) island with you?', I'd say *Super Trouper* has got to be somewhere in the conversation. It may not quite be my favourite ABBA album but it delivers a phenomenally powerful statement of what ABBA, firing on all cylinders, were all about. It offers one of my favourite ABBA album covers too, with the band picked out by the spotlight and surrounded by all manner of circus craziness. We all love a metaphor, don't we?

One-line summary: class, confidence and quality everywhere you look

Rating: 4.5 stars

Favourite track: 'Me and I'

I might hit 'skip' for: 'The Way Old Friends Do'

Hidden gem: 'Our Last Summer' (again, not very hidden)

THE VISITORS (1981)

Track listing: The Visitors/Head Over Heels/When All Is Said and Done/Soldiers/I Let the Music Speak/One of Us/Two for the Price of One/Slipping Through My Fingers/Like an Angel Passing Through My Room

F: *The Visitors* is dark, no doubt about it – I mean, look at the album cover for a hint of what's inside – which is nothing you haven't heard before. Recorded in the immediate aftermath of Benny and Frida announcing their divergence, it reflects a difficult time in the couples' lives and also in global terms. There's a lot of content around loss, sadness and separation. There's also a tension and seriousness devoted to the Cold War, not forgetting that Sweden sits not a million miles from Russia. I loved this album when it came out and played it to death. It was a very significant record for me during this time of my life. I've always loved it, loved the moodiness. Not as good as the previous few albums? I beg to differ, and different it was, with an edgier quality reminding us that no-one can stay still in the music business; not to evolve is not to survive.

The title track is for me the absolute stand-out song, and in fact I'll be awarding no other song on this album more than 8/10, which is most unusual. That said, it's still a rock-solid set of nine songs, with not a dog in sight. The band of course were almost a decade into an incredibly claustrophobic existence and the fault lines had started to open up considerably. If this had been their sign-off album, as it was for four decades, as a fan I would have felt very happy that they'd left on a high.

If ever there was a track to set a scene for an album, 'The Visitors' is it. Unbelievably atmospheric, I remember the shock hearing this new sound from ABBA, this new departure, when I first heard it. 'Head Over Heels' comes second and was a bit of a flop as a single, but then along comes 'When All Is Said and Done', another beautifully written song about separation which must have drawn heavily on the very recent second split within the band. 'Soldiers' is given the task of closing out the original side one, and it's workmanlike and lyrically deep without being truly exceptional.

Side two opens with 'I Let the Music Speak' and it's not just because of the subject matter that I tend to lump it in with 'Thank You for the Music'. Next is 'One of Us', pulling at the heart strings like no other and staking its claim to be ABBA's ultimate break-up song. Then we get 'Two for the Price of One', which I felt a bit lukewarm about when I first heard it, but as you get to know it you realise how cleverly it's put together. 'Slipping Through My Fingers' comes fourth, another track that stakes a claim – this one as the definitive 'rite of passage' song – and is a lovely exploration of loss of a different kind. The original album closes with 'Like an Angel Passing Through My Room', and the symbolism of the ticking clock as an ever-present sound isn't lost on me. What a clever way to end the record!

The Spotify Effect: the 2012 Deluxe Edition of *The Visitors* packs a serious punch and treats us to sixteen tracks, so it's worth taking a little time to cover the seven additional songs that almost double the output of the original album. 'Should I Laugh or Cry' leaks a certain bitterness and cynicism in the lyrics, and it's followed by the slightly pedestrian 'I Am the City' from the 1982 sessions. 'You Owe Me One' is simply filling groove space on the B-side of 'Under Attack', and 'Cassandra' isn't that much better. 'Under Attack' comes next and was new for the release of *The Singles: The First Ten Years* compilation and it precedes the first new release from that album, namely the different and, for me, underwhelming 'The Day Before You Came'. Closing out this bounty of bonus songs is the demo medley 'From a Twinkling Star to a Passing Angel', which had the distinction of being the first previously unreleased ABBA release since 1994

One-line summary: a moody, mature, mesmerising end (or was it?)

Rating: 4.5 stars

Favourite track: 'The Visitors'

I might hit 'skip' for: 'Soldiers', at a push

Hidden gem: 'Two for the Price of One'

G: In my eyes, when push comes to a shove, the verdict is inescapable: this album is ABBA's true masterpiece. Above all the others, it's the one they deserve to be remembered and celebrated for. Yet mega-singles are there none! Nor is there anything you could really imagine yourself dancing to embarrassingly at your niece's or nephew's wedding. But we're talking *albums* here. And albums are different. Album-land is where proper bands go to demonstrate what they're truly capable of. That's where they draw the threads together and (if they've any sense at all, or indeed any sense of ambition at all) strive to weave these together into a compelling tapestry.

Unity of theme or mood is by no means essential. But unity of feel – perhaps even capturing a specific moment in time – most definitely is, assuming you're in the market to create an album for the ages. *The Visitors* is just such a piece of (dare I say it...) art. It's art like the paintings hanging on the wall in the cover picture, or perhaps even like the paintings mentioned by the hunted woman in the colossal title track. Dark, doleful, brooding, even at times disturbing – yes. But *The Visitors* is also much more interesting and complex than that.

The classic ABBA balance is very much alive and well. Alongside the dystopian synth-pop of the title track, a 'dying love' song with a grown-up twist ('When All Is Said and Done') and the crippling, knife-twisting realism of 'Slipping Through My Fingers', we find slightly chirpier (though still neatly double-edged) material in the shape of 'Head Over Heels' and 'Two for the Price of One'. Shoulder to shoulder with the denser stage-friendly textures of the magisterial 'I Let the Music Speak', we find the hyper-elementary tools harnessed to craft the remarkable 'Like an Angel Passing Through My Room'.

There's certainly nothing here that would pass muster as a straight-out happy song. Literally everything that doesn't boot you straight in the gut has a real sting in its tail. But what I *am* saying is that, like any truly great album, this one has breadth that dovetails impeccably with its depth. It also has that unity of feel I mentioned. Everything has been chiselled from the same massive block of prime musical granite – using different tools and techniques here and there, certainly, but all sharing a common spirit and purpose.

And *The Visitors* certainly captures a moment in time, not least in the lives of the band members themselves – reflected masterfully in that phenomenal cover photo. Four individuals, distance between them, but all still in the same room, illuminated by the same other-worldly glow, their long shadows competing for attention with the people casting them. It's an image that puts the seal on this extraordinary, one-of-a-kind record – an album that gives up its treasures slowly, perhaps, but really was built to endure.

One-line summary: an essential listen and an underappreciated masterpiece

Rating: 5 stars

Favourite track: 'The Visitors'

I might hit 'skip' for: 'One of Us'

Hidden gem: 'Like an Angel Passing Through My Room'

VOYAGE (2021)

Track listing: I Still Have Faith in You/When You Danced with Me/Little Things/Don't Shut Me Down/Just a Notion/I Can Be That Woman/Keep an Eye on Dan/Bumblebee/No Doubt About It/Ode to Freedom

F: And so from *The Visitors* we move to *Voyage*. A tiny trip alphabetically (via *Voulez-Vous*, ironically) but a chasm in space and time between those two albums. When it was released, I listened to *Voyage* back-to-back more times than any other album, by any artist, at any time in my life. Certainly more than a hundred times, maybe edging towards two hundred. I was obsessed with it when it came out, because we'd been teased a couple of months before with the release of two superb songs. So the anticipation was palpable. Little did we know that they were the best two songs, but that pales into insignificance compared with a reunion and a new release after nearly forty years.

From the first few bars you're reminded that the artists are much older, but they still haven't lost their artistic touch. The voices are deeper, the sound is more orchestral, the mood is more contemplative, yet still we get songs that are beautifully put together, lyrically fabulous (in the main) and so, so catchy. There's the ABBA trademark undercurrent of sadness running through some of the songs, and this time, inevitably I guess, there's a wistfulness too. Has the quartet got more in the tank? It's hard to see it, but we're so much the richer for *Voyage* existing. If another album comes along of a similar standard, let's hear it!

I don't have a vinyl copy of the album but I'm pretty sure the track listing is the same as for the CD and Spotify. This is troubling for me because track order is an important part of consuming an album rather than shuffling or picking the cream and *Voyage* is front-loaded with the good stuff. 'I Still Have Faith in You' is a dramatic opening; the first few notes are delicious and the chorus is majestic. 'When You Danced with Me' follows and feels like it's from an earlier era, lyrically harking back to the past as well. Third comes 'Little Things', the Christmas 'banker'. I thought it was a shoo-in for the number one slot, but a lot of water has passed under the bridge and pop's current heavyweights have an eye towards the benefits of a yuletide success, resulting in very stiff competition in the seasonal singles chart. Then comes 'Don't Shut Me Down' and it's almost impossible to separate it from 'I Still Have Faith in You' in terms of how much I like them. Closing out the vinyl's side one is 'Just a Notion', predominantly written and vocalised forty years ago, and while it's not my favourite, it's arguably the best song here. No coincidence since it hails from the late '70s. An extremely strong side one, then.

Side two, not so much. 'I Can Be That Woman' isn't the song to open the side, and you have to say it's filler material, and when was the last time you heard that about an ABBA song? Fortunately, 'Keep an Eye on Dan' rescues us with a total earworm that has everything you'd want in a pop song. 'Bumblebee' follows, and is very sweet, with a climate change message so delicately worded you and Greta Thunberg might miss it. Down to the last two tracks, and it's a solid enough finish. 'No Doubt About It' is the pick-me-up to the side, with that inimitable way ABBA have of combining an upbeat melody with emotionally charged lyrics. Last but not least is 'Ode to Freedom', with another oh-so-subtle political message. It really does feel like their signing-off song, doesn't it?

The Spotify Effect: We're now well into the digital era and as a pretty pristine record the Spotify album is the ten tracks, so nothing added, yet...

One-line summary: welcome back, a good trip and well worth the journey

Rating: 3.5 stars

Favourite track: 'I Still Have Faith in You'

I might hit 'skip' for: 'I Can Be That Woman'

Hidden gem: 'Keep an Eye on Dan'

G: In what sane world does one of the biggest bands of all time release a brand-new album after forty years of silence? And in what sane world does that album not only confound those expecting some sort of embarrassing, heavily diluted, pale shadow of a release but also remind everyone exactly why the band were and remain so beloved and what was so exceptional about them? And what madness would it be for that band to have the sheer impertinence to brush once more the dizzying heights of brilliance they once scaled?

Well, luckily, we live in a crazy world and the age of musical miracles hasn't passed. The really weird thing is that, even though *Voyage* clearly isn't just another ABBA album, it is at heart just another ABBA album. In sound, approach and so many of the band's trademark moves, it could have popped out of the cocoon pretty much anytime in the early 1980s. In so many ways, so little seems to have changed.

Yet on the other hand, here's yet another ABBA album that has its own distinctive character, casting the net widely over the creative waters and hauling in a remarkable range of ideas, then meshing them into a tempting chocolate box of an offering. As a result, it never ever repeats itself. Every song is different, the material hitting all sorts of musical and thematic buttons with something that might be thought of as reckless wantonness – except, because it's ABBA, we know it's actually all part of a cunningly constructed plan.

The slight downside is that there's almost bound to be the odd misfire ('Little Things', in particular, seems an opportunity missed). But even when you stumble on a song you find it hard to connect or engage with, for whatever reason, you can't but admire the sheer audacity of the whole project. True to form, ABBA never even LOOK like falling for the temptation of resorting to 'Return of the Dancing Queen' or 'The Winner Takes It All Over Again'. Instead, we're met with the neo-classics 'Don't Shut Me Down' and 'I Still Have Faith in You', plus wondrous stealth gems like 'No Doubt About It' and 'Ode to Freedom'. There's many a small nod to past triumphs overlaid on a gorgeously reflective mood that befits four individuals now advancing in years and pausing to look back just for a moment.

But crucially that doesn't constrain their capacity to look both forward and around them too. Even some of the clunkier lyrics sound just a little less jarring with repeated listens. Tear-jerking, reassuring, inspiring, troubling, sobering, optimistic, comforting, touching, unnerving: it's a long way from perfect but nonetheless *Voyage* is an incredible reaffirmation of ABBA as a musical force that can still fire devastating emotional shots at us even after half a century.

One-line summary: gloriously unexpected, defiantly ABBA

Rating: 3.5 stars

Favourite track: 'I Still Have Faith in You'

I might hit 'skip' for: 'I Can Be That Woman'

Hidden gem: 'No Doubt About It'

The 'Live' Albums:

F: Genuinely 'live' ABBA performances – as in a proper tour or the odd one-off events – were, in the grand scheme of things, as rare as hens' teeth. They simply didn't play 'live' that much. Not as bad as Kate Bush or Enya, but not flippin' far off. So it's perhaps unsurprising that there are only two officially sanctioned album recordings of them playing 'live'. *ABBA Live* from 1986 features fourteen songs: 'Dancing Queen', 'Take a Chance on Me', 'I Have a Dream', 'Does Your Mother Know', 'Chiquitita', 'Thank You for the Music', 'Two for the Price of One' (bit of a surprise to see that deep cut in there), 'Fernando', 'Gimme! Gimme! Gimme! (A Man After Midnight)', 'Super Trouper', 'Waterloo', 'Money, Money, Money', 'The Name of the Game', 'Eagle' and 'On and On and On' (strange one to finish on). This album passed me by, I must say.

Live at Wembley Arena came out in 2014 and was taken from the 1979 tour. Many years later, the 1979 vintage was the one chosen for the *Voyage* show ABBAtars. Pity, as for me their peak was a couple of years earlier. I watched an edited-down (fifty-seven minutes) version of the Wembley show on YouTube quite recently, a version full of shoddy joins between the London event and clips clearly taken in the US. Très incongruous, mes amis.

Of course the real treat of the album is – redundant comment of the chapter – the 'live' sound, of which, as I've already said, we're generally starved. Some songs take on a new dimension when sung 'live' with a full band. 'Voulez-Vous' has tremendous backing vocalist "a-ha"s, an awesome bass sound and a real spirit-of-the-age disco feel to it. The tempo is a bit slow on 'Knowing Me, Knowing You', but Frida's voice sounds amazing. Speaking of vocals, they're immense on 'Chiquitita', from the back as well as the front of the stage. There's good energy on the perennially huge crowd-pleaser 'Does Your Mother Know', and there's a good segue into 'Hole in Your Soul', which is a fantastic, rollicking version, the best song on the album. 'The Way Old Friends Do', with Benny on his accordion, is a bit of a comedown from 'Hole', but the vocals are still awesome.

Despite the benefits of the loud sound, the mix isn't great on a number of songs, a shortfall that would have been eradicated in the painstaking perfection of a studio album. The keyboards are not loud or jazzy enough on 'Gimme! Gimme! Gimme!' and they're too quiet as well on the closer, 'Waterloo'. The biggest travesty is the keyboards on 'Dancing Queen'. The arrangement's not great and you can't hear the keys, and DQ is all about the keys... 'Eagle' isn't rocky or heavyweight enough for a 'live' version. On 'Thank You for the Music' the percussion sounds a bit pedestrian and has dated somewhat. 'Summer Night City' benefits from the longer alternative intro, which is rather nice, but the rendition is too fast, too 'thin'. In the chorus they sound the 't' in "City", which is different to the studio version. Is it because it's a UK audience? Could they have that fastidious attention to detail? Listening to the 'live' album means that we're spared the visual embarrassment of Björn's dancing; the poor lad looks lost without his guitar.

These are minor-ish quibbles, even though the negatives look like they outweigh the positives, words-wise. It's still an album worth hearing, for the true fan.

G: What's the point of a 'live' album? I'm not sure there are all that many examples of this slightly strange genre that I genuinely love. I can probably only pinpoint about half a dozen that I'd regard as an absolutely essential part of my music collection. To focus on the positives, I guess it can be interesting to hear a band operating in the wild, so to speak, and arguably with less constraints than in the studio. I certainly DON'T want to hear straight re-treads of original studio versions, while I most certainly DO want to get just a whiff of the excitement of actually being at the gig, as well as a sense of a band's skill when the pressure's on and they can see the whites of the fans' eyes. Overall, though, stripped of the visual content and the sweaty spectacle, a 'live' album is never going to leave me totally satisfied. For me, perhaps the main pleasure is to hear which songs really flourish and acquire an extra dimension in a 'live' context. So, where past masters of the recording studio such as ABBA are concerned, the potential pitfalls are that much bigger.

It's extremely gratifying, then, to be able to judge the *Live at Wembley Arena* set released in 2014 as a pretty successful exercise – not least thanks to its relative grittiness and lack of too many layers of polish. (Full disclosure: I've never owned a copy of 1986's *ABBA Live* and don't massively care for it, primarily in view of its ragbag, here-and-there, cherry-picked nature – not to mention the overdubs which inevitably erode that vital sense of authenticity.) 'Does Your Mother Know', in particular, takes on a new lease of life thanks to the greater looseness and spontaneity that's part and parcel of performing 'live'.[11] So too 'Hole in Your Soul', which definitely benefits from that extra dose of rawness and energy. I've even got a sneaking regard for the free-flowing version of 'Gimme! Gimme! Gimme!' – especially Benny's piano work – despite the unfortunate jangliness of the synth sound used for the classic riff.

But it's not just all about the up-tempo numbers. The stripped down, back-to-basics version of 'The Way Old Friends Do' sounds vastly superior and more heartfelt than the tinkered-with version rounding off *Super Trouper*. Overall, it's remarkable how well most of the songs hold up, with tracks like 'SOS' gaining an urgency and immediacy that makes the 'live' versions interesting companion pieces to the studio originals – sort of slightly rough-round-the-edges but nonetheless endearing cousins. Very few of the tracks fail to land some sort of punch – perhaps 'As Good as New' comes closest to being a bit of a damp squib. Top to bottom, though, *Live at Wembley Arena* makes for an enjoyable, if only occasional,

---

[11] Which also explains why it's almost inevitably one of the highlights in the set of any ABBA tribute act.

75

listen. For a band that didn't venture out on tour all that often, it's a creditable, three-and-a-half-star effort and, showing a different side to ABBA, a very welcome addition to the catalogue.

The Compilation Albums:

F: These days, making money is all about the touring and the 'merch' for bands. £100 for a ticket, £35 for a shirt, thank you and goodnight. But for a band in the twentieth century who didn't like to tour much, it was all about repurposing the content into compilation albums. These slight tweaks in the recipe were served up regularly to their adoring public. Here's a list of just the main ABBA compilations...

- The Best of ABBA (1975)
- Greatest Hits (1975)
- Greatest Hits Vol. 2 (1979)
- The Singles: The First Ten Years (1982)
- Thank You for the Music (1983)
- ABBA Gold: Greatest Hits (1992)
- More ABBA Gold: More ABBA Hits (1993)
- Love Stories (1998)
- The Definitive Collection (2001)
- 18 Hits (2005)
- Number Ones (2006)

(NB: there were many more compilation albums internationally.)

And let's not forget the mega-compilations, otherwise known as box sets:

- Thank You for the Music (1994, four CDs)
- The Complete Studio Recordings (2005, nine CDs, two DVDs)
- The Albums (2008, nine CDs)
- Album Box Set (2022, ten CDs)

That's fifteen different packages of a body of songs that numbers a little over a hundred. I can't possibly do justice to all of them, especially since the content overlaps so extensively, so I'm going to concentrate on the two compilations I know.

Of course, I should digress here and say that the compilation concept is a bit odd. I do like compilations, a throwback to my youth where I'd be happy with a shortcut to the artist's talent. Of course, it's the best stuff, the stuff deemed most popular. Yet the standard unit of fare is the studio album, a blend of album tracks and hits finely and agonisingly tuned to get the order and the mood swings just right. So then you take all these peaks out of more than one album and you put them all together. You still have to sweat blood deciding on the placement of each song. The compilation album, therefore, is an artificial thing, a chimaera, rather like a dream within a dream that's been decoded, if you pardon the lyric grab.

I used to have this theory that right about the turn of a new decade, the music became inexplicably a bit crap before sorting itself after a couple of years and then blossoming. So it was, then, that after the latest crappy bout of music around 1990-91, and with ABBA's parting a decade in the past, *ABBA Gold* came on the scene. I got the CD for my SONY Discman that I bought in the US, along with a giant transformer that stopped my US 110-volt device from being fried at a whopping 240 UK volts.

I've never done drugs, ever, apart from the occasional moderate-to-heavy imbibition of alcohol in my earlier days. That said, *ABBA Gold* is crack cocaine, pure and simple. Nineteen tracks – an odd number in every sense, when you ponder it – of unrelentingly exquisite ecstasy. There's no time to draw breath between them, nowhere to hide, not a single dip in the stellar standard. It's a constant rush. You know when you play an album a lot and as you reach the end of each track you know what's coming next? It's the same with *ABBA Gold*. You're mainlining on some of the best pop music ever written. The closest thing that comes to this? Probably the Beatles' *1*, with all their number ones.

No wonder it stayed in the album charts for about a gazillion weeks. Plenty of time, then, to capitalise with the sequel helpfully titled *More ABBA Gold: More ABBA Hits*, in 1993. Except that this should really be called *ABBA Deep Cut Gold,* or perhaps *Pillaging the ABBA Gold Seam*, since it's a rare outing for this squad of songs and second-team makeweights. Some of the songs are nowhere near the precious metals of *ABBA Gold*. 'When I Kissed the Teacher', for example, 'I Am the City' and 'Cassandra' appear back-to-back towards the end of the twenty tracks and form a pronounced sag. It's not an album I listen to much, given that its predecessor is the eight-hundred-pound compilation gorilla.

While Catherine Johnson, who penned *Mamma Mia!* the musical, knew the Bs since 1983 through the *Chess* project, the timing of *ABBA Gold* and *More ABBA Gold* must have heavily influenced the confidence to link the songs into a narrative worthy of London's West End. And so it was that the aforementioned stage show debuted in 1999, ushering in two decades and counting of global dominance and spawning the internationally successful film franchise of the same name.

G: Full disclosure time again. I'm not a fan of compilation albums, period. They never feel all that coherent and I always get the impression I'm just flicking through a magazine at a railway-station newsagent rather than reading it properly. Having said that, through my initial decades of ABBA fandom, I owned – at various times – two ABBA compilations. First, there was 1975's *Greatest Hits* (an impertinent title if ever there was one, given the youth of the band and the sketchy nature of the hit status of much of the material). I picked up a cassette copy in summer 1978 from a piazza-based market vendor on a cheapo school trip to Italy (noteworthy for our grim hotel which seemed to serve nothing but watermelon).

Very cheap too. Very pleased with it, until I got back to the hotel and (in between mouthfuls of watermelon) discovered it was a pirate copy. (Should have inspected the goods prior to purchase – I might have noticed that the two little plastic tabs were still in place, indicating that home-taping had been the means of transferring the music onto the tape. And no, I didn't have a receipt...) It sounded OK, quality-wise, but the track list itself was a real rollercoaster job, with dizzying peaks co-existing side by side with some quite deep valleys. I didn't return to it very often, since I was by now fortified by my ownership of *The Album*, *Arrival* and *ABBA*.

Several years later (1984, I think) I succumbed to an impulse buy of a picture-disc pressing of the double album *The Singles: The First Ten Years*, which had found its way into the bargain rack at my local branch of Our Price. ABBA had been deemed by the court of history to be a bit naff by now, so I got it at a comical price. Being a compilation, though, I barely played it. What hit you with a cricket bat was how much stronger the first LP was compared to the second, taking the listener on an extraordinary chronological journey from 'Ring Ring' through to 'Summer Night City'. This only heightened my innate distrust of compilations, of course; any album (for any good or bad reason) so framed that it would only represent *The Visitors* through the presence of 'One of Us' was self-evidently almost criminally flawed.

Sometime, somewhere, my copy of *The Singles: The First Ten Years* went missing. Not sure if I lent it to someone and didn't get it back, or if I gave it to someone in a fit of misguided generosity, or if some other fate awaited it. (Most probably it fell victim to a misguided rush of decluttering zealotry.) If I remember correctly, I think it suffered water damage at some point during a house move between student digs. Maybe that was a factor in its demise, which I didn't massively mourn in all honesty because I wasn't much of a fan of the 'late' photo used to provide the picture for the second disc, even though the iconic white fedora shot used for the first one was undeniably magnificent.

What, then, of that music industry phenomenon *ABBA Gold*? Doesn't everyone need at least one copy in their collection?? Well no, actually. I was immune to its attractions for three long decades. I prefer to experience the songs running wild in their natural habitats rather than safely caged in compilation captivity. I'd heard the album, of course. And it undoubtedly set, so to speak, the gold standard for all compilations by anyone and everyone. Yes, there were one or two tracks I'd probably be keen to swap for others if I could have been bothered to think about it. I could even have tied myself up in futile knots agonising about the running order.

But my only significant bone of contention was that there's not a metal anywhere on the periodic table that adequately reflects ABBA's sheer brilliance and the transcendent place they chiselled out for themselves in my musical firmament. So likening their 'best' stuff to gold really does seem to be underselling them quite a bit. Not that I can think of a better title, of course. *Perfect ABBA*? No, thought not. But overall, I've always been glad this compilation's out there and has been so staggeringly successful for them – and I've been content in the certain knowledge that, if even just a tiny percentage of those who've bought it have gone on to give *The Visitors* or *The Album* a listen at some point, that actually amounts to a pretty respectable number of people.

And then, of course, after all those years, I eventually succumbed. Having seen and thoroughly enjoyed 21st Century ABBA in September 2022, my elation and the associated energy burst had to channel itself SOMEWHERE. Almost inevitably, as noted earlier, it channelled itself in the direction of Amazon. At long last, alongside all those millions of other people, I was and remain an owner of *ABBA Gold*. Absolutely bloody love it.

The Songs They're Singing: Part 1

When it comes to the basic building blocks of musical success, it's the songs themselves that are, of course, front and centre. Over their career, ABBA have released over a hundred. All of them warrant our attention, all of them play their own particular role in the band's story. Everyone experiences them in different ways and none of us has quite the same perspective on this remarkable body of work, with all its quirks and oddities that sit alongside its gargantuan high spots. Here, in traditional A-Z fashion, we give every one of those songs the attention it deserves[12] and provide our verdict on each – verdicts we confidently predict you'll sometimes be delighted by and at other times mystified or even irritated by. And we really wouldn't have it any other way.

Andante, Andante (from *Super Trouper*)

F: Beautiful piano and lead guitar ease us into this sensuous ballad. The rest of the song is beautiful too, as Frida's velvety voice encourages her lover to take it easy, take some time, and be gentle. Can you imagine Frida singing this next to you in a secluded location somewhere? Probably best not to, actually. Luther Vandross made a very decent living with this sort of love song smoochiness, which reminds me of Prince's 'Slow Love' in its theme and treatment. Björn, Benny and Agnetha add their backing vocals to the chorus and the end result is a warm, fluffy blanket of emotions and sweetness, rather like a Glüwein or two in a hut halfway up a mountain after a couple of hours on the slopes. This is surely the song to have playing for that all important hosted dinner date. It hits all the right notes. This one, like the US State of Virginia, is for lovers. 8/10

G: I'm not big on ballads, or slow songs in general. They generally have to work a fair bit harder to secure my affection. My default position involves the wandering of mind followed by the glazing of

---

[12] We're focusing only on the English language versions and we score the songs out of 10.

eyes. So a track literally called 'Fairly Slow, Fairly Slow' really does have warning stickers plastered all over it. Here, though, that absurdly lovely guitar hook lassoes me in from the first moments and the way the verse builds so elegantly towards the chorus – Frida's perfect vocal navigating us expertly through the rising tide of sultry tenderness – leaves me no choice but to clamber fully on board. The superb "I am the music…" sections dangle a tantalising glimpse of future theatricality on *The Visitors* and beyond, while the track's perfect positioning – allowing the album to catch breath between the rumbustious 'On and On and On' and full-throttle 'Me and I' – only enhances its understated impact. The last forty-five seconds are *ridiculously* classy; rounding the track off with the guitar hook repeated, then slowing the song down to a complete stop and sidestepping the all too obvious alternative of a fade-out really is a clever call. I'm left with an overriding sensation of a languid round-trip on a sailboat serenely completed and every stay and cable neatly fastened in its appointed place. 7/10

Angeleyes (from *Voulez-Vous*)

F: Lyrically, 'Angeleyes' doesn't pull any punches. A spurned former lover sees her ex with a younger partner, is noticeably shaken and contemplates giving her replacement the warning before it's too late. What I always find fascinating about this song is that this emotionally charged and borderline vindictive topic is delivered in such a melodious and sweet way. This is the second song on the *Voulez-Vous* album to make liberal use of the odd "a-ha" – or is it "ha-ha" this time? – and yet again it works. If I was to be super-critical, I'd say it sounds a touch manufactured, with the drum machine-sounding percussion, the unremarkable bass and Benny's piano work (faultless, of course) nevertheless resulting in a slightly bland blend. The lyrics and the vocals put it on the right side of memorable though, lifting it to mid-table in the second division of the ABBA league. 7/10

G: ABBA – masters of the art of the "a-ha". Or in this case, the "ah-ha-ha". For me, this track is all about the lightly tripping synth riff and all those "ah-ha-ha"s dropped in at strategic points along the way. To be more precise, it's all about the interweaving of those two elements, instantly staking out a slice of fresh, distinctive territory for the song. The rest is all reasonably straightforward, enjoyable enough but relatively unremarkable. The chorus is perfectly decent, albeit a couple of notches adrift of classic status. But no sooner does my mind start to drift just a little and start reflecting on potential amendments to my latest online grocery order than BACK comes that hypnotic synth riff and some more divinely delivered "ah-ha-ha"s and my full attention is right back exactly where it needs to be. 7/10

Another Town, Another Train (from *Ring Ring*)

F: (First time, by which I mean my first time hearing this.) What's this? Björn leading the vocals; you don't get that very often. A sweet song, this. I wonder if there's a touch of Simon & Garfunkel's influence over the subject matter – and treatment, actually: the idea of needing to say goodbye to someone, heading away, and being between places, perhaps touring and spending a lot of time travelling the trains. Nice, slightly flute-y keyboard work – I don't think it's another woodwind instrument tooting along. I feel very calmed by this one, an early '70s feel to it. I'm liking the acoustic guitar and could see this one going down very well 'unplugged' in front of a smaller audience in an intimate venue. Any song with 'groovy' in the lyrics gets an approving nod from me. Gentle, harmless stuff. 5/10

G: Call me crazy but, generally, I really don't have any problem at all with Björn having the odd runout on lead vocals. One of the big plus points is that it can really tee up a chorus where Agnetha and Frida swoop onto the scene together, maximising the impact of their arrival. Björn's voice also has that natural melancholic quality which helps him slip effortlessly into the role of self-pitying "no-good bum" with utterly convincing results. That makes it a great fit for any material which plays the woe-is-me or I-think-I've-just-made-a-terrible-mistake card. Which is actually quite a decent slab of ABBA material. With its instantly catchy chorus, this track is an early test drive for all these features as it competently, if undemandingly, deploys the trusty railways-as-a-metaphor-for-life trope. For a sad song, it also skips along quite briskly – a trick ABBA were to pull off expertly time and time again throughout the course of their phenomenal career and another defining feature of their work. 6/10

Arrival (from *Arrival*)

F: My first time hearing this, which is a bit odd, let's face it, for a track that gives its name to the title of the album. For me, it starts with the feel of an album track too, a big weighty anchor to the ship in rather the same way as 'The Visitors' was for that eponymous album. I found 'When You Danced with Me' from *Voyage* oddly reminiscent of 'Arrival'; perhaps it's the bagpipe-like keyboard sound, perhaps not. It's perfectly placed at the end of the album, a strong sign-off and an 'au revoir' rather than an 'adieu'. And 'arrival' too: arrival of what, who? As the last track, this messes with me linguistically too, I have to tell you. An interesting song, this one, since many ABBA songs have so many different ornaments in them, yet this is a reworking of a few notes and one essential refrain. But work it does, and I like it too. Definitely makes me feel like someone's saying goodbye, not hello. 7/10

G: Putting to one side the fact that it always makes me think more of departures than arrivals, I've always very much enjoyed this little curio. And quite a departure it is too in terms of style and approach. Benny's synths beautifully evoke the overriding Highland/Hebridean mood, while the wordless, choral-style vocals conjure up visions of gathering dusk on gloomy evenings and small boats heading out onto misty seas lapping against craggy coastlines. This track also delivers an arresting change of direction after the nine preceding it – a little reminder for the listener that, for all their newly found mega-success, this band won't be falling into any predictable pop-by-numbers trap any time soon. Or indeed ever. Fundamentally, it ensures the *Arrival* album ends not with a question mark but an ellipsis… Which of course begged the big question: where would ABBA go next? A tasty twist. 7/10

As Good as New (from *Voulez-Vous*)

F: (First time.) Defying the stereotypes, this song starts out all strings and classical pop and then has a change of mind and gets pretty downright funky. I'm imagining John Travolta snaking across the multi-coloured dance floor with some serious Saturday

Night Fervour. And then, to confound us all, in kicks a chorus so unmistakably ABBA-ish you wonder where you'd been for the last sixty seconds. ABBA have this ability to mix multiple genres into a song and stitch them together like an exquisite patchwork quilt. Not quite so on 'As Good as New', as the funky verse and the gentle poppy chorus don't really play nice for me. The second half is more even and has a melody which seems to hint at what's to come with the *Super Trouper* album. Foot-tappingly decent, yet not one that's ever going to stay within the Greatest Hits sieve methinks. I'm between a five and a six...ah, what the heck. 6/10

G: ABBA always knew how to spring a surprise. And it was almost always a good one – though there are a few notable exceptions, of course. So the jaunty, Mozarty string intro here shouldn't come as much of a shock. Nor should the fact that it's the gateway to a song (and an album) that wears its disco-lite credentials proudly on its sleeve. Bearing in mind the last album track we'd heard from them was the dark-as-dark-can-be 'I'm a Marionette', while the last pre-*Voulez-Vous* single had been the slightly muddy and messy 'Summer Night City', this is the sound of ABBA flinging the curtains back, throwing the windows open and letting some light and air back into the room. ABBA being ABBA, though, it's never going to be totally straightforward and back comes the string quartet for the chorus, bedding down beside the popping bass and a few handclaps. (For some reason I've always had a soft spot for handclaps. Not sure why.) Agnetha is as peerless as ever in her delivery of a trademark walking-out-on-you-but-have-I-done-the-right-thing lyric, while the "ma...ma...ma...ma" bits give what's otherwise a fairly straightforward song a nifty point of difference. ABBA generally knew how to kick off an album with a belter and this track is no exception. The message is loud and clear. It's '79 and it's Mozarty party time! 8/10

Bang-A-Boomerang (from *ABBA*)

F: (First time.) I've heard the title before, but never the song itself. Is that an organ in there helping to kick things off? Wow. The song starts a little slowly for me, a touch meh, but then the chorus kicks in and what we have here, ladies and gents, is the dictionary definition of 1970s Eurovision, yes indeed, complete with nonsensical, no-danger-of-being-lost-in-translation humming. Where would we be without the odd "dum-de-dum-dum"? You can still hear Benny in the background with his little fills and trills, but what I really like is the insistent bassline that runs through this one. Not many idle moments for the bassist on this number, they're kept pretty busy throughout. It's got all the hallmarks of a classic ABBA song, like those intricacies that sound deceptively simple and natural, so it's a surprise to me that this one doesn't get that much airtime. Up against some stiff competition though, in fairness. 5/10

G: No frills, no spills – don't you just love it when ABBA take Route One and knock out a fantastic pop song with seemingly minimal fuss and effort? Even more remarkable, their skill level means that even the most nonsensical of nonsense lyrics won't necessarily impede your enjoyment. In fact, you may not really notice them at all, such is their natural fit with the feel and mood of the music. This song is a great example. The use of the shuffling drum beat to drive the track works brilliantly, and even before you reach the ebullient, irresistible earworm of a chorus you've had to fight off multiple killer hooks. As for that chorus, it's as singalongable as you could possibly want to sing along to, while the bridge is also a little ripper in its gone-before-you-know-it way. Throwaway pop you're very, very glad to keep way past its ostensible sell-by date. 7/10

Bumblebee (from *Voyage*)

F: ABBA's ode to the 2020s environment and climate change – and possibly also about getting old and wanting to capture the fleetingly fast movement of time – with the fluffy, hazy honeymaker as its mascot is a touch twee but on the way towards being a sweet homage from the moment the piccolo or tin whistle kicks things off. It gets the full orchestral treatment and would definitely work as a musical or film number for today's equivalent of *The Sound of Music* or *Mary Poppins* in that sort of parental or pedagogic way. I do love Frida's Swedish accent on this song; it sounds very endearing and seems to come through most strongly on this track, of all the tracks on the *Voyage* list. It's a well put together song, without setting the world alight or resonating to any real depth of emotion, which is why it may well get consigned to the 'filler' box along with 'I Can Be That Woman'. I can't see 'Bumblebee' having droves of fans over the age of twelve and under the age of sixty, but it's light and harmless, and that's OK by me. 6/10

G: 'Eco-Fernando' as I've come to think of it. Cutesy and slightly trite, this song nevertheless kind of works. The main issue is, I don't need this and 'Little Things' on the same album. Too much sugar! But of the two, I've a significant preference for this track. Frida drags it back from the very brink of the perilous chasm of cutesy doom, her affectionate, soothing, rather touching reading of the song ensuring it never quite tumbles out of control into a big green void. This type of song can easily get very irritating indeed in less skilled hands. Maybe it's best experienced sitting in a sunny summer garden awash with banks of blooms and sundry buzzing insects – with the surreptitious wiping away of a sentimental tear from a watery eye almost mandatory, especially if wine is or has been involved. 6/10

Cassandra (B-side of 'The Day Before You Came')

F: (First time.) ABBA delve into the mythological world for this story of the doomsdayer that no-one believed, sticking it on the B-side of 'The Day Before You Came' and in the lower reaches of the later releases of *The Visitors*. I always like a Frida lead, but on this one I find myself obsessing over her pronunciation of some of the words – 'bid' for bed and 'secrit' for secret. Usually I find her Swedish accent so endearing, but on this one for some reason it jars with me. Then the chorus kicks in and I think I'm listening to 'Put on Your White Sombrero'. They're very alike and it's hardly ever you could accuse ABBA of repeating themselves. There are some nice chords going on and the song builds in places but then breaks down again. Slim pickings, then, compared to the usual fare in the ABBA banquet. Not a great song, even if well sung and well played. 4/10

G: A classic game of two halves, this one. I'm really rather fond of the verses, with those lovely plaintive melodies and a great vocal by Frida. But I'm not quite as besotted by the chorus and could even be persuaded to agree to a trial separation. It's perhaps a bit too reminiscent of 'Put on Your White Sombrero' for comfort and leaves me longing for the verse to come back again as soon as it's got availability in its diary. A prime example of the regrettable but unavoidable truth that I'm not massively fond of any of the output from the 1982 recording sessions. 5/10

Chiquitita (from *Voulez-Vous*)

F: Flamenco-inspired Spanish guitar sound, anyone? Yes, it's 'Chiquitita' alright, as the lads effortlessly lead us into their command of the Latin style. Dripping in pathos, it's the stunning vocal and the peerless piano that make it one of ABBA's most loved songs. It builds without so much as a mild strain and leaves you gasping in agony before the two-minute mark. The vocal is so damn good that you almost miss the delightful little ornaments on the piano. Four and half minutes in you get a chance to draw breath in what you think is the post-coital glow of the song, but no, you peaked too soon and it picks back up again in an instrumental finish that many classical composers would be proud of, to leave you sweaty and breathless once more. Bloody hell, I could do with a lie down in a dark room after that one, I'm shattered! 9/10

G: Disclaimer: after forty-plus years I still haven't finally decided what I think about this song. I clearly need just a little more time to come up with a definitive opinion. When it first came out, I felt it was flirting with an ABBA-by-numbers approach, what with its obvious echoes of 'Fernando'. And the oompa-ness of the chorus meant it simply didn't match the almost absurdly high standard set during the band's golden run of singles from 'SOS' through to 'Take a Chance on Me'. Following on from 'Summer Night City', I was left to grapple with the chilling thought that ABBA might not scale such heights again. On the other hand, there's so much to admire here: a lovely lead vocal by Agnetha, that interesting, almost baroque flourish in the verse melody, Benny's marvellous ripply piano, the dramatic instrumental bom-BOM after "sure of yourself", and that ethereal backing vocal as we head for the chorus. Plus there's the outro with its pub-piano-at-closing-time singalong feel, which I enjoy hugely even though I know I probably shouldn't. In fact, for me, the chorus is arguably the weakest element in the entire song and — conflicted as I am and probably always will be — that's probably why I'm never quite going to file this track under Top-Drawer ABBA. 7/10

Crazy World (B-side of 'Money, Money, Money')

F: (First time.) What is or was the point of a B-side? Filling up space? Throwing in a rubbish song as a freebie? Have there been that many great B-sides from any artist? Anyway, 'Crazy World' finds itself on the Deluxe release of the *ABBA* album and is a pretty inoffensive effort. With Björn doing the heavy lifting, it tells the story of a bloke who thinks he's being two-timed by his lover, with a clever twist towards the end. ABBA's story songs always seem to narrate so smoothly and with such control. I found myself sucked into what might happen next. Meanwhile the song itself tootles along pleasantly enough and the main hook is catchy too. On second hearing I further appreciated its quality and liked it even more. I suppose you'd call this a deep cut, but if I'd bought the MMM single I'd definitely have been glad to get this on the reverse. 7/10

G: Sometimes a song's so naff you're obliged to have a sneaking affection for it. This isn't one of them. But it does have a kind of dumb charm and Björn's voice really is absolutely perfect for this sort of hard-luck-story-with-a-happy-ending stuff. Perhaps this could have been a pretty solid song with just a little more work. But they probably had another classic on the boil and were eager to crack on with it. As for the storyline of 'Crazy World', the girlfriend's brother sounds like he's going to end up being a right pain in the arse — the sort of in-law you fervently pray will never drop by to see you "just because I was passing". 5/10

Dance (While the Music Still Goes On) (from *Waterloo*)

F: (First time.) Much as I love Agnetha's dulcet tones, I can't help thinking this song should start at Björn's bit, fifteen seconds in. Then, when Mr Ulvaeus does start, the melody and lyrics are so familiar to me, so redolent of another song later in the ABBA canon, yet I can't put my finger on it. Maybe it'll come to me later. What it also reminds me of is Nat King Cole's 'Smile' ("...though your heart is aching" etc.), though that's not the mystery song I can't index at the moment. The more of 'Dance' I get through, moreover, the less confident I am in my Big Nat assertion, and by the time of the pause and the key change I'm doubting I have all my marbles. Another key change as the chorus takes us to fade, and I'm warming to it. I've since given it a multitude of further listens, and have yet to source the echo of its pesky, elusive sibling. 6/10

G: This track starts unpromisingly, those first couple of lines prompting the unwelcome and frankly terrifying thought that we might be heading back into the quagmire of 'Hasta Mañana' territory. But, thankfully, Björn's arrival nudges us in a slightly different direction, more akin to 'Another Town, Another Train'. Panic over! A decent chorus and a bit of modulation ensures we veer another notch or two away from the foaming rapids, even though this track doesn't threaten to pack any sort of real punch at any point. It's just an OK pop tune. But I do still have a bit of a soft spot for using brackets in a song title. I blame the 1970s, when it almost became mandatory and was probably enshrined in some sort of United Nations Charter. 5/10

Dancing Queen (from *Arrival*)

F: This is another all-time-great, how-can-you-not-have-this-in-your-top-ten classic that's so hard to write about objectively without a moistening of the eyes. ABBA have this ability to subvert the music-composing norm yet come out with something that feels so right and so, well, normal. I mean, who starts a song with the chorus for heaven's sake? The piano 'sweep' and then the "aaah-aah-aaaah, ah-ah-ah-aah-ah-aaaah" is so indelibly marked on the psyche. And then the verse! It's as good as the chorus, for goodness' sake. The one thing that always hits me about this song is the balance; everything in its right place, to borrow from a Radiohead track title. It's all so beautifully complementary. You know you're in the presence of an astonishing song when you've already hit your allotted words for its review and you're barely a quarter of the way through. And the lyrics, hinting at the boundless possibility and yet fleetingly narrow window of youth, my oh my. A longish song by the strict three-minute mega single benchmark, with lovely strings at the end, but you wish it were even longer. 9/10

G: A quintessentially perfect pop song, isn't it? I'm not really a disco beast so DQ is never going to be one of my absolute ABBA favourites. Specifically, the relentless hi-hat – which places the song as firmly in the summer of 1976 as memories of the UK's infamous Big Drought – dampens the magic for me just a touch. But further nit-picking would be as churlish as it'd be unwarranted. Heading from the intro directly into the chorus is one of the best decisions ABBA ever made. And I realise I'm not giving Agnetha and Frida's vocals nearly enough focus in these song reviews – their brilliance is almost invariably a given – so let me redress the balance just a little right now. The way they lock together here is simply sensational, both in the shimmering verses and the force-of-nature choruses, ratcheting up a curious blend of euphoria and drama but dowsing them with an indefinable air of insecurity that conveys the inescapably transient nature of each and every 'good time'. Quite simply, this song is iconic for a bloody good reason. It almost dares you to have the effrontery to feel miserable while it's playing. They'll still be dancing to DQ when the clocks chime twelve and the twenty-first century eventually gives way to the twenty-second. See you there. The only downside I can think of is that its enduring popularity will probably mean we'll never entirely free ourselves from the ominous possibility of yet another instalment in the *Mamma Mia!* series of films… 9/10

Disillusion (from *Ring Ring*)

F: (First time.) A ballad lamenting love's loss and the anguish of separation. This song sounds very much of its era. Agnetha on the lead vocals this time and it's also co-written by her good self of course, for the only time in the entire ABBA studio corpus. It's fair to say that our blonde chaunteuse is a dab hand at the melancholic stuff, the classic example being 'The Winner Takes It All'. And if anyone can carry a song on their own, it's the fiendishly talented Ms Fältskog (Swedish names sometimes look a bit clumsy written down, with their Germanic clustering of consonants, don't you think?). This one's got a bit of a country feel to it, especially the strains of the grieving guitar. Speaking of which, the guitar gets the best bits; I'm thinking in particular of the delicate melody that introduces the verses and closes the song. Left me a bit down in the dumps if I'm honest. 5/10

G: Great Unanswerable Questions of Our Time: Part 2,427. How might ABBA's career trajectory have differed if Agnetha had written more of the material? As the only track on a studio album not entirely composed by Benny and Björn – and Stig, as appropriate – this track is quite the curio. But it's actually a good deal more than that. It's a pretty impressive composition in its own right: nice intro; strong, varied verses; effective chorus; plus, of course, a pretty quirky title guaranteed to stick in the memory and stand out on an album sleeve. The whole thing has a well-judged musical theatre vibe that Agnetha was clearly very comfortable with (unsurprisingly given her experience of treading the boards), reflected in her totally assured vocal performance here. A track that deserves to be much better known, I'd say, and not just as a matter of historical curiosity and what-iffery. 7/10

Does Your Mother Know (from *Voulez-Vous*)

F: In these hyper-aware days of levelling the political correctness playing field, 'Does Your Mother Know' raises a few eyebrows. That said, it's probably the best ABBA song with Björn on the lead vocal. From the stonking bass-synth intro to the lead guitar riff you're left in no doubt that this is going to be a high-energy ditty and you're not disappointed. The ladies' deliberately youthful-sounding backing vocals sound tremendous too. You can do pretty much any kind of upbeat dance to this song; me, I fancy a bit of a polka to 'Does Your Mother Know', whipping round the floor like a sweaty whirling dervish with my partner. Yes, the song's basically saying 'you look pretty young to me and I don't mind dancing with you, but that's about as far as it goes, and you'd better have a plan for getting home'. For consenting adults, however, this is musical foreplay, no question. 9/10

G: Dumb songs. Don't you just love them? Or perhaps not... This is a track I never particularly look forward to listening to – and in a strange way I'm not at all sure I actually WANT to enjoy it. But, somehow, I always DO enjoy it immensely whenever and wherever it ambushes me. And even though I invariably feel slightly dirty as a result. I simply get shanghai'ed by the pulsating intro and then dragged on board the good ship Dumb Party, with no danger of disembarking at any point during the journey. The only option is to surrender to the madness, lie back and think of Sweden. The real credit for pulling this one back from the precipice of ultra-corny, slightly dodgy rock must go to Agnetha and Frida, whose supercharged backing vocal performance adds at least two dimensions to a track that could oh-so-easily have sounded like a massive misstep (and, with the passing years, has only sounded more likely to). Those electrifying yelps of "chaaaat!", "fliiiirt!", "daaaance!" are undoubtedly the highlight here. Awesome. Still not at all sure I'd have plumped for this as the second single from *Voulez-Vous*. On the other hand, the song was absolutely tailor-made to come to life on stage, the 'live' version from the 1979 tour really taking the brakes off and letting the song motor ahead in top gear and open-top configuration to savour the cool, liberating air of the freeway to Rock City. Sort of. 7/10

Don't Shut Me Down (from *Voyage*)

F: Co-released with 'I Still Have Faith in You' in advance of the full availability of *Voyage*, 'Don't Shut Me Down' tells the story of a former lover stalking (in a nice way – if there is a such a thing) and doorstepping her lover before asking to be a key part of their life again. Staying with the lyrics, they reflect an incredibly articulate command of the language: take "I'm like a dream within a dream that's been decoded", to marry "reloaded", for example. It's an excellently crafted pop song, with the usual ABBA ingredients such as piano sweeps, violin-heavy flourishes and catchy-as-a-mother-dog chorus in a heady blend of musical loveliness that has the ABBA hallmark stamped all over it. It's almost the best song on the album (and the biggest trigger for hope that the guys aren't finished yet). For me, however, it's not quite residing on the hallowed 'nine-out-of-ten' ground but rightfully occupying a seat at the 'pretty-bloody-good-all-the-same' table. 8/10

G: For ABBA to pull such a rabbit out of the hat so late, late, late in the day is, I'd argue, one of the most remarkable things to have happened in the pop world for a very, very, very long time – and quite possibly ever. It's one thing to hear the years roll away. But it's another altogether to hear the *decades* do so. Top-class ABBA. No more, no less – and a sophisticated, beautifully constructed song masquerading as quite a simple one. Agnetha's delivery here is nothing short of logic-defying. Totally assured, she's got this material right in the palm of her hand. And what material it is, leavened with any number of lovely touches harkening back to the glory years, with everything built to frame one of the band's best-ever choruses. This is a track teeming with musical imagination and harvesting the fruits of long, long experience in the best possible way, its non-stop cavalcade of great ideas dropping off the end of the production line with machine-like regularity and precision. It's the very epitome of effortless brilliance – and all done exclusively and defiantly on ABBA's own terms. It's as if the band, after all these years, are saying to us: "Oh – you want another classic? Let's see... Will THIS do???" As for us, we're left to wipe away a crafty tear and thank whatever power we pray to that it did all actually come to pass and isn't just some kind of weird dream after an inadvisable late-night toasted cheese and chutney sandwich. 9/10

Dream World (from the *Voulez-Vous* sessions)

F: (First time.) 'Dream World', of all the ABBA deep cuts, has had a very circuitous gestation and chequered history, and indeed I'm listening to the version on disc four of the 1994 *Thank You for the Music* mega-compilation. The song certainly opens in a dreamy way, with the barrel-organ-like sounds that remind me of an old-fashioned music box or a merry-go-round at the funfair. Then the drum machine kicks in and you feel like you're being treated to the mixing-by-numbers pop equivalent of 'Hooked on Classics'. It's easy to pick out the bits that were lifted for the far superior 'Does Your Mother Know', and perhaps because of my close familiarity with DYMK, 'Dream World' does feel like it's been cobbled together rather than a seamlessly woven blend of complementary elements. Not bad at all, but not great either. 6/10

G: I always find it hard to believe that this could potentially have appeared on the *Voulez-Vous* album – until the bit quarried for 'Does Your Mother Know' comes along, of course. The track sounds like a band limbering up before getting on with the proper business of the day. I quite like the fairground keyboard that tops and tails the piece, but everything else I can quite happily live without. The song doesn't really land any sort of blow, glancing or otherwise, and you can absolutely see why Benny and Björn chose to move on to other material before the morning coffee went cold. 4/10

Dum Dum Diddle (from *Arrival*)

F: (First time.) I'm not averse to a bit of nonsense in a song title and a chorus, let me tell you, The Police's 'De Do Do Do, De Da Da Da' being another good example. Any excuse to get something to rhyme with 'fiddle' – surely there's a missed opportunity with the word 'middle'? – and the cheeky rhyming of smilin' and violin made me smirk too. I like the idea of the song, that a woman laments the fact that she can't be as close to the man as his fiddle. Musically, I like the bass guitar line as it bombs along, and there's some lovely keyboard work that gives the whole song the feel of a reel or a jig, which I'm sure is the intention with a song about a fiddle. Perfectly pleasant, if slightly unprepossessing and unambitious, but then again every song on an album can't be a belter. 5/10

G: Dumb, dumb fun 'Dum Dum Diddle' may well be, but I don't feel even slightly guilty about finding it a real, real pleasure. I absolutely adore that slightly jarring synth riff and from that point on I find myself, in every sense, hooked. I mentioned earlier how adept ABBA were at chucking in a nonsense lyric without you really noticing and that's very much the case here. Or it is for me. I know many fans disagree bigtime. I'm not a particular fan of 'alternative' interpretations of the meaning of this song either. Why won't people just let it be about a bloke and his violin? With no strings attached (so to speak). And you can't but admire the attempt to rhyme violin with smilin' and then the sheer audacity to actually pull it off. While ABBA are without peer when it comes to delivering the happy-sad goods, they certainly never sounded chirpier or more chipper when conveying a lyric saturated in unfulfilled longing. 7/10

Eagle (from *The Album*)

F: What's the dictionary definition of an album track? 'Eagle' from *The Album* is the answer, I believe. What a way to open the album. Not a single but, rather like 'The Visitors', a slightly longer but oh-so-excellently crafted piece that hints at the serious composing abilities under the hood that would find their milieu post-ABBA-part-one. Soaring, majestic, inspiring, just like the subject of the song, and therefore so appropriate. I imagine paragliders have this on infinite loop as they float on the thermals at two thousand metres, the perfect audio accompaniment. If I'm not mistaken, the ladies sing duo all the way through this song, and I'm struggling to think of another example of a band that can match this kind of sound. It sounds so good, then it's thrown into relief by the superb instrumental breaks. This is a song from a band at the height of its powers, having reached full maturity, and what a maturity it is too. 9/10

G: Who's up for a game of Pick an Adjective? Majestic. Imperious. Panoramic. Regal. Celestial. Or that trusty old standby 'ethereal'. And who knew that, inside one of the world's most successful-ever pop acts, there was a fledgling prog-rock band battling to get out? Is it too much of a stretch to imagine this song nestling somewhere on a solo album by the great Jon Anderson of Yes? Ever since Year Zero of my ABBA fandom, this track has made its nest at (or very near) the very top of the tree, never falling out of my top three ABBA tracks, as far as I can remember. And why would it? This is ABBA fully embracing a more mature, adult-oriented sound – something they'd only occasionally toyed with up to this point. I love the sense of space the song gives you and the way this cleverly combines with a sense of striving to shake off the shackles. And I particularly adore the pre-intro intro – a very clever touch – plus the way Agnetha and Frida really do sound as if they're mesmerised, and even fired with an almost religious inspiration. Although the synths dominate, the acoustic and electric guitars provide any number of crucial interventions, while the backing vocal interjections ("I'm an eagle...!", "what a feeling...!" and that deliciously delayed "...high!") launch the track to even greater soaring heights. Climbing, climbing – as the song unfolds, they pull us up with them into the wide blue yonder, where the view really is quite astounding. And you know what? I'm delighted this was never released as a single back in '78. Sometimes you need to keep your most valuable jewels away from too many prying eyes. And an eyrie at the top of a massive mountain is as good a place as any. 10/10

Elaine (B-side of 'The Winner Takes It All')

F: 'Elaine' is a song I don't know too well, since I bought the original *Super Trouper* album and this one only snuck in under the radar with the 2001 re-release. It's pretty inoffensive stuff, but it's not going to set your pants on fire either. For me the word 'Elaine' isn't something you can really hang a song or a chorus on. Apart from rhyming with 'train' it's not got too much going for it. The result is a song that comes over lyrically as too repetitive, a touch stilted, and how many ABBA songs can you say that about? It's fingers of one hand stuff. Musically, I don't mind it at all, it's got some nice touches like the keyboard solo stuff towards the end, and the backing vocals at the very end, but by then it's too little too late to save the song, especially when it's competing with some stellar stuff that precedes it on the re-released album. 6/10

G: One of those slightly frustrating nearly-but-not-quite tracks. There's nothing wrong with any of it but it lacks that little bit of magic dust which would have transformed it into something more than flipside fare. To my ears, it's always sounded more like a demo than a full-fat, fully fledged ABBA number, with the synths doing pretty much all the heavy lifting. It's a bit of a shame because the words are pretty good and stand up quite well in comparison with ABBA's other modern-woman-in-a-modern-world lyrics. Having said that, I've never been averse to hearing a song on a B-side that (I assumed) I'd never get to hear anywhere else. A hidden semi-gem. 6/10

Fernando (standalone single)

F: True story: last year we were having our bathroom retiled and a ludicrously good-looking Brazilian bloke called Fernando called by to give us a quote. The only Fernando I've ever met. It was all I could do to stop myself asking if he could hear the drums. Anyway, 'Fernando', which was originally included on *ABBA's Greatest Hits* and got lumped into the expanded version of *Arrival*, is bloody great, obviously. You can't help but be drawn to the marching band drums, which, along with the fife-y, flute-y bits, are instantly recognisable. It's an almost perfect song about one old soldier-friend reminiscing to another about their fighting days. I say almost perfect, because the lead is sung by Frida which I've always thought a bit odd since it feels to me more like a natural Agnetha anthem, and the line "And since many years I haven't seen a rifle in your hand" is awkward – you want the word 'for' in second place, surely? – but these are very minor quibbles. I used to be nostalgic, but, ah, they don't do nostalgic songs like 'Fernando' anymore. 9/10

G: One of those songs I've sort of made peace with over the years, after years of fighting it (although without a rifle in my hand). Yes, we've agreed a kind of armistice, 'Fernando' and I. It always used to be the one and only BIG song of ABBA's that I absolutely couldn't abide. Just not my sort of song. A bit slow. A bit cosy. A bit drippy, basically. Worse than that, it was the sort of song your elderly relatives would say they liked – and (if the pale ale and advocaat were flowing at a family do) might even insist on singing along to. Or just singing, even if it wasn't actually playing at the time. At a musical level, I never much cared for the faux-campfire schtick or the whole whistle-and-drums vibe. Truth be told, I was actually pretty relieved it never infiltrated itself onto a 'proper' ABBA album. That meant I didn't have to go to all the trouble of picking up the needle when the song started and plonking it down on the next track, risking vinyl damage in the process. But now I'm older and it's many years since I held a trifle in my hand at a family do where 'Fernando' was likely to be playing. So how does the song stack up now? Well, I can listen to it. It's OK. I can't say I positively warm to it, but I can see it does a job in the ABBA catalogue. That's about it, though. Peace in our time. And not, I trust, just a prelude to a resumption of hostilities. 4/10

Gimme! Gimme! Gimme! (A Man After Midnight) (standalone single)

F: Where to start with this one? Perhaps visually first, as for most males over the age of forty this is the song which most calls to mind the white spandex outfits and the bottoms on the 'live' performances. Let's try to park that image as we contemplate this aural masterpiece that, like a few other songs in the loftiest of company, sees a new lease of life when it's embedded in a musical or gets the sample treatment from the queen of pop herself on Madonna's *Confessions on a Dance Floor* album. Blimey, I'm speechless, or wordless I guess, since you're reading this. There's so much quality I don't know where to go with it. It's almost perfect. Pick me, pick me please, I'm your man after midnight! Give me a time machine set to 1979, make me taller, plonk me on stage and don't come back for me. It makes you weep with envy that you didn't conceive this work of genius yourself. Can a man gush any more than this? I'm going to stop now, it's getting embarrassing. 9.49/10 (to avoid rounding)

G: ABBA's best intro! Maybe even pop music's best intro!! Maybe even MUSIC's best intro!!! To say it shows ABBA at the top of their game feels like underselling it. The metallic ringing of the guitar strings. The drama-drenched swirl of the string synth. The mwowww of another synth. Sensational. And the intro's still only halfway through! In comes the full band and we're hit by arguably Benny's most iconic keyboard riff – with just a touch of panpipery giving it the golden glow of airy space. Utter genius. If the rest of the song stayed on that same lofty level, we'd quite probably be talking about the best song ever, by anyone. As it happens, it just slips down a bit from that pinnacle. The chorus is very good and the verses are fine – but this song really is all about the intro and the keyboard riff. It's also great that ABBA sound like they're genuinely having FUN in the studio. But I think I'd like a bit more guitar driving the verse and, perhaps, a bit more beef overall. On the credit side of the ledger, I've always had a soft spot for the long-ish, somewhat under-loved instrumental section in the middle, which has a great Kraftwerk-y (specifically 'Trans-Europe Express') feel. But oh – that intro... 8/10

Gonna Sing You My Lovesong (from *Waterloo*)

F: (First time.) I hate the title of this song. It sounds so American and un-ABBA-like to me, so I wanted to dislike the song intensely as well. The verses give me reason to feel justified in my initial thoughts; they're decidedly meh lyrically and melodically. But then doesn't the chorus win you back almost instantly? You just know they're going to pull it out of the bag; it's so lovey-dovey and 'upbeat' that you can't help but be taken along with it and feel that they're the worthier suitor. The bridge is as meh as the verse, but it's a top chorus. As I said, I'm not crazy about the gonnas and the wannas, and so much of the song is filler, but the chorus singlehandedly keeps the finger off the skip button. It would be a stonker if the chorus kept better company. A missed opportunity for a classic? 5/10

G: Gonna? More like goner. This very American-sounding song struggles to hit home with me, though at least the first half of the chorus is relatively memorable and Benny coaxes some interesting sounds out of his keyboards. But the track lurches into oversentimentality and lacks the emotional depth of ABBA's later work, meaning it can't really keep its head above water in terms of listenability. And to my dodgy ears, the bridge doesn't sound right at all. 4/10

Happy Hawaii (B-side of 'Knowing Me, Knowing You')

F: I think this is my first time hearing this, or is it? Am I missing something here? This is 'Why Did It Have to Be Me?' from the *Arrival* album, no? Same song, different lyrics, with a bit of not-very-wave-sounding wave noise at the beginning. The B of B-side stands for bollocks on this one. 2/10

G: Daft, undemanding and paper-thin it may be, but sometimes you've got to just reach out and embrace the foamy froth, haven't you? Sometimes a slab of feelgood hokum really hits the spot. I do like the way this track trips along, those snare-drum shuffles giving it just a little shove forward every couple of lines. And I really enjoy the intro and the way it builds, with the bass guitar jogging along on that single note, impervious to any and all distractions. As a whole, the music actually strikes me as a little bit Jean-Michel Jarre-y – a definite plus in my book. And who doesn't, from time to time, like to imagine they're on holiday with ABBA? Exactly. Large rum and coke please, Benny. And do have one yourself while you're at it. Another plus point: this song gives me happy Hawaiian flashbacks to those surreptitious early morning under-the-bedclothes listens to 'Junior Choice' during my 'tricky' apprenticeship as an ABBA fan. 6/10

Happy New Year (from *Super Trouper*)

F: In contrast to my bad self, me' ol' mate Gaz really likes the first month of the year. His January go-to album is *Super Trouper* and his go-to song is 'Happy New Year'. A slow start to the song, echoing the slow start to the year after the excesses of the previous week, and then we're into the chorus. And how refreshing it is to hear a world-class song about the New Year, instead of the tens of great and hundreds of average songs about Christmas flippin' Day. Is it a travesty to suggest it belongs next to 'Auld Lang

Syne'? It's probably a bit of a stretch, but for me it's a great pick-me-up. If we don't have hopes we might as well lay down and die, you and I, to quote the ladies. Quite so. A simple, beautiful song, with lovely harmonies and backing vocals and a delicious sprinkle of flute-y keyboard in there too. Suffers from lack of play due its seasonal nature, but always worth a play nonetheless. 8/10

G: Trust ABBA to deliver a classic song about the post-Christmas dip and the January blues. How very like them to dovetail positive and negative sentiments so seamlessly, and leave you feeling pessimistically optimistic, optimistically pessimistic and more than a little bit conflicted and confused. This song takes the 'Thank You for the Music' template, cranks it up a couple of levels and ends up gift-wrapping a timeless, should-be-better-known singalong anthem with the potential to speak to pretty much each and every one of us. I'm also totally comfortable with the reference to 1989. OK, it dates the song – but in a good way, nostalgia being part and gift-wrapped parcel of the Christmas season. Listening to this track, I'm always struck by ABBA's incredible knack of making it look and sound ridiculously easy to be this brilliant. Which, of course, it absolutely isn't. 9/10

Hasta Mañana (from *Waterloo*)

F: Simple, sweet little tootsie roll of a song is 'Hasta Mañana', a sort of Mary Hopkin-Vera Lynn mélange that you put in the oven and out comes something like Tony Orlando and Dawn's 'Tie a Yellow Ribbon'. It works though! The slightly twangy guitar carries a laid-back tune, ably supported by lots of instruments that would work well in a small 'live' venue to an audience of a couple of hundred. The only displeasing part for me is the bit where Agnetha speaks the lyrics rather than singing them; I'm not sure what that conveys or what it adds to this lovable-ish love song. There's not too much to it – and, you're probably thinking, there's not much to this review, and both are better for that. Multilingualists that they are, you'd expect them to execute the hasta without the 'h' too. Yes, it's a touch saccharine but I don't mind a small dose of that. 6/10

G: Stand well back. In fact, take cover! Hide behind a settee or something! This ain't gonna be pretty. Because this is comfortably my least-favourite ABBA song. I just can't salvage anything at all from it, I'm afraid. In the world of ABBA counterfactuals, the one where they decide to enter this into Eurovision instead of 'Waterloo' is the one that's been known to wake me up at night in a cold, cold sweat. Its syrupy sentimentality and lack of any sort of musical or emotional edge means there's nothing whatsoever for me to grip hold of. It's so middle-of-the-road, it simply can't fail to get run over. And just when you think it can't spiral down any further, you get a gratuitous talky bit. As soon as this song starts (which, in my house, it very, very rarely does), I just want it to stop. And never start again. 1/10

He Is Your Brother (from *Ring Ring*)

F: This one fraternally follows 'Me and Bobby and Bobby's Brother' and continues with Björn leading the vocals. The guys were arguably more established writers and performers, and on this first album it feels a bit like the ladies are the sideshow – backing vocalists – until the later albums when it was pretty much 'pretty faces up front'. A bit of a country vibe to this one, lyrically and musically, until the chorus comes in, which is a bit of a surprise to me. It sounds very like Cliff Richard's 'Power to All Our Friends' from Euroviz '73, and the ABBA song came before it. Very interesting, Mr Bond… I'm liking it though, there's some super harmonies and it trots along like a spruced-up pony, glad to be alive and sucking in the fresh air. Some understated but quite stonking saxophone makes a welcome entry too. A dark horse for me, this one. 6/10

G: A track that consistently leaves me feeling stupidly happy. It carries great connotations of that eye-opening, life-changing trip to see *ABBA: The Movie*, of course, partly accounting for my profound affection for it. But that's not to underestimate the fact that this is a box-ticker for me in strictly musical terms too. I'm a big fan of that opening guitar riff, the superbly balanced he-says/she-says vocal and the general swagger oozing from every pore. Great tempo for this type of rocker, too, while the sax adds some terrific little punctuation marks during the chorus. The great thing, though, is that this song's not just a (mild) rock workout – it's also loaded with singable, hummable melodies, right through the verses and then right through the choruses too. An early ABBA belter where virtually every line's a hook. I wonder if they were ever tempted to go down a slightly harder-edged route, as opposed to just occasionally dipping their toes into the rockpool (so to speak)? They'd probably have made a pretty decent fist of it. A rocky road not travelled. 8/10

Head Over Heels (from *The Visitors*)

F: 'Head Over Heels' starts lightly and joyfully, and has always reminded me of the simile about a cat on a hot plate. It's one of those rare songs where you can dance in pretty much any kind of style too, from a serene, sweeping waltz to a crazy pogo as you freak out in an extreme fashion like the subject of the song. Something for everyone, you might say. You also get the bonus of the double chorus for some back-to-back deliciousness, because it's too good to be only heard one go at a time. Let's not ignore the verses either, which for me are delivered with a lovely tongue-in-cheek irony, and a great counterpoint to the spin-me-round giddiness of the chorus. All in all, then, it's a very solid album staple that's not going to find itself on too many ABBA top tens but nonetheless is a very good example of just how good ABBA's songwriting had got to at this point in what we thought was the twilight of their pop career. 8/10

G: Another song where my appreciation forms a fairly contrarian counterpoint to most fans' opinions. To my ears, with only two exceptions ('Gimme! Gimme! Gimme!' and 'Eagle'), no song in ABBA's catalogue offers a finer intro than this one. And what a song to back it up. Never have ABBA done happy-sad better than this. It's absolutely chock-full of great melodies and sublime musical touches. That falling, then rising keyboard pizzicato effect in the intro. That backing vocal on "and with no trace of hesitation...". Those acoustic guitar flourishes. That pseudo-Hispanic keyboard fanfare after the chorus. That perfect, wryly amused commentary vocal from Agnetha. Her vibrato on the final, gorgeously elongated "heeeeeeeeeeeeeeeeeels...". That final piano ripple. Far, far too good for the UK Top 10. Knickers to the record-buying public. Let them gorge themselves on the Goombay Dance Band and other 'big songs' of 1982. ABBA should take it as a back-handed compliment that most people steered clear of 'Head Over Heels', its top-notch, understated yet overwhelming song craft and its total, seemingly effortless mastery of the recording process. There, I've said it. 10/10

Hey, Hey Helen (from *ABBA*)

F: (First time.) Nice, rocky guitar opening, reminds me quite a bit of the riffs in Garry Holland's work, but then I might have that the wrong way round... It's all rather rocky, actually, and sounds very un-ABBA-like to me, I wasn't expecting this at all. I like it though, it feels pretty laid back and cool. I wonder if it was the inspiration – at least vocally – for 'Eagle' from *The Album*? They're not alike as songs but some of the chords and vocals feel similar. It gets quite funky in the bridge towards the end, and I still like it. The vocals sound full on this, especially in the chorus, where it sounds like there might be two Agnethas and two Fridas singing, but alas we can only dream of a world with cloning. I digress. Style-wise, I'm not sure how it sits within the album, making it remind me of the somewhat eclectic two albums that preceded it. Enjoyed it though! 6/10

G: One of my fondest memories of ABBA fandom is the first time I played the *ABBA* album. It was the summer of '78, I already had *The Album* and *Arrival* in my collection and I was eager for more as soon as I was sufficiently solvent. I knew plenty of the tracks already, mainly thanks to their prominence in *The Movie*, so I was confident I was on pretty solid ground in terms of this use of precious, pretty scarce teenage financial resources. But what about the handful of tracks I'd never heard before? Would they let the side down? Following in the glory-streaked wake of 'Mamma Mia', 'Hey, Hey Helen' would provide the first acid test. As soon as that stompy, glammy drum pattern kicked in and that meaty, grindy, growly guitar riff slotted in over it, I knew ABBA had come to play on my home turf. Everything about the song was – and is – right up my street. I love the vocals' slightly steely, somewhat judgemental, on-the-outside-looking-in quality as Agnetha and

Frida skilfully lift the lid on poor old Helen's plight, before climaxing in those lovely, dismissive sustained high notes near the end. And how about those pinpoint Stevie Wonder-esque clavinet interventions? This track zips itself up in its big glam boots and flaunts them to perfection as it struts its mighty stuff down the pop pavement. And from that very first play through to, literally, this very morning, I've never, ever remotely tired of hearing a song which is very much right in my personal musical wheelhouse, ticking every conceivable box. 10/10

Hole in Your Soul (from *The Album*)

F: How is this my first time hearing this gem?! From the very first bar, this is rock 'n' roll as it should be – and in case we didn't know, the chorus tells us so – and demonstrates rock 'n' roll's almost unique ability to shock you out of your reverie and pull you up by the lapels. I love the Björn low-voice chorus, and only Björn's lyrics can inject a touch of pathos into the typically light and airy genre with the classic lines: "It's gotta be rock 'n' roll, to fill the hole in your soul...". This song really tests the vocal abilities of the ladies, with loud top-of-the-register stuff one moment and then angelic softness the next, and of course they carry it off with aplomb. It sounds like there's about ten people in the band on this song, and while there probably were about that number in the recording studio it's hats off to the lads for making all the elements work together so well. Rousing, get-out-of-your-bed stuff, love it. 8/10

G: Yet again! THAT's how to start a song! The first thirty seconds are off the chart. The last forty aren't too shabby either, from the moment Benny finds his inner Rick Wakeman and chucks in a very tasty synth solo to see out the track. Plus, of course, there's Agnetha's iconic wine-glass-shattering scream somewhere in between. It's a bit of a shame, then, that the nuts and bolts of the song – the verse and chorus – don't quite live up to those outbursts of brilliance. I think it might be the drums. To keep someone like me happy on a high-octane track like this, they need to thud and pound a bit more; here, they seem to pop and shuffle. But it's still a pretty good rock workout and it was always satisfying to hear ABBA reach enthusiastically beyond their and many of their core fans' primary comfort zones. So I'd say this song's very good but it could oh-so-easily have been great. And it really should have opened the second side of *The Album*. Imagine hearing the last strains of 'The Name of the Game' ebb away, then flipping the vinyl over and getting hit straight in the mouth with that opening ker-UNCH! Opportunity slightly missed. 7/10

Honey, Honey (from *Waterloo*)

F: A lovely little flower, this song. I imagine it shifted a few copies among the girls and ladies back then, and I reckon quite a few boys and blokes would have harboured a secret crush on this song too when it came out, since it's such a guilty pleasure. I have the feeling with 'Honey, Honey' that its influence on ABBA's future work is sizeably underestimated. It has the hallmarks of a deceptively simple song that requires a ton of work to get to this stage. Or maybe it was conceived like this and kept its shape; it's the same pleasing result. Some of Björn's best vocal work is on this song, backed up by Benny's gorgeous keyboard work, and the ladies sound so butter-wouldn't-melt-in-our-mouths, which, together with the "ba-ba-ba-ba-oo"s, is perfect for this song about the birds and the bees, and the bees' end-product. The one black mark? The odd heavy breathing mid-way, what's that about? 7/10

G: ABBA counterfactuals part 6,138: alarmingly, ABBA don't give this song away to be covered by Sweet Dreams, who have a decent international hit with it. Instead, they keep it for themselves and have a decent international hit with it. Seduced by this success, they steer their songwriting in the same super-frothy, cotton-candy-pop direction and never arrive at the fertile, sunlit uplands where classics like 'SOS' and 'Knowing Me, Knowing You' are shimmering in the breeze, waiting to be harvested. I can see why the song sold, of course. But there again, I can see why 'Tie a Yellow Ribbon Round the Ole Oak Tree' sold. It's just not the sort of thing I would ever want to buy or even want to hear on the radio. Not at all sure about the heavy breathing effects (on 'Honey, Honey', not 'Tie a Yellow Ribbon'); a bit odd. 4/10

I Am Just a Girl (from *Ring Ring*)

F: (First time.) Love this! A slow-dance smoochy, dreamy dance hall song in a similar vein to 'She's My Kind of Girl' era-wise. What a delightful waltztastic number, and I can't even waltz for goodness' sake! Take your partner by the hand and feel a restrained closeness to them that you can only really experience with the old-time genres. Loving the strings and the brass on this. It's making me imagine my Mum and Dad taking to the town hall on a Friday evening in the early '50s, paying their shilling and sixpence and mixing this treasure with a bit of Glenn Miller and a bit of swing, a pale ale for his Lordship and a lemonade for the Duchess. Beautifully sung, beautifully accompanied, in fact a beautiful song from a bygone era. I Am Just a Convert! On first listening it's my fave song on *Ring Ring*, and not even my style, that's how good it was. 8/10

G: The only serious competition for 'Hasta Mañana' in the race to the coveted title of my least-favourite ABBA track. Fair play to ABBA, though, for exploring all the side streets before hitting the highway to their ultimate destination. But, as they say, if you can't say anything nice, don't say anything at all. So I'll just say this specifically about 'I Am Just a Girl'. Nothing. (Note: I didn't even mention how dire the "la-la-la-la-la" bridge is.) 2/10

I Am the City (from the 1982 sessions)

F: (First time.) Nestling towards the end of the *The Visitors* Deluxe Edition, 'I Am the City' isn't too bad. I don't mind it, but it's not quite setting my tracksuit bottoms on fire either. What I mean is, the verse is a bit plodding, there's a nice "oo-oo-oo-oo/oo-oo-oo-oo" hook which sounds like it's been ripped off by somebody else in the '80s, and the synth sirening and the chorus are alright too. It's just not quite firing the synapses the way most other ABBA songs do. Maybe it's a grower, it certainly has the potential, because there are enough bright little shoots popping up from the roots. They can't all be great songs, it's just not possible with such a high (and wide) bar set. Unlike 'Happy Hawaii', which was on the bench for the *Arrival* album, this one's the better for existing in the first place. 5/10

G: I mentioned a little bit earlier that I'm not big on the post-*The Visitors* material, recorded just before the lights flickered out. In some ways that stuff reminds me of the first two albums as it casts around for a direction to head in. You can hear ABBA almost trying too hard to tap into what was 'happening' in Musicland, to see if it might bear fruit for a band pretty much dying before our eyes and ears. This turned out to be a recipe for some fairly unconvincing forays, all of which sound a bit half-hearted to me. This track is a classic case. I'm not sure I see the point of it at all. It doesn't even sound much like ABBA. Catch me on a bad day and I'd argue that this slightly tinny old thing is barely of Bucks Fizz B-side standard. (I'm not knocking Bucks Fizz here btw.) The melodies neither move me nor stay with me. And bottom of the pot is the very strange "funny smells" lyric. Some bands, perhaps, were born to sing about nasty urban niffs. The Damned or Stiff Little Fingers, perhaps, or maybe Motörhead. ABBA was most definitely never, ever one of them. 4/10

I Can Be That Woman (from *Voyage*)

F: I grew to appreciate 'I Can Be That Woman' after listening to it more than a hundred times in the months following *Voyage*'s release, but I can't honestly say that I like it. It's not a bad ballad, but it's not a good one. It's not Agnetha's best work either, but lyrically she'd been handed a sow's ear and does the best she can to render a silk purse under the circumstances. It feels wrong to write this, but in telling the story of redemption the lyrics are not good. Well, at least not ABBA good. They're clumsy, awkward and on the first listen or two I winced inwardly. I can't think of a single ABBA song from '75 to '82 that does that to me. Bear in mind that if you shelled out big bucks for the *Voyage* vinyl version, this song opens side two, and it runs the risk of you reaching for the stylus and unceremoniously plonking it down on 'Keep an Eye on Dan'. It's a bit like a soap opera for me, a song you don't like at first but you persevere with to give it at least a fighting chance, and in today's world of short-attention-span song-skipping it takes commitment to do that. A song that started out as a two or a three out of ten but because I still have faith in them I gave it repeated chances which raised it a tad. 4/10

G: Not for me, this one. It sounds painfully slow (even though it actually isn't when it gets going), so that leaves it with quite a bit of ground to make up to get me onside. Added to that, the lyrics have a few hard edges and tricky angles that I really struggle with. Nor am I keen on that low-key Country & Western vibe sprinkled over the track. I can sort of understand why some people would like the song (and some people do seem to like it a LOT), but I haven't remotely found a way into it yet. And believe me, I've tried. Send me directions. Lovely vocal by Agnetha, though. 4/10

I Do, I Do, I Do, I Do, I Do (from *ABBA*)

F: The jaunty sax of 'I Do, I Do, I Do, I Do, I Do' ushers in the most sing-along, clap-along, dance-along song of the album. How can you not feel good listening to this one? It's an anthem to optimism, the anathema of downbeat. Take your partner, ladies and gentlemen, and join us in a spot of set-dancing, will you please? And what's not to like about Aggie and Freeds telling you they love you, repeatedly? They're singing it to you, you know that. A simple melody, built on and layered, built out and complementary to the core, gives you a glimpse of a formula for songwriting where the end-product can only hint at the effort that must have gone in to make it so simple, yet so good. It's probably not in many people's top five or top ten ABBA songs, but it's a rock solid example of the craft of writing a song to sing along to. 8/10

G: Like 'Fernando' but unlike 'Honey, Honey' and 'Hasta Mañana', I've mellowed on this one just a little in the last few years. I used to find it pretty much unlistenable. It felt like an unwelcome throwback to some of those one-dimensional, wafer-thin songs on the first two albums, and on *Waterloo* in particular. And its schmaltzy 1950s stylings left me ice-cold – that's not a decade I've ever really locked onto music-wise, Frank Sinatra excepted. In that sense, 'I Do x5' is probably a bit too good a pastiche. But these days I can tolerate it if I zone out just a little bit while it's playing. At least I'm not actively irritated by it anymore. Which is progress. 4/10

I Have a Dream (from *Voulez-Vous*)

F: I have a dream too, ABBA-related, but one that I can't commit to print, I'm afraid. What is the sitar-like sound that the synth kicks off the song with and drops in now and again for a bit of continuity? I'm not sure, but it's another example of a uniquely recognisable introduction. Frida's sultry vocals should make this song come with a fire hazard warning. On the surface it's a ballad, and ballads can sometimes be a bit of a Debbie Downer, but this one's so upbeat, so optimistic that it restores your faith in humanity, if only fleetingly. Then the choir kicks in and you feel that lots of other people are feeling the inspiration and aiming for the stars. Yes, we can all cross the stream, cross our own Rubicon and chase our dreams. A wonderfully uplifting number that never feels hackneyed or cliched, at least to this writer whose stuff you've so nobly put up with so far. 8/10

G: Inexplicable. There's absolutely no universe, parallel or otherwise, where I should be able even to remotely stomach this one. Modern nursery rhymes aren't my kind of thing. Nor are children's choirs. Strange to relate, then, that I've never had an issue with 'I Have a Dream'. I'm not sure there's much more to say. It just works, gliding along nicely and carrying me along with it, as if I'm sitting on a sturdy raft on a gently flowing river in fairly pleasant weather. I do like the full-circle trick of kicking off a verse with a song title and then using the title to round off the chorus too. The lovely descending synth riff also makes a massive contribution to the song's success. Most of all, though, Frida's mature, matter-of-fact vocal neatly sidesteps the obvious trap of trying to sound young and innocent. Even grown-ups can have dreams, she seems to be saying, and not just about having more, owning more, buying more. If you're going to have a dream, have a proper dream, as the iconic Dr King almost said. 7/10

I Let the Music Speak (from *The Visitors*)

F: If you look inside the word 'ballad' you can see most of the letters in ABBA, which is very apt since they do ballads so well. If you've never heard it before, you'll find that 'I Let the Music Speak' is yet another example of how comfortable they are in this territory. This is a song for a Sunday morning and letting yourself slip as deep into a comfortable cavernous couch as you can, with one hand free for a coffee cup. Both hands free actually, as the song moves into another gear with a beautiful section of orchestral loveliness that makes you want to conduct it with your other hand. How do they do it? This song sounds late eighteenth century and late twentieth century at exactly the same time. This is an ode to music, both lyrically and musically, and showcases how accomplished the band is at pretty much anything it turns its hand to. Pop music, disco music, one or two-trick ponies? Utter tosh. 8/10

G: You know how most stage musicals last a couple of hours or more? Well, this prodigious song manages to encapsulate pretty much the whole experience in a little over five minutes, so rushing from the theatre to catch the last train home wouldn't be an issue. Even *The Girl with the Golden Hair* needed four songs to get to where it needed to be. This is the sound of Benny and Björn flexing their ambitions and proving they've got an instinctive touch for this kind of music. But it's also the sound of Frida showing how 'leading lady' was a role she was born to play, while the gorgeous orchestral and choral arrangement is complemented superbly by Benny's piano and synth interventions. Not a song you can remotely digest fully over the first few – maybe even the first few dozen – listens. It's one that needs to be peeled away layer by layer, gradually and methodically, before you can embrace it enthusiastically like an old friend. An outstanding pastiche and a brilliantly successful warm-up act for the mighty *Chess*. 8/10

I Saw It in the Mirror (from *Ring Ring*)

F: (First time.) Young Björn puts in a serious vocal shift on *Ring Ring*, and this one sails perilously close to the 'whiney bullcrap' wind. He's going to throw his back out, or his throat out anyway. Bit of an album filler, this one, buried in the middle towards the end of the old side one. The bass guitar is the best part of the song for me, thwamping out the sad lament of another love's-got-away-from-me-again-dammit number, closely followed by a tasty touch of hi-hat on the percussive front. The ladies' echoing of Björn's "this boy cries" and the "ooh"s are pleasant enough, and the harmony is nothing less than you'd expect from the angelic duo, but it all sounds a bit stodgy and unambitious. The bridge feels like it's in there like a naughty school child who doesn't really want to be there. I'll give it the benefit of a second listen and see if I missed anything worth a mention. Nope. 3/10

G: Fair warning. You may need to give yourself a moment after you've read this review. Because I'm most definitely not a member of the 'I Saw It in the Mirror' lynch mob. As mentioned earlier, I rather like the *Ring Ring* album because it's so experimental. Here's a new band testing the water in an almost dizzying number of directions to see where their future may or may not lie. While being very un-ABBA, this song is a perfect example of that intrepid spirit. It's a decent song of its type, elevated by memorable backing vocals from Agnetha and Frida. Björn's 'limited' lead vocal works well too, adding to the song's hangdog realism and frank, self-pitying vibe. Most hardcore ABBA fans detest this track. This one doesn't. 6/10

I Still Have Faith in You (from *Voyage*)

F: 'I Still Have Faith in You' bridged a forty-year gulf since the band had last released material. Released in September 2021 along with 'Don't Shut Me Down' to tease the hugely anticipated *Voyage* album released two months later, this is a song that impresses and informs in equal measure. Lyrically, we're treated to an ostensibly general theme which is clearly the story of how the band's members feel about each other after all these years. It also opens with a Freddie fave, which is their fondness for starting a song with its title. Musically, it's a beauty of course, from the unmistakeable and moving opening notes and the deeper, richer, more mature voice of Ms Lyngstad. The song builds confidently into an astonishingly good chorus which serves to remind us that the lads have officially not LTTed, otherwise known as Lost Their Touch. And we still have faith in you too, so much so that I'm in between an eight and a nine out of ten for this one. Emotionally it's a nine but when I set it objectively against the total sum of their work I knock it down a point. Bravo! 8/10

G: For me, that initial run of six notes opening this song – later repeated at strategic and tactical key points throughout the track – is perhaps the biggest eye-mister in the whole ABBA catalogue. It absolutely presses my 'totes emosh' button. Of course, it's impossible to detach this song from that incredible global premiere in September 2021 and all the emotions it conjured up. But that's not a problem, is it? Isn't every great song loaded with associations of some sort or other? And this is a great song, make no mistake about it, ascending gradually and purposefully to that higher ground – that mighty monster of a chorus – with that six-note run returning every now and then just to help re-moisten the eyes. The whole track is drenched in an almost unfeasible degree of musical dexterity, in terms of composition, arrangement, production and delivery – a fitting encapsulation of everything ABBA learned along the way. As for Frida's vocal, crammed with experience and insight, yet also an astounding lightness of touch – wow! Just WOW! This song feels like a five-minute opera, let alone a five-minute musical. Could it be half a minute shorter? Perhaps. But it's a classic, no question, and it's a song I sometimes have to stop playing too much because it is, appropriately, really almost too much. 10/10

I Wonder (Departure) (from *The Album*)

F: Frida gets a go on this song from the mini-musical *The Girl with the Golden Hair* that ABBA would close their 1977 tour performances with, and boy does she do a great job, cultivating just the right level of emotion on this teary number that would belong comfortably on the theatre – rather than pop concert – stage. The band seems very at ease with the transition from pop songs to musical songs, with the extended piano contributions and full orchestral sound, a clear sign that the lads would be fine moving to the full stage production demands of *Chess* in the 1980s. By the end of the song you're rooting for Frida as her character heads in a new direction. Fun Freddie Fact: this song is home to one of my longest-ever misheard lyrics; always thought she sang "I don't even...dry-eyed like a poet", which is a bit different to "I don't even try, I'm not a coward", only discovered a few moments ago... 8/10

G: I may not be much of a ballad fan but I can spot a slightly underrated specimen a mile off. Frida sounds made for the stage here. I love the arrangement too, which helps bring out every detail in her outstanding delivery. Nice touch to strip the instrumentation back as the chorus starts, while the drums come in at precisely the right moment. I also love Benny's piano fill between the chorus and the second verse. But when it boils right down to it, this track is really all about the sentiments it conveys and Frida's flawless expression of them, extracting every last micro-crumb of dramatic impact. At times it's effortlessly Sondheim-esque. Moreover, this track has surely proved its anthemic worth over the years, emboldening many, many listeners to gird their loins, take a plunge and make a bold step forward in their lives. And that "who the HELL am I..." bit, where you're completely convinced that Frida is rounding on the less courageous part of herself and giving it a bloody good talking to, really is rather magical. 8/10

Masters of These Scenes: Part 1

ABBA's extraordinary success has been firmly and fundamentally rooted in the unrelenting excellence of their music. But this always went hand in hand with their recognition of the role that both small and big screen could, should and would play in underpinning, extending and consolidating their appeal. The way they embraced these opportunities forms a pivotal part of the ABBA story – from their insistence that the world sit up and take notice of a group from unfashionable Sweden; through the glory years; on to choppier late-career waters where personal relationships changed and were put, often uncomfortably, under the spotlight; and finally when ABBA were on their forty-year career break but their flame continued to burn with the arrival of the hugely successful Mamma Mia! movies.

Eight Key TV Appearances:

1. **First TV appearance together, singing 'California, Here I Come' (variety show, Swedish TV, 1970)**

F: Ah, the sixty-two seconds that launched a thousand, erm, hours of recorded ABBA video material. So much to trawl through, so much to choose from, and the springboard is this fleetingly short but delightful rendition of an earlier twentieth century classic. The uploader of the video I watched on YouTube felt the lads were off key; they sounded pretty good to me! What comes across to me from a visual point of view is what an acting and performance presence all four of them have, especially Frida. It seems a surprise that none of them ventured into a world of celluloid that went beyond music videos and *The Movie*. I've got the benefit of the rose-tinted spectacles of hindsight here, but don't they gel as a quartet? They're already romantically inclined at this point, and have been doing a few bits and pieces together musically, but you can't help nodding sagely and pronouncing to yourself that, yes, of course they were going to be huge. They look like a supergroup in waiting. Who knew that a brief stint in a US Western-themed production would lay the template for the most successful proponents of European pop, period?

G: Very much pre-ABBA, but it's still quite a thing to see them all together on the same TV screen, sort-of performing this Al Jolson classic. I know we're looking at it very much through the wrong end of history's telescope, but to me they really do already look like a tight little foursome here. There's a kind of natural balance about them – maybe that's partly to do with their shared demeanour and how comfortable they clearly are in each other's company, as well as their similar height and build. But it does feel like a travesty that it's not Benny playing the piano. Agnetha really steals the show here, though, putting her acting talents to good effect as she delivers a performance that almost convinces me she actually is at least three and possibly four sheets to the wind. And I know I'm wilfully deluding myself but (amid the raucous din) there's definitely more than a hint of that magical fusion of voices destined, very, very soon, to become one of the most famous and familiar sounds in pop.

2. **Performing 'People Need Love' (Swedish TV, 1972)**

F: Not quite ABBA yet, but now billed as Björn and Benny, Agnetha and Anni-Frid on *Festfolket*, this was their first song to make the US charts. They're all consummate performers in their own right by this stage and together they look a tightly woven group, which belies the fledgling status of the quartet. It appears easy-peasy for them to mime. At least I think they're miming, unless there's a mike just above their heads, off camera. You can see why their appeal was so visual, even at this early stage. They look so damn wholesome, so '70s, and this is certainly a big part of the appeal if we're to trust the vox pop sections of *ABBA: The Movie*. They look like they're having a lot of fun performing, as if they can't believe their luck to be getting this chance to showcase their talents.

G: ABBA's first single. Or kind of, seeing as the name 'ABBA' is still marooned in the future, just out of reach. Again, I'm struck by how relaxed and comfortable they seem while they're miming to this song – like Agnetha and Björn have dropped round to Frida and

Benny's for a Friday night takeaway and, on the spot, they've improvised a very serviceable pop ditty as part of an impromptu songwriting session. I think it's easy to underplay how important that sense of ease and comfort in each other's company was to ABBA's initial success. I'm not at all sure a group like ABBA would have been able to withstand an awful lot of internal creative friction. That sense that they're all basically pulling in the same direction was part and parcel of everything they delivered for a good slab of that first ten years.

3. Performing 'Waterloo' at the Eurovision Song Contest (Brighton, UK, 1974)

F: Spoiler alert: this ain't just a key appearance, it's *the* appearance, appearing at number one in Freddie's fave five on-screen ABBA bits, as you'll see towards the end of this book! It's hard to come up with something new to say about the three minutes that defines the future course of practically the only loved European institution. The legendary David Vine introduction, referring to them as "the ABBA Group", is regularly borrowed by impersonators I'm sure. The conductor's donning of Napoleonic gear is a genius move, especially when you think how staid Eurovision was in the mid-1970s. It's easy to forget too that Sweden had never won Eurovision until this year. I wish I'd met my 'destiny' in quite a similar way. Björn's sounding good on backing vocals and Agnetha looks pleased as punch in the victorious reprise. Her blue upturned-funnel plus-twos are still wrong though, half a century later. It's good to see the original – late and great – Stig take a bow too. Top TV, seminal moments.

G: Impossible to watch this with truly fresh eyes, of course. We know it won and we know what it lit the touchpaper to. We even know the conductor's going to walk on dressed like Napoleon. I love Björn's half-strangled yelp of "yep!" as Frida and Agnetha pile down towards the front of the stage, the pounding intro triggering an almost visceral sense of excitement and anticipation. I think we can call this a nerveless performance, even though it almost certainly wasn't. Not a hint of over-rehearsal or over-confidence, it all feels so natural. They're having an absolute ball, as if the most important thing isn't the eventual result but being there, on that stage, right there and then, performing that song with each other.

The biggest accolade I can offer is that, by the standards of Eurovision 1974, it's like watching a song that's been entered for the wrong contest. More than that, ABBA don't remotely come across as an early-career band at all, all those years of individual experience pooling together to deliver something that, in Eurovision terms, comes from somewhere so far left-field it's still hard to process what's actually happening out there on that stage. Consummate songcraft, consummate delivery, consummate presentation, consummate everything. Still not sure about Frida's hairstyle, though. A historic clip, in its way.

4. **Performing 'Waterloo' and 'SOS' on Seaside Special (BBC, 1975)**

F: I tell you what, it's a tough musical act to follow Lulu. She was huge in the mid-'70s. I remember my folks taking me and my brothers to see her perform the year before while we were on holiday on England's south coast, and she was a top draw, like Mike Yarwood was. Mind you, that evening ended badly as we were in a car crash – not our fault! – and spent the night in hospital. Anyway, ABBA following Lulu, a tall order. I'm not sure what Tony Blackburn's going on about in his intro, it was last year they won the Eurovision Song Contest, not "a couple of years ago".

They start on safe ground with 'Waterloo' of course, and again you have to say the vocals sound so damn good. Then they're inside the big top for 'SOS' which was to buy them at least another few months at the top of pop's roll call. Agnetha's sporting her readjusted gnashers, looking very well, as is Frida. They're wearing their animal print outfits made famous by the tours and copycat bands the world over, but boy they're really short! It must have been pretty risqué clothing back in the mid-'70s. Their performance is true quality though, evidenced by the fact that it's dated so much better than most of the other acts on that show. Sheesh, were the '70s really that naff?

G: For some reason, I've got a soft spot for the clips where Benny straps on a guitar. And that's exactly what he does here in the knockabout outdoor version of 'Waterloo' that gives the audience both outside the circus tent and tucked up in their living-rooms at home a gentle reminder of who the hell ABBA are and were, in case they'd forgotten during the band's post-Eurovision dip in fortunes. Looking at that crowd, I wonder how many of those youngsters (as the 1970s would have termed them) dined out later in their lives on the fact that they'd been "that close!" to ABBA.

Moreover, here ABBA are basically their own support act as we move inside the tent for the top of the bill: ABBA again, with a song that's not just new but also absolutely critical to their ability (i) to shake off the dreaded Eurovision nine-day-wonder tag and (ii) to be seen as much more than mere purveyors of throwaway pop. When you think about it, it's kind of apt that we get both 'Waterloo' and 'SOS' in this guest slot. Both songs were, in their own very different ways, real statements of intent. And as 'SOS' unfolds, you're struck by the undeniable fact that ABBA's whole look and feel has changed substantially since Eurovision, the first hint of a slick pop machine perhaps starting to sweep into view – assuming they can nail that second big international hit...

5. ABBA in Studio 2 (TVP2, 1976)

F: I love any TV where we get an insight into the real people, and there's so much to appreciate in this show. It's so revealing that Agnetha and Björn try to fly separately when their young child is travelling with them. Studio 2 must have been a pretty big deal in Poland to get this gig. Of the four parts of the programme now on YouTube, part one is my fave, containing loads of stuff I didn't know, rather like the research the journalist is doing on the plane in *ABBA: The Movie*. In part two, the Studio 2 stage made out of letters looks very cool. And the band look like they're genuinely enjoying it – there's less pressure miming I guess – while the audience look really into it too. They're having so much fun, the crowd and ABBA, with the ABBA-branded cushion-balloons on stage and in the audience during 'Tiger'. The 1920s outfits in 'Money, Money, Money' are really good too. The beginning and closing bits of part four are strangely reminiscent of *Voyage*'s 'When You Danced with Me'. Super stuff!

G: You can look at this Polish TV special in one of two ways: an intrepid expedition behind the Iron Curtain, or a quick hop across the Baltic. Whatever the case – and once you put Frida and Björn's misspelt names in the captions to the back of your mind – it shows plenty of ambition, I think, to see ABBA starting to embrace the possibilities of the international TV special. Interesting to see that two versions of the band's name are now co-existing – the one with the mirrored 'B's now beginning to vie with the earlier one comprising the conventional 'ABBA' spelling. It's like seeing evolution in action, with natural selection about to determine which of the two competitor strains will become dominant and which one will represent a dead-end. Talking of evolution, this show has the feeling of something of a dry run for *ABBA: The Movie*, with its fly-on-the-wall element, the madcap press scrums, the airport/airline scenes and a little bit of fan mania thrown in. There's even the odd awkward interview moment and a little gratuitous Kenny Everett-style zaniness chucked in for good measure.

Most importantly, though, there's a whole lot to enjoy once ABBA actually arrive in Studio 2. And the slightly precipitous staircase entrance to 'Dancing Queen' (in heels/platforms, mind, and with Benny back on acoustic guitar) is a nice touch. As ever, as they mime their way through most of *Arrival* and a couple of other classics, there's a warmth and ease about their relationship with both the audience and the cameras. More than that, ABBA almost routinely seem to glow in this sort of setting. They perform with such easy mobility and phenomenal charm, it's tempting to forget that working a crowd and a camera at the same time isn't necessarily the simplest thing to do. Not quite sure why Frida's *quite* so chirpy during 'Knowing Me, Knowing You' but what do I know? All thoroughly enjoyable and yet another reminder that ABBA were far from being the recording studio recluses they were slightly stereotyped as in some quarters as their career progressed. You could even argue that the TV studio was their most natural habitat of all. Strangely, the highlights for me are 'My Love, My Life' and 'When I Kissed the Teacher', two songs I'm generally a touch cool about. It's nice to see them come alive in the (mimed) flesh, benefiting from that trademark ABBA dynamism, zest and panache. Prime ABBA.

6. ABBA in Switzerland (BBC co-production, 1979)

F: This winter-cum-winter sports show is a Michael Hurll production, he of Eurovision Song Contest fame. There's some cheesy muzak to start but the quartet skiing to 'The Name of the Game' and 'Mamma Mia' works well; a little Scandinavian time on the piste in their youth methinks. They're not bad skaters either, as we see during 'Hole in Your Soul'. The band is back in the tent for 'Kisses of Fire' and 'Lovers (Live a Little Longer)'. There's a ripple of recognition applause for the emblematic 'Chiquitita' and the clapping along for the closing bit is great; you can sense a genuinely giddy feeling in the tent. It's not all golden though. I'm not at all sure about Björn's dancing on 'Does Your Mother Know', even though the song sounds 'live'. When he lets the genie out of the bottle you kinda wish he'd put it back in again. I find myself being distracted by trying to figure out if they're singing 'live' or miming. It's so hard to tell since they can sing with feeling so effortlessly. As an aside, Kate Bush is certainly singing 'live' (great performance too!), and ditto Roxy Music. It's weird that Kate and Roxy don't appear in the credits though...

G: This really should be a slam-dunk for me. ABBA in their absolute pomp, bolstered by guest spots from the sainted Kate Bush and the mighty Roxy Music. To be fair to Kate, she absolutely delivers what you want Kate to deliver. Roxy Music, though, are giving 'Dance Away' a run-out and, speaking as a big Roxy fan (indeed, a fan for even longer than I've been on the ABBA fan bus, though not nearly as intensely), that's my least favourite major hit of theirs by some margin. And it's symptomatic of the whole Swiss show, from my point of view. I'm not quite comfortable with it. It doesn't quite hit the right note for me. The cheesy, 'show-busy', Saturday night light entertainment intro sequence gets me off on completely the wrong foot and, as radiant as ABBA themselves are throughout the programme, I never quite recover from that. (Nor am I saying anything I didn't 100% feel at the time.)

Actually, that's not strictly true because 'Take a Chance on Me' is a decent enough opening number. But I much prefer ABBA when they seem closer to the audience, are less static and are generally much more dynamic. Showcasing some of the (for me) less convincing material from the *Voulez-Vous* album also leaves me wanting quite a bit more. (Glad they changed the intro to 'Does Your Mother Know' for the album, by the way.) The outdoor sequences don't add an awful lot and indeed end up driving ABBA off the screen for much longer than was surely necessary. It all just lacks that bit of excitement, strut and swagger that ABBA's best TV performances were accustomed to delivering. It's a bit too safe and unthreatening. Teatime TV for all the family. And that's not really 'my' ABBA. I like them with just the hint of a whisper of a suggestion of a trace of a bit of an edge and that's more or less completely absent here.

7. Dick Cavett Meets ABBA (Swedish TV, 1981)

F: While not quite 'iconic', this is an important appearance and one of my favourites too. Actually, I wish the interview had lasted a little longer; I could listen to them being interviewed all day. I love watching Benny skilfully covering his face with the song sheet so we can't see him 'singing' 'Don't Fence Me In' in Swedish. It's the endearing wholesomeness of their public personas that strikes me, in parallel with their playing performances. It's also the point at which they or their designers lost their fashion mojo and the hair and clothing started to miss the mark, in my opinion. There's some priceless visual stuff though. The full concert, according to the accompanying blurb, contains five songs sung 'live' for the only time. I don't know which five, though one of them must have been 'Two for the Price of One'. 'Summer Night City' sounds sensational.

G: So we arrive at ABBA's last big TV appearance and performance. Fin de siècle ABBA, if you will. I actually quite enjoy Dick's deadpan, slightly self-deprecatory interview technique, which somehow puts ABBA at their ease – or at least as much at their ease as could be achieved at this tricky moment in their career trajectory. The exchanges are all very low key and understated and that's probably just as well. In fact, it's all extremely relaxed and good-natured, with the reversing of Frida and Agnetha's 'natural' seating positions presumably applied as some sort of insurance policy against any awkwardness.

Of course, all the chatter is just the prelude to the main business of the evening: the gig. Again, it's all a little static but there's loads to savour, especially for the minority cult I belong to comprising the tiny proportion of humanity which rather enjoys 'Two for the Price of One'. Added to that, I absolutely love ABBA when they adopt a tougher, rockier sound with a bit of attack, so the versions of 'Gimme! Gimme! Gimme!' and 'On and On and On' are right up my alley. It would have been nice if they'd found room in the main show for another favourite of mine, the routinely overlooked 'Me and I', but there you go.

8. The Late, Late Breakfast Show (BBC, 1982)

F: I really can't watch this clip again, or write too much about it. It's too painful. Would I have been as nerdy-looking as the superfan who got to join them if I'd won the competition? Probably. The timing of the Benny-Frida split seems pretty apparent here; there's a definite frostiness between them that gets verbalised – so rare for the ultra-professional team and symbolic that they were really going through the motions at this point. It's hardly surprising then that they split soon after this. How do you work so closely with someone you used to be famous for being married to? I find Noel Edmonds a bit fawning and saccharine too, but there are hardly any talk show hosts who haven't been, with the possible exception of Parky and Cavett. This is another production by Michael Hurll, who probably died after this show...

G: I don't think it would be much of an exaggeration to describe this interview with Noel Edmonds, fleshed out with a brief run-through of 'Thank You for the Music', as notorious. How else should I describe this, ABBA's final public appearance before they went on a forty-year sabbatical? You just know I'm going to use the word 'frosty'. You just know I'm going to use the word 'awkward'. Or am I? Is it really as bad as it's gone down in folklore as being? I'm not actually sure it is. Personally, I could do without the chat about sexy bottoms and the slightly cool exchange between Frida and Benny (whose folded arms don't radiate a feeling of any extreme comfort, that's for sure).

But generally it's OK, when we try to put all the band's personal baggage out of our minds for a moment. They handle themselves in a mature and pretty affable manner, I reckon. The main problem is that they don't really seem to having an awful lot of *fun*. There's that sense of turning the handle, going through the motions and a race almost run. That air of excitement and joy which we saw at Eurovision or in the Polish TV special, for instance, seems to have vanished almost without trace. Goodnight and thank you for the music indeed.

Three Key Movies:

F: *ABBA: The Movie* came out in December 1977, documenting a supergroup at the zenith of their powers, fame and relationships. Lasse Hellström, who did most of the band's music videos, directs it. My trusty Wikipedia also tells me that in May 2022 the film had a theatrical re-release to mark the group's fiftieth anniversary, its first wide release in North America. So there you go. Personally, I hadn't seen this film since it first came out. Not an owner of the DVD, nor actually these days an owner of a DVD player on which to play said DVD, I had to look far and wide to find it, eventually settling on a dodgy Polish streaming site which just about did the job.

I found myself enjoying the film immensely, although it remains challenging to try to park everything we know now about the guy who played the DJ and his despicable crimes. I was really getting sucked once again into the dramatic tension of the story. But there's more to it than that, which takes the conversation into the realm of the, well superfan isn't quite the right word. But let me explain. This film remains essentially the greatest archive of what the band members were like when they weren't on stage, and is arguably the closest they appear to us as real people. As I watched the film, I did imagine what it would be like to have the good fortune to know them personally. As a marketing person, I'm trained to put myself in the minds of other people, so to me it's not that difficult to imagine myself being around them at that time, or indeed now.

In terms of the drama, I must say I find the dream sequence a bit awkward, with the wives openly flirting with the journo in front of their husbands. I know it's supposed to be him dreaming, and we've all had idle thoughts about being a friend to one of the ladies (OK, just me then), but even so…

The 'live' sound (in places 'helped along', shall we say, in the movie's production process) is really, really good, providing a slightly wistful reminder that I've never seen the band 'live'. Is it true that Benny has his mike muted because he doesn't rate his voice? I've no idea, but the performances are a tour de force (and what a great name for a band's tour that would be!). 'Intermezzo No.1' is my least favourite ABBA track, a real hotch-potch of a number, but there's good use of it during the sequence where the journalist travels to Perth.

You really can't beat 'live' music, even a video recording or TV version of it, and some of the songs sound better 'live' than on the studio albums, like 'I'm A Marionette'. The backing vocals on 'Get on the Carousel' (only available on the film, nowhere else, and a 9/10 song for me by the way) are outstanding, and I don't know what to make of the fact that the backing singers get almost no visual love in the film. In the audience at the concerts, meanwhile, you see for yourself the multi-generational appeal that ABBA had and indeed still has. You also get a nice advertisement for Stockholm in the credits. Super stuff, and it's a mark of ABBA's greatness that the presence of a subsequently disgraced actor doesn't totally ruin it. 7/10

Like Garry, I've not seen any 'official' version of the *Mamma Mia!* musical which debuted in 1999 and is still going strong. I've seen a recording of a US school performing the musical, so I guess that counts as some class of familiarity, as well as an on-screen performance, but that's pushing it, I realise.

I want to say up front that any imitation of an original is simply that, an imitation, a facsimile. Often, well-known artists will put their slant on some other well-known artist's song, as a kind of homage to the inventor. But they're professionals doing other professionals' work, not amateur singers having a bash. As for *Mamma Mia! The Movie,* from 2008, which I re-watched on Amazon Prime the other day – well, it isn't quite karaoke, but it's not a set of proper cover versions either. But I find the film entertaining because it's a well-knitted-together story and the actors can act, most of them at any rate.

The arrangements of the songs are modernised and 'musicalised' – even 'movified' if you like. It's still like watching a tribute band, admittedly a decent one. Are they going for 'carbon copy' or 'our take'? You find it impossible not to view the performances through the lens of the majestic originals. The songs are woven quite nicely into the storyline; it does work, in my view. I did find myself wondering how the songs would have been staged in a theatre setting, so that remains a yet-to-be-ticked item on the FH bucket list.

The singing is quite painful, shaky in parts and often pretty cringeworthy. In general, the men cope better than the women. I find Pierce Brosnan passable, except for 'When All Is Said and Done', which he strangles. Amanda Seyfried can sing, though, no argument there. 'Waterloo' is an anti-climax left until the very end, glammed up excessively, and can't even be saved by the presence of His Royal Björnness. Decent, harmless fun nonetheless. 5/10

Ah, the sequel. So often the shameless run to the cash machine, and so rarely an improvement on its predecessor. In which camp does *Mamma Mia! Here We Go Again* pitch its tent?

The film came out in 2018, but I didn't see it until it found itself padding ITV's summer schedule one unfashionable evening in mid-2022. It opens with a rewind to 1979 and a young Donna Sheridan, so you see early on that this is clearly going to be the back story for meeting the three 'dads'. The C factor – the Cheese factor – is set on high, but when the opening number drops – 'When I Kissed the Teacher' – the cringeworthiness is so epic that I found myself reaching for the remote, which took huge resolve not to follow through on. Björn is on the stage as a don, presumably wondering what on earth was going on, in more ways than one…

So where to begin? Of course, I have begun, but was having to relive the horror as I wrote this. In the restaurant scene Benny plays on 'Our Last Summer', which segues into an utterly awful 'Waterloo' – and I never thought I'd see those three words together. The singing is just not good enough. It's a tortuous plot too, which doesn't help.

Andy Garcia turns in a wooden performance for the ages but, Mr G notwithstanding, the film does get better when the heavyweight actors come in, far too late to lift the score very far up the scale. 'Why Did It Have To Be Me?'. Why indeed, murmurs the whole audience. You're trashing the legacy, lads, careful how you go. At the time of writing, rumour has it that they're threatening a third film in the franchise. Please make it stop, somebody. 2/10

Going slightly away from the brief here (let's call it three-and-a-half key movies for my bit), I also want to give a quick mention to *Muriel's Wedding* from 1994 since ABBA's music figures quite prominently there. Wikipedia tells me that Björn and Benny allowed the music's use in the film and also the adapting of 'Dancing Queen' as an orchestral piece. This overall permission, however, only came a fortnight before filming was due to start, so it's no surprise that the filmmakers had a plan B for the identity of

Muriel's favourite band (The Village People, in case you were wondering).

There are some very good sequences in the film, which I re-watched recently, having not seen it in full since it came out. I remembered a lot from the first time I saw it, which is a good sign, and also a good sing too, as my typo reminded me. I also envy Muriel's poster collection in her bedroom... The rendition of 'Waterloo' is simply brilliant and there are some lovely comedic touches by Toni Collette. Using 'I Do, I Do, I Do, I Do, I Do' for the wedding aisle walk is genius. You can see where *Mamma Mia!* got some ideas from, I'm guessing... Enjoyed it again! 6/10

G: It's utterly impossible for me to be anything other than utterly subjective about *ABBA: The Movie*. As I've already explained, it represents the point of origin of my fandom. So I'll kick any notion of objectivity firmly into the long grass and just remind you (and myself) why, to this day, it remains such a firm favourite of mine - despite the pall that inevitably now hangs over the film for the reasons Freddie's outlined above. The reliance on 'live' footage, with plenty of those harder, slightly abrasive musical edges that I've got such a soft spot for, plus the excitement and spontaneity of concert performances where ABBA are clearly having a down-and-slightly-dirty ball, means the film pushes on a wide-open door for me.

Even the naff narrative has its uses, with the trite, tedious stretches of the DJ's interview quest simply making ABBA's reappearances all the more welcome and exhilarating when they come along. (Apart from the DJ's 'The Name of the Game' dream sequence, that is; I've never been able to watch this through anything other than semi-closed fingers, it's so cringey and ill-judged.) Nor do the fans' incessant cries of "WE WANT ABBA!!!" irritate me especially. (One day I'm actually going to count them.) To be honest, when the goddam DJ's hogging the screen, I feel like joining in.

Regarding the music on display, there are plenty of highlights – particularly where some lesser-known tracks get their moment in the sun (and, at times, the teeming rain, of course). I'll just pick out 'He Is Your Brother' and 'Why Did It Have to Be Me?' on this occasion, though it could equally well be 'Tiger' or (don't tell Freddie) 'Intermezzo No.1'. But all roads lead to 'Eagle', don't they? It's the song that brings proceedings to their kind-of climax, with the soaring elevator adding a neat bit of orgasmic symbolism to the movie's ultimate moment of resolution and fulfilment.

I'm sure I should be much more critical of *ABBA: The Movie*. At no point does it ask difficult questions and at no point does it really threaten to draw the public veil to one side. But that's not the job of films like this. It really isn't. As anyone who went to see it twice in a week back in February/March 1978 will be only too happy to tell you. ABBA have fun and so do I – and not even the presence of a disgraced actor can change that unalterable fact. 8/10

Of course, we can't produce a book about ABBA and not grasp the prickly old nettle presented by the whole *Mamma Mia!* phenomenon. Full disclosure: I've never seen the stage musical. Even fuller disclosure: I've never remotely *wanted* to see the stage musical. I think I'd even pass up on free tickets. You see, I'm only really interested in seeing/hearing ABBA songs sung by ABBA (or a 'proper' ABBA tribute act). It's that simple. I struggle with the basic concept that anyone else could do them anything like justice. I may be wrong to feel that way, but I'm happy to take the risk that I'm somehow missing out. Having said all that, I *did* find myself magnetically lured to the cinema to see *Mamma Mia! The Movie* when it came out in 2008. Call it part curiosity, part an inability to successfully deflect months of media hype.

And, wouldn't you just know it, I sort of quite enjoyed it a bit to some extent within reason to a degree, more or less. Put it another way, I think they got away with it. Just. I bought the DVD later in the year and watched it, possibly twice – so it must have had a few saving graces. The main one, for me, was the prominence given to some of the hidden gems of the ABBA catalogue, not least that huge favourite of mine 'Slipping Through My Fingers' and that slightly smaller huge favourite of mine 'Our Last Summer'. The 'Gimme! Gimme! Gimme!'/'Voulez-Vous' sequence on the night before the wedding is also a bit of a barnstormer, while the ensemble cast all seem pretty comfortable in their roles, even if the singing duties aren't always discharged a hundred percent convincingly (shall we say). Bullet dodged, just about, even though it was travelling quite fast. 6/10

So it's completely factual to say that, when I rolled up at exactly the same cinema a small matter of eleven years after the first *Mamma Mia!* film to sample the follow-up, *Mamma Mia! Here We Go Again*, my guard was completely lowered. I was simply expecting more of the broadly tolerable, reasonably entertaining same. As the 'entertainment' unfolded, however, I'm afraid I was as close to walking out of a cinema as I can ever remember being.

I genuinely cannot remember a single redeeming feature offered by the first half of the movie, which had me literally squirming in my seat and not quite knowing where to look or where to put myself. The original film had come across pretty much as an affectionate, if light-hearted, tribute to ABBA's music. To me, the follow-up just felt like it was on the cusp of ridiculing it. To my mind, it was a massive succession of grotesque musical missteps.

Thankfully, the second half picked up. A bit. I could at least shelve any plans to bale out, judging that I could probably just about make it all the way to the end with the help of my big bag of Maltesers. To be fair, Cher's appearance helped almost as much as the confectionery – things definitely took a bit of a turn for the better when she took control of the screen.

Overall, though, I was left with the dreadful feeling that ABBA's legacy was in grave danger of being severely tarnished – or, at the very least, trivialised – by this bizarre film. And no, I didn't get the DVD. And no, I've never watched even a bit of it again when it's popped up on TV from time to time (generally on ITV2, which is probably the right place for it and tells you everything you need to know about it). The thought of any potential third film in the series is quite literally unthinkable. Ironic, then, that sometimes I can't stop thinking about it. Again, let's move on. 1/10

The Songs They're Singing: Part 2

I'm a Marionette (from *The Album*)

F: I don't know this final song in the *The Girl with the Golden Hair* mini-musical particularly well, so much so that I didn't know the brooding, foreboding bass line when it first comes in, but the tension is established very early on. In fact, I only really know the chorus. You can see why they close the mini-musical with this one, though. It's a superbly masterful effort and could easily double as a dramatic soundtrack to a blockbuster film. And, just like a marionette, we're pulled in all directions by the sharp and deliberately jerky passages in this emotional rollercoaster. Sorry for the cliché, but it has that anthemic quality to it that makes such a platitude entirely justified. And the ability to render the word 'pirouette' as a musical echo to the sung lyric is top drawer, along with several other little jewels to list without going overboard. What a crescendo at the end too, reminding me of the raw emotion of epics like *Les Mis*. Astounding. 9/10

G: That rumbling bass... It's like the sound of distant thunder heading your way. Then those little glockenspiel touches pave the way for the strings to swoop down on you, first from on high and then, it seems, from near-ground level. And when the storm finally arrives, it delivers one of the most unsettling listening experiences in the entire ABBA songbook. This track is no warmly enfolding blanket. It's like lying on a bed of nails. This is all good, by the way. The air of menace and disorientation instantly and expertly eradicates the cosy complacency of 'Thank You for the Music' and the fragile optimism of 'I Wonder (Departure)' to leave a gaping emotional black hole and a sense of icy numbness where they once stood. Perfect! A cheeky reference to King Kong (providing a possibly unintentional flashback to 'King Kong Song') even reminds us just how far and how fast ABBA have evolved from purveyors of ultra-disposable pop to masters of a much wider, much more challenging musical palette. And that minute-long guitar solo underlines emphatically the fact that compromise really isn't on the agenda. This is grown-up music. The toybox has been padlocked, the key placed on a high shelf. And as the track finally reaches its disturbing destination, the last half minute provides a quite sublime finale, with Benny's wildly rippling piano and that dying synth note closing out song, mini-musical and album with an unmistakable air of foreboding which, as with 'Arrival', asks the unavoidable question: where on earth do we go from here? 8/10

I'm Still Alive (from *Live at Wembley Arena*)

F: (First time.) Always a treat to hear ABBA 'live', for two reasons: one, I never got to see them in person; two, they didn't really tour that much so it's a rare treat anyway, relatively speaking. So, as Benny says, Aggie the writer and also on the keys, nice one. And nice the song is too, a bit schmalzy and sugary-sweet, but of course I'm assessing it against the century of songs penned by the best pop-writing duo of all time, probably. Speaking for Agnetha, not that she needs me to, it seems slightly odd and perhaps a bit galling for her that it was only played 'live' for a couple of months and wasn't released until 2014. I scooted over to YouTube for a quick search of 'live' video of her playing, and there's one little-viewed and pirated video where it's so blurry it could have been my granny playing. Never knew Agnetha played the piano, so that's a bonus point from me. 6/10

G: As someone who's often wondered how Agnetha's songwriting might have evolved if she'd been given a Ringo slot on every ABBA release, this song's eventual appearance on an official album was extremely welcome. Of course, its pretty low-key, stripped-down character is a bit of a double-edged sword, giving the piece an intimacy that contrasts nicely with ABBA's big-sounding stock-in-trade but also making it a little bit harder to imagine how this, or any partly Agnetha-penned song, might have worked on, say, *Super Trouper*. A bold counterfactual would see 'The Way Old Friends Do' relegated to B-side status and 'I'm Still Alive' taking its place as that album's closing track, complete with sweeping orchestral accompaniment and some liberally sprinkled power chords to build towards a massive 'wow!' ending. We'll never know. Even though I think I kinda do. 6/10

I've Been Waiting for You (from *ABBA*)

F: (First time.) This is a sickly-sweet ballad with very little to commend it. Actually, that's not fair. Agnetha sings it very well and the harmonies are good, but it's not a very memorable song. There's no part of it that I can remember after the first hearing. It can't even be saved by a few "na-na-na-na-na-na-na-na-na"s. Don't get me wrong, I'd be thrilled beyond bits if I'd written this myself, but we're talking ABBA here and the bar is very, very high. It doesn't stand up remotely close to the stuff we've grown up with. Maybe it's a grower, who knows, which is why I tell you when it's my first time hearing a song, as opposed to the songs which are practically part of everyone's DNA. Well executed but not well conceived or crafted, in my humble opinion. Heresy, I know, but that's my view. Whose were you expecting? 3/10

G: This is another of those high-quality tracks on the *ABBA* album which pretty much popped out of nowhere. Whatever their various merits, the slower, ballad-y songs on the first two albums only really gave the vaguest possible hint that ABBA would pretty much nail it on the third. Composed and assured, with a perfect lead vocal from Agnetha and a glorious full-throttle power ballad chorus, this song falls decisively into the category 'unknown gem' and surely deserves wider appreciation and recognition. Plus I've always had a soft spot for the occasional well-placed, well-executed "na-na-na" in a song. The only problem with this track isn't of its own making – it simply can't fail to be overshadowed by 'SOS' as the album's heartstring-tugging highlight. 7/10

If It Wasn't for the Nights (from *Voulez-Vous*)

F: I've only heard 'If It Wasn't for the Nights' a couple of times before, and I don't mind telling you I had to check I was listening to the right song. I thought I was listening to 'Dancing Queen', to be brutally honest. Then the song settles down nicely and eases into a chorus that's, well, epic, the sort of chorus you instantly think must be a cover version, so snuggly does it pick a lobe-shaped orifice and lodge in your brain as the archetypal earworm. This isn't '70s disco, this is '70s R&B with much more longevity to it, and man it's catchy. Move over Rose Royce, there's a new kid on the block. I could see this song sitting comfortably on the Tavares side of the *Saturday Night Fever* soundtrack, rather than the falsetto-flailing boys from the Isle of Man side. Where has this song been all my life? An undiscovered – by me – gem nestling in plain sight in the cleavage of *Voulez-Vous*. Love it! 9/10

G: Well now. Here we come to the epitome of the fan-favourite deep cut. But this track has never really got past second base for me. It's pretty zippy and zesty, of course, and there's absolutely nothing wrong with any of it. But it never really stays with me once it's faded away. That's probably because it veers a little too much towards the dreaded 'easy listening' for my liking. It's perhaps a little too polished, a little too smooth. And I'm not really sure why it's a five-minuter; four, or even four and a half, would have been ample. It's an absolutely rock-solid album track and it might even have had double A-side potential somewhere down the line. But could/should it have been the lead single from *Voulez-Vous* as originally planned? Not in my book. Not in this book. And I guess (and it IS just a guess, of course) Benny and Björn ultimately had some reservations about it, plonking it second on side two – a place where they never tended to put the absolutely frontline stuff. 6/10

Intermezzo No.1 (from *ABBA*)

F: (First time.) Didn't like it at all. WTF! Am I at the circus? It's the musical equivalent of trifle: too much going on that doesn't belong together, and ends up a mess. Trifle is the only food I don't like. Do not play this at my funeral. That is all. 2/10

G: Time to hit the contrarian button again. Initially, I just knew this track as that neat instrumental Benny played quite early on in *The Movie*. It took a serious, high-risk research effort to find out what it was actually called. (This involved asking a mate of mine to ask his younger sister, who was a big ABBA fan, as she'd probably know. Always risky to drag others into your nefarious schemes in case they blow your cover before you're ready to go public.) It had been a bit of a bolt from the blue when it popped up in the film – simply not the sort of thing I'd been expecting from ABBA. As one of their rockier – and slightly proggy – numbers, it was always going to be pushing on an open door where I was concerned. And just because it's an instrumental doesn't make it a filler track; just ask Emerson, Lake and Palmer. I still hugely enjoy 'Intermezzo No.1', I still wish that a later ABBA album had found room for an 'Intermezzo No.2' and I still get happy flashbacks to that intrepid, credibility-busting visit to the cinema whenever I hear this barnstorming party piece. 8/10

Just a Notion (from *Voyage*)

F: Do yourself a favour next time you've got some vacuuming to do: get your headphones on or your earbuds in and fire up 'Just a Notion' a few times. You'll be singing along to it and actually enjoying doing chores to this song's heroic honkytonk tones. My knowledgeable co-writer Garry H tells me that JAN was recorded during the *Voulez-Vous* sessions and never released, despite the plaintive pleas of fans over the years. It certainly feels like it's from that era, with its foot-tappingly catchy keyboard work and the higher vocal register of the ladies compared to the other stuff on *Voyage*. Beautifully expressing those giddy butterfly feelings when you think someone might have the hots for you, this is not, as I thought when I first misheard it, an anti-environmentalism chant – "just an ocean, that's all". On a much more serious note, I wrote this review on a coach in Ireland during the early days of the Russian invasion of Ukraine, and accidentally typed the song title as 'Just a Nation', which gave the song a poignancy that could never have been foreseen or intended. Back to the music: one of the best songs on the album for me, nearly a nine, which is ironic given when it was first recorded. 8/10

G: Here's an odd admission. I've never been keen on the word 'notion' in songs. Sounds like one from the rhyming dictionary. For this and other equally good reasons, I wasn't at all sure about this song when I first heard it. I suppose 'I Still Have Faith in You' and 'Don't Shut Me Down' had set the bar impossibly high, so whatever followed as the third single from *Voyage* could scarcely avoid disappointing me just a little. But the song shone in a completely different, more radiant light on the album, tucked in behind the second of those new-era classics. Quite the feelgood number, letting us all (ABBA included) wear our years just a little more lightly. The Wombly intro creates a jaunty air of birthday party jollity which shows no sign of relenting over the next three and a half minutes. And Benny's trusty old pub-piano vibe keeps the party spirit motoring with glorious ease, leaving me with the feeling that Chas 'n' Dave would have given their eye teeth to get their hands on this number. Two Bacardi Breezers when you're ready, bartender... 7/10

Keep an Eye on Dan (from *Voyage*)

F: I immediately warmed to 'Keep an Eye on Dan' the first time I heard it, with its oo-oo-oo-oo-oo melody and its percussion on the off-beat, an initial feeling that hasn't diminished over time. Staying with the musical side, the song for me is a microcosm of the overall ABBA corpus: loads going on – funky keyboard bits, delicious synth work, several catchy melodies, lush strings, super verse and chorus vocals – yet all fitting together seamlessly into a song that sounds deceptively simple. Plus, we get the bonus of the lads on backing vocals, which I think adds a lot to the second half of the song. It tells the story of the pain of sharing the parenting duties following separation and tells it pretty well too, written by the ex-husband Björn and delivered by the ex-wife Agnetha. As always, I home in on the lyrics a lot and I find myself asking the question why Agnetha would "bang a wheel" rather than "bang *the* wheel", as in the steering wheel? That would have been so much better, no? Probably just me then. 7/10

G: The title jars a bit (would 'Keep an Eye on Sam' have been a little smoother?). But once you get past that, you're rewarded with a crafty, spritely little song that quickly burrows into your memory banks and absolutely insists on multiple repeat listens. A massive dollop of trademark ABBA light and shade deposits you right in that limbo state between emotional extremes – territory where so many great songs plant their flags. Cracking intro, while the beat-free arrival of the first chorus provides a sure-footed touch of drama and a sense of things that are not only unresolved but probably unresolvable. As I say, there's that classic ABBA trick of handcuffing conflicting emotions together: in this case, fear and determination. Plus there's a genius decision to drop in a few backing vocals from Björn and Benny as the song weaves its way towards its conclusion, taking it in a slightly different direction while reviving a few fond memories of classics like 'Lovelight' and 'Kisses of Fire' where a similar trick has a sensational impact. Loads and loads of hi-hat here but it's never intrusive. A grower and a stayer – and, for me, a highlight of the second half of *Voyage*. 7/10

King Kong Song (from *Waterloo*)

F: (First time.) A rocky enough effort from the quartet, this one. It sounds very much like Elton John's 'Saturday Night's Alright (for Fighting)' with its relatively raucous guitar sound and the singalong-stompalong keyboard work. The vocals feel a bit forced from the ladies and the growling bits from Björn don't really work for me. This feels like one of those early ABBA songs where they're feeling their way, trying a few different things, and looking for a reaction or some fan traction that might send them more positively in that direction. Thankfully, this one turns out to be a bit of a cul-de-sac for them. Don't get me wrong, ABBA can do rocky, especially when they're on tour and are smashing their pop hits, but this feels a bit amateurish and basic, one of the early crap ones you have to try and get out of the way. Leave the glam rock to Slade and Wizzard. 4/10

G: It's glammy. It's rocky. It's quirky. It's got a bit of punch and attack about it. By rights I should be able to get something out of this one – maybe even award it dreaded 'guilty pleasure' status. But the song doesn't work for me at all. In fact, it's really only notable for being even dafter than the dire song preceding it on the album ('Sitting in the Palmtree'). Just as the song struggles way too hard to be wacky, that lead vocal you can hear is the sound of Björn trying way, way too hard to salvage something from the chaos and carnage. And then the Showaddywaddy-esque backing-vocal "bom-boms" put the bloomin' tin lid on it. A song to keep your Non-ABBA-Fan Friends (NAFFs) well away from, unless you want to be the butt of cruel jibes for the rest of your natural life. The song's single greatest sin? It barely sounds like ABBA at all. The most positive thing I can say is that at least they didn't stick it out as a novelty single in the desperate quest for a big post-'Waterloo' follow-up hit. 3/10

Kisses of Fire (from *Voulez-Vous*)

F: I've only heard this song a couple of times before, and in fact I didn't recognise it until the chorus kicks in. Normally I'd be praising the lads for their production values, since forty-nine times out of fifty they'll get the balance spot on in the mixdown. Not on 'Kisses of Fire', in my opinion, since it starts so quietly and placidly, before the chorus explodes. And the explosion is unwarranted too, it's too much of a step and it's simply too damn loud. In the later renderings of the chorus the balance feels fine, so maybe it was just the first chorus that made me spill my tea when I thought I was in for a gentle one. Presumably, since it's the last song on the original *Voulez-Vous* release, they wanted to leave us fired up and ready for more. By the end of it I think they've done that, just about, after recovering from a misstep and causing me to recalibrate my pacemaker. Little shout-out to Björn on the backing vocals at the end too, nice. 6/10

G: Ah, the arcane art of the album-closer! Or is it a science?? Finishing an album with a whimper really is one of the cardinal sins of music-making. Fortunately, ABBA generally had the knack of filling the final grooves with an absolute belter. And this track is one of their very best LP-enders as they save one of the highlights of *Voulez-Vous* right till the last knockings. 'Kisses of Fire' is classic ABBA. But it's also secret ABBA, known really only to initiates. A hidden treasure, then. Brilliance is strewn and scattered about almost casually. The breathy vocal in the second verse is a great touch, building to the punch of "losing YOU!". But the song's really all about the chorus – one of ABBA's very finest. And even that has a trick up its sleeve, with the intrusion of Björn's mixed-back backing vocal as the song heads to the fade-out – his voice's vulnerability providing a perfect contrast to the urgency and general chutzpah of Agnetha and Frida's stunning lock-stepped vocals. My only real gripe is that the song's a bit short. Another half a minute or so would have been gratefully received.

In fact, they could have pinched thirty seconds by making 'If It Wasn't for the Nights' a bit shorter... 9/10

Knowing Me, Knowing You (from *Arrival*)

F: There are uplifting tremendous love songs, and there are distressing tremendous love songs. This one is – obvious statement of the book – in the second camp. You only have to listen to the first few lines to wonder what kind of a place Björn had to get himself into to write this, sheesh (not forgetting Stig's co-credit, of course). And then there's the "a-ha" in the chorus, clearly a filler but, depending on your own interpretation and state of mind, either so emotionally charged that you can just imagine the heaving sobs of some poor sensitive soul, or else the affirmative acknowledgement that we're done. Björn's backing vocals are great on this song, a great contrast to the ladies' plaintive chorus. Damn, from the first bar there's so much going on here, and you want it all. Delicately melodious, musically accomplished, instantly memorable. It's the ultimate break-up song. Pass me a tissue, I've something in my eye... 9/10

G: I'm not at all sure how or where to start describing the epic qualities of this faultless song. And I'm not one to bandy the word 'genius' about lightly. But using it here is surely warranted. Put it this way: this song is so good it makes 'Money, Money, Money', which follows it on *Arrival*, sound like a bit of a second-rater – even though 'Money, Money, Money' is an out-and-out classic in its own right. But back to this track. The sheer *drama* in those opening six notes/chords is quite remarkable. Frida's story-telling – all wrought emotion and weary resignation – is a marvel too, sharpened still further by Agnetha's superb whisper vocal. But top billing has to go to that barnstormer of a chorus, which strains every sinew to put you through the emotion-mincer. I'm also very partial to the little bass guitar touches littered all over the song and the superb way the lightly fuzzed electric guitar chords shadow the acoustic guitar which bonds everything together like superglue. Then there's that wonderful outro, with the electric guitar throwing an extra flourish into the riff that rings in your ears as the song eventually dies away. Incredible. You can make a very good case indeed for this song being ABBA's towering achievement – and that, singles-wise, it was all very, very slightly downhill from here. 10/10

Lay All Your Love on Me (from *Super Trouper*)

F: What. A. Song. If this song carried a wallet you'd find an ID card with 'Anthem' written on it. It's in the same league as 'Gimme! Gimme! Gimme! (A Man After Midnight)' for crying out loud! The opening synth chords signal that you're in for a belter, and when the drum beat kicks in behind it, you know there's no going back. You're propelled forward by the astonishingly good lyrics, pure poetry. And there's something so sexually charged in the chorus and the beseeching title of the song. I put 'Lay All Your Love on Me' in the same category as 'Eagle': not on the casual ABBA fan's top ten radar but massive all the same. Benny gets in on the act with some awesome synth work towards the end, a perfect complement to the chorus to fade. Another track that would have sounded absolutely flippin' amazing 'live'. Heavy-duty disco that sounds as good as it did forty-something years ago. 9/10

G: Sad disco – is that even a genre? Well, if there was one band capable of making a brilliant success of infusing a classic disco track with a big dollop of Nordic noir, it was always going to be ABBA. This song really is mature pop of a very high calibre indeed. It always reminds me (though not musically) of The Police's 'Every Breath You Take', with its real meaning and essential darkness almost inevitably evading the casual listener carried away by its driving rhythm and memorable chorus hook. Neatly adding to the withdrawn, even mildly creepy feel, the almost robotic beat conjures up overtones of a Kraftwerk-y 'tanzen mechanik' vibe – further fanning the flames of an obsession-fuelled compulsion to dance away the pain. I'm almost tempted to give this remarkable track an extra point for infiltrating a six-syllable word into the lyrics. But that would be incomprehensible. 8/10

Like an Angel Passing Through My Room (from *The Visitors*)

F: The ticking clock sound that closes the can't-stop-time 'Slipping Through My Fingers' continues seamlessly and ushers in 'Like an Angel...' in this side two ballad from *The Visitors*, staying with us for the duration of the song as a constant reminder of the fourth dimension. Agnetha passes the baton to Frida for this one, and it's clear (to me at least!) that you can view these two songs as a couplet, as the deeper, more mature-sounding voice of Ms Lyngstad suggests an older person reflecting once more on time's inexorable march. Speaking of dimensions, and very rarely for ABBA, this is really a one-dimensional, one-paced song, but still has the beauty and sadness of a slowly fading flower. Since the two songs, I believe, are meant to be taken together, it's also hard for me to separate them in scoring them, reflecting each other as they do, better together and somehow diminished without their twin. 7/10

G: Isn't there something in the International Convention on Human Rights about this sort of thing? I mean positioning a song like this straight after your soul's been put through the wringer by 'Slipping Through My Fingers'. It's very much the second instalment in a one-two punch to the emotional solar plexus like no other I can think of by any musical act on any album I've ever heard. Softened to a pulp by 'Slipping...' and left to survey the emotional wreckage wrought by the reflections it invites on the inescapable passing of time, we're now ambushed by a gently ticking clock and a child's bloomin' music box! Brutal! Merciless! Even as a standalone, 'Like an Angel...' homes in on that innate sense of nostalgic longing, grasping you in its deceptively velveteen grip and refusing to release you until long after the tick-tocks evaporate into the darkness at the end of the song. Images of idyllic childhoods; softly glowing candlelight; comforting, whispered words. Genius concept flawlessly delivered – and all the more powerful as a result of its ultra-stripped-down nature. The ultimate in modern nursery rhymes, coaxing us into a dreamless sleep yet with a scent of forlorn hope and resigned regret hanging in the air as the firelight fades. Amazing! That wreckage in the corner is me, by the way. (Additional comment:

'From a Twinkling Star to a Passing Angel' is interesting but doesn't really bear repeated or frequent listens.) 9/10

Little Things (from *Voyage*)

F: ABBA pressed the Wholesome Family Entertainment button (apart from the heavy innuendo of the breakfast tray delivered as barter for sexual favours) with 'Little Things', a sweet Christmas ditty released as a single from *Voyage* about a month before SBD – don't worry, I'm referring to Santa's Big Day 2021. I thought this was a shoo-in for the Christmas No.1 but I hadn't counted on it falling a full sixty places behind another septuagenarian called Elton John, aided in no small way by the physically small shape of E. Sheeran esquire. Did anyone manage to pick up any 'Little Things' merchandise before it sold out? Shelf, meet hot cakes. It's got all the ingredients of a good Christmas song – appropriate lyrics, yuletide sounds, kids singing carol-like bits – yet it lacks a melody memorable and catchy enough to propel it into the highly competitive stratosphere within this genre. Nevertheless, it makes a welcome contribution to this diverse album. 6/10

G: Well, you wait nearly half a century for ABBA to record a Christmas song. Then it finally arrives and you wish it wasn't about Christmas. The delicate tunes are pretty sumptuous. But I struggle with some of the lyrics. I just can't warm to them. Maybe the problem is that the song spends too much time describing things people are doing and not enough describing the things they're *feeling* – which is surely the essence of Christmas? It all seems a little flat-footed as a result, which is a shame. But I won't let it spoil my Christmas. 4/10

Love Isn't Easy (but It Sure Is Hard Enough) (from *Ring Ring*)

F: (First time.) I should be forgiven for thinking there was some kind of salacious double entendre in this one, but no, this is the innocent early '70s, and again it's got that feel about it. There's a hint of country in the intro but then it moves back into the US-influenced pop mainstream. I quite like the first half of the chorus but the second half housing the title of the song doesn't quite do it for me on first listen. And that single bass drum sticks out like a sore thumb too. This is going to sound sacrilegious, but some of the ladies' vocals are a bit shouty-screechy for me. Yikes! The redeeming feature is Benny's work on the piano, which ties the song's somewhat disparate pieces together and reminds me of Elton John's work around this time. I have a sneaking feeling this one might be a 'grower' though. (Author's note: it didn't really grow on further listens to be honest, I probably didn't prune it right.) 4/10

G: Simple, even primitive by ABBA's standards. But this works really quite well. Agnetha and Frida's rock-tinged intrusions into Björn's verses are executed brilliantly and the chorus is very nicely constructed. The track certainly flirts with quirkiness and at times you almost sense it wants to stake a claim to novelty song territory. But it pulls back from the brink sufficiently to make it one of the most successful of ABBA's early attempts to nail the throwaway three-minute pop song format. It's one of the early tracks where you can definitely see the band's potential starting to shine through. I even don't mind the big 'BOM!' of the drum in the chorus. On the other hand, I don't need a xylophone. I rarely do. 7/10

Lovelight (B-side of 'Chiquitita')

F: (First time.) Let me break this down for you. I loved the first fifteen seconds and immediately felt I'd have to dash back home for my technicolour dream coat. Then everything went a bit gloomy and dreary like the room in the opening lyrics, before the song shifted gear and the room got brighter, in fact just like the song and probably just like the band intended me to feel, clever so-and-sos. And then the chorus, oh what a chorus! I loved it. Why change a winning formula, so 'Lovelight' repeats it again, toying with our emotions. What a great concept 'Lovelight' is too, calling to mind Cream's 'Sunshine of Your Love', as we lucky ones bask in the warmth of someone else's affection. So, ultimately an uplifting song, further lifted by Björn's late-on backing vocals and some nice twiddly guitar work. Definitely a grower. 8/10

G: Sometimes a band you love comes up with a song that they clearly don't rate especially highly but somehow zeroes in on the epicentre of everything you love about music. It's as if your heroes have been walking round a hitmakers' hypermarket plucking things off shelves and shoving them in their trolley, only to slightly regret buying them when they've been through the checkout – and completely oblivious to the fact you're absolutely cock-a-hoop that they chose them. And so it is with 'Lovelight'. I remember when I first found it, skulking out of sight on the flipside of 'Chiquitita'. I had to give it a spin, of course. It would have been rude not to. Good call! What a revelation! I do love a nifty guitar riff – and, for my money, this is a monster, ABBA's finest. Did someone let Ted Nugent into the studio??? I was instantly on board. Then the song simmers down just a touch with that lovely acoustic-guitar-driven verse, tilling the soil for that killer chorus to burst out of the ground with the girls belting out the words and those great back-up, distant cries of "lovelight shining..." from Björn, plus a few perfectly placed tom-tom thuds to add even more oomph. Then, as the girls hold those last notes of the chorus, back comes the killer riff. I'm in heaven! And let's not forget the lovely, minimalist "I feel so good..." bridge with its sumptuous piano intervention just before the chorus fires up the rocket launchers again. Sublime! But, incredibly, the best is yet to come! As the chorus repeats to fade, back comes the riff again – but this time DURING the chorus. EXACTLY what I want to hear. In fact, the first time I listened to the song, the thought crossed my mind how awesome it would be if the riff were, later on, to come back during the chorus. And blow me down – there it was! They actually did it! How this track was deemed surplus to the requirements of *Voulez-Vous* will remain in the Big Box of Unexplained Mysteries until every star in the night sky has burnt itself out and the cosmos has faded away to cold nothingness, in desperate need of some lovelight. 10/10

Lovers (Live a Little Longer) (from *Voulez-Vous*)

F: (First time.) Well, never mind a pastime paradise or a gangster's paradise, this one's a crooner's paradise! I could definitely see a grizzled lounge lizard singing this one, admittedly an octave or so lower perhaps for a male vocal. It's one of a few songs from the *Voulez-Vous* album that feels like it could belong quite naturally in the *Saturday Night Fever* or *Grease* pantheon, and was perhaps inspired by them. On the whole I liked it, though I was left slightly unsatisfied with the chorus, which feels a bit forced, a bit compressed, and a bit screechy. It sticks out a bit like a sore thumb on what is a decent hand of a song. The strings are nice and the bassline funks along nicely too; in fact, everything is pretty peachy apart from the jarring chorus, which is a very un-ABBA-like weak link. Pity, since I like the idea and the lyrics too. 6/10

G: I've never been able to warm to this song. It sounds like ABBA following current musical trends (and being buffeted somewhat by their crosswinds) rather than absorbing them on their own terms. From those first descending notes, immediately reinforced by the generic-sounding disco strings (yuk!), it's a grating listen. And I could do without the over-insistent hi-hat. I'm not keen on the unusually shouty vocals on the chorus, although you've got to give Frida and Agnetha credit for going at it full welly. At least Frida (as ever) manages to pull off 'sultry' with great aplomb, while the Eric Clapton-y lead guitar work beds down quite well. Plus there's a bonus point for squeezing the word 'longevity' into the lyric. But did I mention how much I hate the strings? If they'd been dropped down in the mix a little, there certainly wouldn't have been any complaints from me. 4/10

Mamma Mia (from *ABBA*)

F: Blimey, where to start with this one, the song that spawned a musical, two films (to date) and introduced ABBA to millennials everywhere? Talk about seminal. The start is so recognisable, the high-pitched glockenspiel-y clip-clop and then the oh-so-familiar guitar riff, the riff that returns to fade after what seems like thirty seconds, but it's in reality over three minutes in. This is yet another almost perfect pop song. There's so much going on, so many lovely little trills and ornaments, yet it all fits together so delightfully you hope it's like one of those Willy Wonka sweets that never ends. And of course the ladies are now in the 1975-1979 phase when they too were, well, almost perfect. I realise I haven't talked much about the song, really, but then again you know it, you all know it so well. Ludicrously good, achingly catchy. Monster track. 9/10

G: Take 'Waterloo' out of the equation and, in terms of conception, ambition and execution, this song is so far ahead of any track on the first two albums it's almost bizarre. Talk about a great leap forward. Finally, ABBA find the sweet spot and, so assured is this track, they somehow manage to look and sound like they've been doing this kind of stuff of this stratospheric calibre for years and years. Here's a band that's more than found its feet – it's striding forward with confidence, panache and just the right amount of swagger. Agnetha and Frida have got the melodies right in the palms of their hands and instilled their vocals with precisely the right feel – and of course their voices lock together perfectly. Meanwhile, every component of the musical backing is so well-judged – from the ticking-clock-style intro and lovely overlaid guitar riff to the satisfying snare drum thwacks announcing the arrival of the verse and the second half of the chorus – that it's quite impossible to imagine the track sounding any other way. This is a band that now sounds like they know exactly where they're going and how to take us with them – and simply can't wait to get there. 9/10

Man in the Middle (from *ABBA*)

F: (First time.) It's deeply funkadelic this one, '70s tough Americana oozing out of it. "I'm talking about *Shaft!*", Björn taking the vocal lead and the ladies providing the backing vocals in the same '70s groove. I'm not sure I like the repetition of 'the middle' in the middle – ironically – of the song; it feels like metrical padding to me. What you can't deny is the artistry of the instrumentation, however. The lead guitar, bass guitar, saxophone and percussion sound very accomplished. I wonder how the song would go down with no vocal at all, as a purely instrumental version? Pretty nice I would have thought. Not a genre that would continue to preoccupy ABBA all that much, but a classic example of the fact that they can turn their hands and voices to pretty much any musical style. 5/10

G: Derided and dismissed by many ABBA fans, this track poses me no particular problems. I'd go as far as saying I enjoy it without any serious reservations. It tells a story neatly enough while the backing, dominated by the entertainingly funky electric piano and modestly raspy brass, would grace any stakeout scene in a '70s cop show. The backing vocals give the chorus the little bit of extra heft it needs and the net result is a perfectly respectable, professional period piece that keeps the album moving along, even if it never threatens to be a contender for any *Best of* collection. 6/10

Me and Bobby and Bobby's Brother (from *Ring Ring*)

F: This would have been a 'my first ever time hearing this!' for sure, had Garry not sent it to me for a listen a few months ago, if I remember correctly, because of the funky song title. Don't mind this one, the idea and lyrics have a got a whimsical, reminiscing feel about them, harking back to the innocence of youth and time gone by. This and 'Love Isn't Easy...' from the same album remind me of The Monkees somehow; must be an early '70s thing. More of Benny coming into his own, and if your tunesmith is composing on the piano then you'd expect that, I guess. My favourite part of this song is actually the fade-out, with no sarcasm intended. Stripped back and chilled, with the driving piano and the Björn/ladies vocals answering each other, all delivered with a completely appropriate 'ah, those were the days' vibe. Not bad. 5/10

G: Straight into the chorus, this one, without any fannying around. And that's not a bad strategy. The verses don't offer an awful lot, so whatever charm this song has got definitely resides in the chorus. Not quite clear why Frida can't remember the name of Bobby's brother if they were such great mates, but that's children for you. Not keen on the panpipe-type effect. Granny-friendly pop with a vaguely West Coast feel that doesn't do an awful lot for me or for most other people, as far as I'm aware. 4/10

Me and I (from *Super Trouper*)

F: What an intro to this song! It sounds like the calling card of a TV channel or movie company. And the anthemic keyboard chords kick in and you think the band might be straying into prog rock territory, but no, it veers back into the land of perfectly crafted pop music, with the delightful chorus echoed by the keyboard chords from before. It really is rather synthtastic electro-pop with the computerised voices, a good couple of years before this kind of treatment was considered almost compulsory. Frida's voice is great for this execution and it flummoxes me somewhat that this song never became a *Greatest Hits* staple; it could quite easily sit within a musical too. The song could just as much be about multiple personality disorder as it is about our different moods, and it's yet another example of the classic ABBA split between sadness and happiness that seems to underpin a lot of their songs. Another rock-solid resident of the second division within the ABBA league. 8/10

G: Where vinyl (or cassette) albums were/are concerned, I've always thought that the way you end side one was/is at least as important as the way you open and close the whole show. Does the listener flip the album buoyed with excitement and expectation? Or are they left with a slightly deflated feeling and a hope that, with a bit of luck, things may pick up a bit on side two? For me, as well as being a fabulous standalone, 'Me and I' was/is an ideal side one closer. From those very first synth notes, it simply brims with high-class melodies, terrific ideas and a tidal wave of point-perfect touches. The treated vocals in the last line of the chorus are an obvious masterstroke. But so are the clucking electric guitar, the clever accentuation of offbeats, that intermittent tom-tom thud, the way the acoustic guitar joins the party during the chorus – I could go on and on and on... The outcome is a peerless platform for characteristically brilliant lead and backing vocals, a cracking set of lyrics and some of Benny's most memorable keyboard work – a lovely final flourish beautifully embellishing the exquisite outro. I'm still surprised this song lasts five minutes; it seems to absolutely fly by much more quickly every time I listen to it. Who'd have imagined a dip into the murky world of Sigmund Freud could be so joyous and life-affirming? 10/10

Medley: Pick a Bale of Cotton/Old Smokey/ Midnight Special (B-side of 'Summer Night City')

F: (First time.) This is the only ABBA recording of material not written by the band's members and was originally recorded for charity. It gets a second lease of life on the *ABBA* album Deluxe Edition. I'm not into my folk (of the musical rather than the human variety) but found myself instantly taking to the driving piano and vocals of 'Pick a Bale of Cotton'. It transitions very nicely into 'Old Smokey', the original of which I've heard before of course, and again the arrangement and vocals are top quality. Another nice transition and we're into 'Midnight Special', which takes the pace back up to 'Bale of Cotton' levels and again reminds you how good the band are in pretty much every department. Not a 'proper' ABBA song, then, but nonetheless it gets the magic pixie dust and sounds really good. Probably an eight if it was their own stuff, but we're the richer for it being in existence. 7/10

G: I'm not completely sure what Peter Powell thought he was doing when he gave this a spin on his Radio 1 show when 'Summer Night City' came out and he resolved to play the B-side as well. I often wonder whether he had any idea what was on it. Surely, if he'd realised it was a medley of traditional American folk songs, he may well have had second thoughts. As I listened – and on the rare occasions when I listen to this track today – I was impressed with how ABBA tackle the first bit. It's all very jaunty and swaggy and actually works quite neatly, with Benny's clanking piano working overtime down in the boilerhouse. Then things go off the rails a bit (despite Frida's very best efforts) as 'Smokey' just sounds unremittingly naff, dated and pointless. Fortunately, it doesn't outstay its non-welcome and 'Midnight Special' covers over the traces in its non-essential but kind-of-entertaining way. And it's always nice to hear Agnetha and Frida's voices lock together as they belt out a vocal – even if this track is substantially inferior to the vast majority of ABBA's own stuff. 5/10

Merry-Go-Round (B-side of 'People Need Love')

F: (First time.) Lurking towards the lower reaches of the 2001 Deluxe Edition of *Ring Ring*, which on Spotify contains a veritable trove of different-language songs, 'Merry-Go-Round' has the early 1970s written all over it. The first few bars had me thinking about Jethro Tull, which is a bit weird, and then later on I heard what could have (in another life) influenced Snoop Dogg, which is possibly about as weird a connection as you could imagine, I know. After that mental hiccough it all gets a bit long hair and flares and is nice enough without being overly memorable for a killer hook or an outstanding chorus. So all in all, then, it's a touch bland and a touch limp (two band in-jokes there that only Garry will get, so it'll be a miracle if they survive the edit. Mind you, we're self-publishing so it's got a decent chance of self-indulgently staying in). 5/10

G: Back into the time machine for this one. Again, the backing track actually sounds like it could do a pretty serviceable job as the incidental music for a late '60s or early '70s detective show like *Jason King* or *Randall and Hopkirk (Deceased)*. Unfortunately, the vocal melodies don't do it any favours and the low-octane backing vocals (which barely sound like Agnetha and Frida at all) don't bring too much to what's a very low-key party. The last half minute isn't bad. 3/10

Money, Money, Money (from *Arrival*)

F: How do they do it? How *do* they do it? Who said writing pop music was to music what heating a tin of beans was to cooking? In the first ten seconds alone there are two melodies so mouth-watering they'd be the single stand-out element of any other 'good' song. The idea is of course breathtakingly simple yet powerful, telling the impossible dream of the woman who realises if she can't marry into money she'll have to make it herself. The rhyming of money, funny and sunny conveys so easily in a handful of words the illusory qualities of being wealthy that would take mortals like me a page to try and explain. And then there's that "a-haaaaaa-ah-ah-ah", straight after we've had something similar in 'Knowing Me, Knowing You', and meaning something completely different! Again, you have to ask how they do it. Was it blood, sweat and tears or flashes of inspiration? It's chock full of musical chocolate nuggets too. Bloody great song... 9/10

G: Of all ABBA's mega-famous songs, I think this is possibly the one that never really gets the full credit it deserves. From a UK perspective, perhaps that's because it just failed to hit the number-one spot in the mad frenzy of the Christmas 1976 singles chart. Hard to believe that, in the prevailing economic crisis of the time, people preferred to shell out their hard-earned cash for 'When a Child Is Born' and 'Under the Moon of Love'. Then again, perhaps the real problem was that 'Money, Money, Money' was sold what the sporting world would call the ultimate hospital pass. And not once but twice! First, of course, it was chosen as the follow-up to 'Dancing Queen' – a deeply unenviable task in a world where critics, DJs and many, many others simply can't wait to tell you your latest song is nowhere near as good as your last one. And as if that wasn't burden enough, it had to slot in straight after 'Knowing Me, Knowing You' in the *Arrival* album's running order. Added to all that, did the song's tongue-in-cheek cash-grubbing cynicism go against the grain for that part of the fan base who routinely lauded ABBA's wholesomeness? Not sure, can't remember. To my ears, though, it's brilliantly successful, with that iconic piano intro drawing back the curtain for Frida to stride into the spotlight, Sally Bowles-like, and assume an utterly convincing would-be conniving gold-digger persona. Giving more than a passing nod in the direction of *Cabaret*, perhaps this is actually the first song where Benny and Björn's ambitions in the direction of musical theatre really start emerging from the mist. Sort of *Abbaret*, if you will. 8/10

Move On (from *The Album*)

F: (First time.) ABBA does popped-up Johnny Cash! Well, this one's different, you can't deny that. It's still got that unmistakeable ABBA timbre to it, even in the first spoken part, and so it's no surprise when Björn steps down and the song moves on, as it were, to the more traditional format of the ladies vocally leading the way. Even though the theme is about never standing still, there's something very relaxing about the chorus that ironically makes you want to stay where you are, put your feet up and ease into the moment. There are some nice touches in this song, with the high pipe sound, the lush acoustic guitar and the "la-la-la-la-la-la"s. That said, it feels like this song has a bit of an identity crisis going on. It doesn't quite seem sure of itself nor of what it wants to be. Not a bad song per se, but I'm not sure I could be pressed to remember the chorus without a prompt. 6/10

G: Always a big call to throw a talky bit into a song – and a REALLY brave call to kick off a song with one, not least at the start of an album side. And I'm really not at all keen on Björn's effort to crack the genre here, to be honest. Nor do my problems with this song end there, all the wide-eyed wonder and innocence layered over it kind of sending me in the opposite direction in terms of buying into its message. But I suppose it's pleasant/harmless enough and the melodies are perfectly serviceable – I don't even mind all the "la-la-la" bits – although the faux piccolos do get quite annoying. Another issue I have is that there seemed to be an awful lot of songs around in the '70s called 'Move On' or something very much like it, saddling this track with a bit of a bland title. Over the years, I've actually heard a few people argue that this should have been a follow-up single to 'Take a Chance on Me'. I just don't see it at all. I'm not even confident it would have broken into the UK Top 5 and, had that catastrophe come to pass, it would have been slated as a flop. So at least I've got that small crumb of comfort to be thankful for. Let's move on. 5/10

My Love, My Life (from *Arrival*)

F: (First time.) Many ABBA songs have a lot of variety within them, but this one kind of trucks along, and I'll be honest, it's flatlining a bit for me. I'm not warming to the melody; it's not really taking me anywhere. It's a proper, well-thought-out composition, don't get me wrong, but the collection of notes isn't striking a chord with me, no pun intended; it's not going to be one I'd remember anything of if I never heard it again. Lyrically, it sounds a bit heart-wrenching, and while we need some of the bad to remind us how good the good can be, this one's a bit of a downer, not something you want to play after a tough day at the office, a reversal of fortune, or a rubbish date. Not a bad song, but on first hearing it's a touch so-so for me. Maybe it's one of those that grow on you though, as it gets more of a chance to seep into your veins. 4/10

G: As I've said before, slow songs typically have to put in just a bit more graft to win me over. This one falls frustratingly short of really ticking the box. Objectively, I can appreciate its many musical merits and the subtle effectiveness of Agnetha's magnificent vocal delivery. I also quite like the clanging of the bells, which gives the track a handy point of difference. But overall the track's just a tad too slow and slushy for me. More specifically, I do find the "possess you/God bless you" rhyme quite annoying and hearing it once in the song would be more than enough. A beautifully composed track I admire but can't profess to love. 6/10

My Mama Said (from *Waterloo*)

F: (First time.) I quite warmed to this off the bat. Though the lyrics don't support the comparison, when I heard it I immediately thought of '70s US TV shows like *Kojak*. Yes, I could definitely see it as the musical backdrop to a criminal caper with the good guys and bad guys. I do like the way the bass guitar pops up for a little flourish before disappearing back down into the song's bedrock. In fact, now I listen more there's a lot of guitar work going on that I like. The instrumental showmanship works well with the vocals too, and together it's a very pleasing sound to me. The lyrics haven't aged well, and the victimisation theme of the fairer sex jars quite considerably. I'd definitely want to redo those if I was giving this the update treatment, which I think it deserves. That said, it's got something, this one. 7/10

G: Following in the slipstream of what are, for me, three mahoosive clunkers, this song gives the *Waterloo* album a bit of a bunk-up. And, boy, is it needed! I like the track's insistent, mildly hypnotic groove and its slightly restrained, held-back-a-bit tempo. A very neat bass guitar glues it all together, the jazz-funky lead guitar touches boost both chorus and instrumental section, while the whispered backing vocals are quite a nice feature too. But easily my favourite bit is the "I wanna live…" bridge, revisited right at the end of the song. Lightweight, inconsequential but enjoyable stuff. 6/10

Nina, Pretty Ballerina (from *Ring Ring*)

F: I wonder if this was the thematic inspiration for 'Dancing Queen'? This one sounds like it's from the steam age… I've probably only heard this song once before, but warmed to it straightaway. For some inexplicable reason it also calls to mind 'Chiquitita' for me. Once more the guitar catches the ear, chugging gently away as a nice counterpoint to the vocal. I like the idea of this one, the day-night contrast of Nina as an office nobody commuter nine-to-five and a dancing queen in the Friday dark hours. Really catchy chorus, though I'm not sure about the crowd effects that usher it in and then continue with the encores; they feel unnecessary to me. Also not sure about the high and insistent 'bing' – or is it me? – vocal in the background of the verse either. I wonder what the lads would do with this song if they revisited it these days? Nevertheless, a lively enough optimistic number which I enjoy listening to. 6/10

G: It's a 'no' from me. And rather a big one. This song can be completely forgiven for being formative and I do quite like the first ten seconds (naff sound effects and all). But from that point on I'm left behind at the station with my half-eaten cheese and onion baguette in my hand. Having said that, the basic melodies strike me as pretty decent. I think it's the arrangement that does my head in. Not a fan of that clucking guitar in the verse – I find it really quite irritating – and that fairground-y keyboard absolutely vandalises the chorus, to my ears. The crowd noises are way too intrusive and even the backing vocals (almost uniquely for ABBA) really get my goat. 3/10

No Doubt About It (from *Voyage*)

F: Hiding towards the end of *Voyage*, 'No Doubt About It' gives us a pick-me-up in the same way as 'Just a Notion' did, and indeed it does sound like it also comes from an earlier, less complicated era within the ABBA productivity timeline. You can't tone down a tonic for the senses and the relentless positivity of it never fails to put me in a good mood. Lyrically, well, it's a rare ABBA song for me because I'm not sure what the words are supposed to mean to me. She messed it up, has come clean and apologised, so what happens next? The chorus has the quality of an instant ABBA classic and perhaps suggests why the lads flip the song and lead with the chorus before the verse comes in, which is good, actually pretty damn good in the way that it builds. There's some lovely keyboard work going on in the background and it makes me wonder how this song would sound with just Frida and Benny doing their thing in a small, intimate, 'live' venue. Probably rather nice. 7/10

G: This track arguably nails the quintessential ABBA sound better than anything else on *Voyage*. Had they been minded to, they could comfortably have passed this track off as a lost classic from the early '80s. Excellent chorus, leading to a clever two-part verse that effortlessly builds-in a big tempo change before unleashing the killer chorus again. Lovely contrast between the attack of the vocals in the chorus and Frida's more reflective delivery of the verses. Great rhythm to the words – Björn really hits the sweet spot here in terms of lyrics. This track is yet another highlight on the greatest-ever comeback album in the history of pop music. No doubt about it. 7/10

Ode to Freedom (from *Voyage*)

F: ABBA close their last album (to date) with a 'political' song in the same gentle mould as 'Bumblebee'. Garry the Erudite One, or GEO for short, will tell you which classical tune ABBA use as the basis for 'Ode to Freedom', or maybe you know it already. Even if you don't need to go to the internet the melody itself is instantly recognisable and elegantly tees up the all-important questions about this album-ending – and possibly career-closing – song:

what's it all about, music or freedom, and what next for de fantastika fyra, or 'fab four' in Swedish? We're left with a good vibe as this solitary nod to a centuries-old genre closes on an aspirational note after threatening to leave us in the doldrums with its allusions to the uncertainties of life that we still haven't solved in the twilight of our lives. The musical foundation of 'Ode to Freedom' is obviously rock solid, and the harmonies of the fab two are tremendous as well. It leans heavily on its musical ancestry but is still a pretty strong closer. 7/10

G: What a characteristically bold and ambitious way to close out an ABBA album! The first few bars create an atmosphere reminiscent of 'My Way' before being swiftly nudged aside by a stately melody, which is then superseded by *Chess*-style musical theatre. Plus, of course, there's the nod to *Swan Lake*. This track feels like a meandering river, gracefully winding towards the shoreline to disgorge its sparkling waters into the eternal ocean. It's the gentlest anthem you could imagine. You can almost feel it brush across your face like a light summer breeze. The vocals sound as if they've been laid down by divine beings on Mount Olympus, viewing human events from afar and discreetly steering them in the right direction. But the song really does need to be just a little bit longer to let us have a good old-fashioned wallow – especially as it provides the terminus on such a logic-defying album which leaves us with so much to ponder on and so much to be thankful for as it reaches its serene and understated conclusion. 8/10

On and On and On (from *Super Trouper*)

F: I love a bit of 'poppy' rock 'n' roll and I like this song a lot. 'On and On and On' has such a catchy chorus, so why not lead the song with the chorus melody? That never hurt anyone. The verses tell the story of chatting up different guys at a party, and the narration is clever, witty and yet has some serious undertones too. The idea of putting the serious stuff in life to one side and partying through the night is for me echoed by the song itself, where you feel 'never mind about the verse, let's just focus on the chorus, it's great'. And how can you not get into the right mood for it, sing along to it, and feel good at the same time? The lead vocal and keyboard are the main stars, but I also like the way the bass, the twangy guitar and the backing vocals complement them. I bet this song could have been a whole lot of fun to perform 'live', and to experience too. 8/10

G: In terms of my personal tastes, this type of track is almost invariably right on the money. Even though it isn't exactly a full-blown rocker, there's more than enough attitude and energy on offer to root this one right at the edgy end of the ABBA catalogue. A skilful concoction of simple but interesting melodies, modestly risqué lyrics, lightly synth-treated vocals, deceptively languid synth splurges, a basic but relentless bassline – it all adds up to a song I've loved since the very first listen. That was when *Super Trouper* first hit my turntable on Christmas morning 1980. I'd just wallowed in the two number-one singles and had now reached what is, for any album, that make-or-break moment: what would the first track I didn't know sound like? Well, I was absolutely elated as 'On and On and On' ripped out of the speakers, its loose-limbed, throwaway feel masking endless hours almost certainly spent crafting, honing and perfecting the song in the studio. How does the old saying go? If you can fake sincerity, you've got it made. In music, substitute 'spontaneity' for 'sincerity'. Faking spontaneity – now that's a real skill! 8/10

One of Us (from *The Visitors*)

F: The opening bars of 'One of Us' transport me back to Christmas 1981 when I listened to this song back-to-back-to-back, gorging on it and wallowing in the emotion, even though I was scarcely old enough to guess at the pain of loss and misaligned relationships. Yes, it's a kind of 'slowy', but it's got a funky undertone to it as well in the bass guitar line which has got a great po-po-pomtastic way of easing the song along. Everything but the bass tugs at the heart strings on this one: the lyrics, the vocals, the strings, the keys, even the flippin' percussion, all backing up the anti-climactic bathos of a Christmastime hit that's sad, not mad. Do they know they're dragging us over the emotional hot coals with this beautifully penned stuff, toying with us, reeling us in and casting us out into the swirly brine, the buggers? Pass me a tissue, runny eyes and nose... 8/10

G: The massed ranks of ABBA fandom and me. One of us is out of step on this song. I'm genuinely surprised how high up it stands in so many fans' rankings. Personally, I just can't go further than saying it's pleasant but a tad obvious. Catch me on one of my less charitable days and I might even admit that I find it a bit boring. The track re-treads old regretting-I-let-you-go terrain but without bringing any particularly fresh aspect to the landscape. Even the reggae-lite feel just seems like an arbitrary way of adding some sort of point of interest. As I've said earlier, I was monumentally disappointed when this came out as the first single from the album – prompting thoughts that ABBA might have grown a bit stale and jaded. *The Visitors* was to put paid to those fears in spectacular fashion – but for me 'One of Us' is still the one comparatively weak spot on the album, even though it works quite a bit better there where it's not exposed as a standalone track. 6/10

One Man, One Woman (from *The Album*)

F: (First time.) A slow-set ballad, and the tricky meat in the sandwich of 'Take a Chance on Me' and 'The Name of the Game' on *The Album*, and it just about carries it off too. This feels to me like a throwback to the earlier albums of the mid-'70s, except everything about it is a little more mature: the vocals, the arrangement and the musicianship. A bit of a Benny-on-the-boards tour de force on this song, and Frida's sensuous, lush voice, that bit lower than Agnetha's, gives this one a bit of extra resonance. A really good song, and one I enjoy, 'One Man, One Woman' would be a standout on other albums, and one of those songs that Billy Joel would have been proud to call his own, yet it feels slightly unremarkable set against the towering company of other tracks on this stellar album. Torn between a six and seven out of ten for this one, so rounding up, because, well, Frida. 7/10

G: On the face of it, this track is the victim of the musical equivalent of a particularly nasty hospital pass. Its unenviable job is to ride in the slipstream of 'Eagle' and 'Take a Chance on Me' and plug the gap before 'The Name of the Game'. No pressure, then. Thinking of the job in hand slightly more positively, its role was to provide a bit of a breather and to add a bit of ballast in the engine room of side one of *The Album* – which was/is an exceptional side of vinyl, by any standards. In fact (again looking at it positively), it's probably just as well that 'One Man, One Woman' delivers a relative dip in proceedings. I'd possibly need oxygen if the standard set by the two previous songs had been maintained. On closer inspection, though, this track does a good deal more than simply make up the numbers. Songs exploring the ups and downs of long-term relationships became one of ABBA's trademarks, of course, and they do it with such surefootedness here – never losing sight of the need to back up the sober realism of the lyrics with excellent melodies and a very hummable chorus. Frida, naturally, is on prime form, infusing her awesome vocal with multiple emotions, the slightly tremulous way she holds on to that final "to the end…" gorgeously combining hope, belief and nagging doubt. Mission accomplished. 7/10

Our Last Summer (from *Super Trouper*)

F: ABBA have this ability to pinpoint exactly how vanishingly fast life passes, and what better place to relive the heady days of summer past than in the city of love, or is it the city of light? Anyway, they capture the nostalgia so well in 'Our Last Summer', and it's an interesting mélange this one; a traditional ballad but with an unusual – for ABBA – and rather excellent guitar solo, moving the song into the odd genre known as 'pop rock'. Frida takes the lead on this one, and the ladies team up as usual for the top-quality backing vocals. The chorus has a timeless feel about it, with the sort of melody that immediately feels like the cosy armchair you've had for ages. But you can't shake the sadness of time gone by, time you won't get back. Day-dreamy. 7/10

G: The big question, where this song's concerned, is of course: why 'Harry'? But let's leave that imponderable right there and reflect instead on how a well-judged, well-placed magic moment can lift an average song – or propel a good one even higher. In 'Our Last Summer', the second applies. Overall, the lyrics may be a tad treacly and less than light-footed here and there. But there's more than enough to compensate in the music's stately majesty and the excellence of Frida's delivery, brimming with all that hazy, heartfelt reminiscing. I love the no-nonsense, straight-in-with-the-vocal opening and the chorus is a little gem, the clever intrusion of the second "our last summer" before the last line cranking up the eye-misting nostalgia which seeps from the song's every pore. Plus there's the guitar solo, a nice abrasive contrast to the gloss and polish of the rest of the instrumentation. But what was I saying about magic moments? Well, here you get two for the price of one (so to speak). There's that gorgeous, disruptive guitar scrape plus power chord just before the chorus reprise, cutting across "how dull it seems..." (I literally never tire of that sort of trick!). And then there's the plaintive "hand in ha-a-hand" in Agnetha's wistfully distant backing vocal, later mirrored by "re-ma-a-ain". Compelling candidates for any list of top ABBA moments I feel moved to make in the future. Which, at some point, I almost certainly will do. 8/10

People Need Love (from *Ring Ring*)

F: Here's the foot-tapping 'People Need Love' to give us a shot in the arm. Not heard this one too many times before. I like Benny's rousing work on the ivories and the way Björn comes in on his own with the ladies counterpunching in their usual flawless harmony. It keeps the interest levels there, and then they reverse the order in the second half, nice. You've been hearing this a lot from me, but I've always liked the way that ABBA often start a track with the title of the song. So many artists save the title for something within the chorus, but ABBA have never been shy about diving straight in with the money shot. This for me has an American west coast feel to it, something you might have heard from The Mamas and the Papas a few years before. And who doesn't love a bit of la-la-la-la-ing and gratuitous yodelling? Upbeat, clap-along fun. 6/10

G: The sort of song which sounds like it took around twenty minutes to write and not much more to record – and absolutely none the worse for that. You often read about bands who are asked to go away and write a song that will garner plenty of radio plays. In this case, regardless of who was calling the shots, we get an instant, immediate, slightly anodyne three-minuter that's essentially just a collection of decent hooks. But its substantial oompf definitely demands your attention and it's always good to hear a band clearly having fun. Nice modulation and some gratuitous yodelling give the track a timely boost just as it emits the first hint that it might be about to outstay its welcome. This has gone down in history as the first real ABBA track and it does a pretty solid job of living up to that exacting mantle. 6/10

Put on Your White Sombrero (from the *Super Trouper* sessions)

F: How do they do it? I mean, it's not everyone's cup of tea, but how do they find it so easy to step into other styles and nail them? With a song title like this you're guessing that it's going to have a Latin American feel to it, yet they still nail the brass sound and the rhythm of that part of the world without having to reach that far. The vocals, melody, instrumentation and arrangement are all solid, and so it's no surprise that the end result is solid too. It's not going to find its way into the all-time ABBA list, languishing as it does as an afterthought in the 2001 edition of *Super Trouper*, but for me it's better in than out. I don't mind it at all, and if you got some castanets, some stompy heels and a swishy dress then you're going to have a lot of fun with it, and that's no bad thing. 7/10

G: This isn't my sort of thing at all. I read somewhere that it had the working title 'Pig Party on Mallorca'. I think I actually might have preferred that – just for the shock value. The combination of Latin American musical styling and a kind-of waltz rhythm is intriguing for about a minute but pretty soon tests my patience. Probably one of those tracks that was a lot of fun to write, rehearse and record, but it's certainly way less than an essential listen. At least it didn't claw its way onto the album, where it would have been a bad, slightly flippant fit, even though it does do that classic ABBA thing of marrying a superficially chirpy tune with a downbeat, relationship-gone-wrong 'farewell' lyric. Definitely one of the ABBA songs I look forward to listening to least. To go a bit further than that, it's actually one of those songs you hope those Non-ABBA-Fan Friends (NAFFs) I mentioned earlier will never get to hear. They'd never miss an opportunity to bring it up in conversation, not least if you'd just put on your white sombrero. 4/10

I <u>DO</u> Wanna Talk: ABBA Jabber

As inveterate music-lovers, we spend far too much time thinking about music and grabbing each and every conceivable chance to jabber about it with others who share our passion. The very least we can do is air our unscientific, highly personal and extremely unreliable opinions and generally pontificate on matters we're not remotely qualified to pontificate about. Just like everyone else, in fact. So we thought we'd let you eavesdrop on one of our recent chit-chats about one of our favourite bands. If you actually find yourself agreeing with any of it – well, now...that really would be a bit of a bonus!

G: Personally, a lot of the interest in this project has been in taking a band that, almost by stealth, became an important part of my life and then stepping back to think "what is it about them that's so special?". Basically, why did ABBA have that traction only shared by a handful of other bands I'd consider myself a massive fan of? I've found it really enlightening, putting into print – literally – just how and why ABBA cemented themselves as a part of who I am and how I see myself, I suppose.

F: For me, when I was researching and writing the book, a key question was "to what extent am I being revisionist here?". In other words, was I imposing current views or feelings rather than nailing down what I genuinely thought and felt at the time? If I'm totally honest with myself, I don't have a very clear primary recollection of ABBA winning Eurovision in '74. But I feel it MUST have lit the touchpaper of my fandom. I couldn't say, hand on heart, though, that my memories are terribly clear. I've found it quite challenging to distil what I felt not just at that time but also later, when I was dipping in and out of ABBA down the years.

G: Well, being a couple of years older than you and cursed with a bit of a flypaper memory, I've got an advantage in that my recollection of the Eurovision win, for example, is absolutely crystal clear. I've found it pretty easy to transport myself back to certain points in time, to certain songs, albums or ABBA-related experiences, and I've managed to convince myself I know how I felt back then. And when I'm thinking about the Eurovision win and indeed everything that followed, one question that always pops into my head is the extent to which there was an element of right place, right time in ABBA's emergence in the '70s. A bit like The Beatles in the '60s, perhaps. Was there something about the musical conditions particularly conducive to a band like ABBA – and four individuals with their specific skillsets and experience – springing out from the pack and elbowing their way to the front?

F: It's a tough one. When I look back to ABBA's performance in Brighton in '74, it very much appears a case of right place, right time. They'd embraced the glam rock look and some of their early music apart from 'Waterloo' had embraced the glam rock feel while still incorporating a kind of pop purity. And Eurovision-wise, they really were this breath of fresh air, just like 'Poupée de Cire, Poupée de Son' had been when it won the contest in '65. It's easy to forget just how different 'Waterloo' was compared with some of the desperately dull fare going on all around it. But what you're looking at with early ABBA is a collection of individuals who've each been plying their trade for a good few years and have become very accomplished in their own right, but who then spot the bigger opportunity and seize it. Coming up with exactly the right song at exactly the right time was key, of course. Does that count as lucky? Yes and no, I suppose.

G: And of course that created the necessity to replicate the success of 'Waterloo', or at least back it up with something credible. That would have been a massive challenge for anyone.

F: Yeah, they sort of bobbed along for eighteen months before delivering two or three more songs that were really, REALLY good, and all of a sudden everyone was talking about them as the Eurovision stars who'd broken the mould.

G: I suppose I feel that, in a similar way to when The Beatles emerged and a lot of the pop music around them was pretty dire and tired and music desperately needed The Beatles, so Eurovision in the early/mid '70s desperately needed ABBA – even if Eurovision didn't particularly realise it. And notwithstanding the fact that the previous year Anne-Marie David had come up with one of my all-time favourite Eurovision winners. But in terms of pure popness, Eurovision was desperate for ABBA's arrival, so to speak. Yet as with The Beatles, you've still got to ask "why ABBA?". More than that, lots of bands get lucky with one hit, sometimes build a whole career around it and often it becomes a bit of a pension for them, reliably delivering royalty cheques down the decades. 'Waterloo' could have been one of those on some level. So I DO feel there's a strong right place, right time element to ABBA but I also feel that unless you can back that up with genuine talent it's not going to amount to much more than those occasional royalty cheques. But there's always going to be an element of chance, I suppose.

F: And the chance element is always really hard to define and quantify. For every ABBA there are probably at least another ninety-nine acts who've plied their trade diligently and skilfully but never break through, let alone consolidate that big break.

G: Again, though, by focusing on chance, are we missing a big part of what it takes to be successful in music – and particularly on the scale that ABBA achieved? It's not just about musical decisions. It's about business decisions, it's about having the right people around you. Someone we hardly mention in this book is Stig Anderson. I'm not sufficiently conversant with all he did in terms of the largely non-musical hard yards and nudging the band in the right direction, but it's certainly easy to underestimate how important that stuff is to a band getting beyond being a talented bunch of people. It's not just about writing great music, looking good, gelling well and all of that – there are so many other aspects to it in terms of getting the planets to align and putting yourself in a position to burst out onto the world stage. The question is, what were the other ninety-nine acts NOT doing which meant they didn't put themselves in the right position for their potential to be realised? That's a vital part of the story and, even with half a century of ABBA fandom on the clock, I still haven't really got my head around it where ABBA are concerned.

F: I think you're right. It's hard to overestimate Stig Anderson's value to ABBA's emergence, bringing as he did colossal experience in multiple aspects of the music business.

G: When you think about the range of things that underpin success in the music industry, like talking to the right people across the business, knowing the best session players or recording producers or engineers, having the right contacts in the media and the rest of it, there's so much more to making a breakthrough than just knowing your way round a good tune or being able to hold a note. This project's made me want to dig a bit more deeply in terms of how all that stuff played out in the ABBA story.

F: And I'm sure it was every bit as important after 'Waterloo' as before it.

G: Which brings us back to that eighteen-month period after Eurovision, when they're beavering away, thinking "where do we go, where do we take this next?". When you look at that period on its own terms, they didn't do too badly, actually. The 'Ring Ring' re-release, like 'I Do, I Do, I Do, I Do, I Do', did really well in certain territories. Personally, I love 'So Long' even though it bombed and most ABBA fans don't give it the time of day. The thing is, they maintained a certain level of profile and maybe the whole Eurovision thing just means we're setting the bar too high for them. They weren't in the wilderness by a long shot. In some senses, after 'Waterloo', they just went back to being normal. A normal band, doing OK – more than OK, arguably – and striving for that next big breakthrough.

F: Well, 'Waterloo' was undoubtedly a giant blockbuster. But yes, immediately after that, they DID have other hits, near-hits and other songs that made them a force to be reckoned with, albeit not yet a world-conquering one. I mean, like you, I even love 'So Long' and I also do like 'Honey, Honey' – I know you wouldn't give it house room – but it was just a little while before they hit the motherlode again. It's not that common for one album by ANYONE to have two absolutely colossal songs on it. ABBA had to wait until the *ABBA* album to achieve that and, in every sense, make the big leap up to the next level. That was what cemented their momentum and, in the great scheme of schemes, waiting eighteen months or so for that to happen isn't that long a time – though it no doubt felt like an eternity for the band and their fledgling flock of fans.

G: I do sometimes feel it's too easy to glibly bandy the phrase 'Eurovision stigma' around and claim that the contest has sounded the death knell for people's careers. Well, maybe it's only the death knell for people's careers if they've only got limited talent. With ABBA, though, you could argue that to some extent it was a too much, too soon scenario and they had to go back and serve a kind of apprenticeship as a band before they could achieve full lift-off. To put it another way, did people really not go into a record shop in the UK and buy 'Ring Ring' or 'I Do, I Do, I Do, I Do, I Do' because ABBA had won Eurovision and were a bit naff? I'm not sure I believe that. You'll always find an excuse to buy a record if you like it – even if you're kidding yourself you're only doing it for a laugh or whatever.

F: And looking through those first two albums, *Ring Ring* and *Waterloo*, I don't think they missed any slam-dunk hit singles – at least from the narrow UK perspective which is the one we've written this book from. Of course, I only got to know and love those albums much, much later, but in retrospect I don't think they missed out. But what I've found, listening to the extended versions of those two records, is that there are some Swedish language and slightly more obscure songs that were maybe products of their earlier careers that I think are just fantastic. But did any blockbusters pass them by? No, I don't think so. But there's certainly some lovely stuff hidden in the folds of *Ring Ring* and *Waterloo*.

G: I've got a soft spot for *Ring Ring* perhaps because I came to it very, very late, having been frightened off it by *Waterloo*. For me, it's a kind of selection box of partially formed nuggets. But with *Waterloo*, take that first track out and I've really no reason to listen to that album. Is there a sense that, as a Swedish band, with that early stuff they're not being true to themselves? They're looking at what's going on elsewhere and I wonder whether learning how to dovetail some of that with their identity as specifically *Swedish* musicians was the key step in terms of them producing the kind of material that would ultimately propel them right up to the pinnacle.

F: To my mind, the whole Swedish thing is another red herring, neither a help nor a hindrance to them. When you strip it all right down, it was all about the songwriting, regardless of who they were, where they came from, what contests they won and all the rest of it. They happened to be Swedish and, while it was quaint, from a UK vantage-point, listening to them singing and being interviewed in their Swedish accents, it really all boiled down to the quality of the music and their visual impact, in terms of providing the platform for their success.

G: I still think being Swedish gave them a freshness and a point of difference which certainly didn't hurt, in markets like the UK anyway.

F: Maybe. But at its root I think you can go back to the hackneyed old ten thousand hours thing – the idea that it takes ten thousand hours of doing something to get really good at it and be considered an expert at it. When you look back, Agnetha and Frida were both in their teens when they started out. And Benny and Björn too. I mean The Hep Stars and The Hootenanny Singers toured and toured and toured, often playing four hours a night, honing their skills. Even when they were singing other people's material, they were still serving that apprenticeship and, with two or three albums under their belts, it was like "do you know what? It's time to try our own hand at this. We no longer need to survive on Swedish versions of English-language originals".

G: And that, of course, was a common enough process back then, with people like The Beatles and The Rolling Stones coming to the same sort of conclusion. Although again touching on the whole Swedish thing, here's a country that, in musical terms – well, the phrase 'punching above their weight' doesn't nearly do it justice, does it? Would Sweden be the music machine it's become if ABBA hadn't achieved what they achieved back then?

F: That's another million-dollar question. You have to make an assessment around ABBA's role in paving the way or making it easier for the Roxettes and whoever came along later. But I'd have to say, hand on heart, that the ABBA precedent was an irrelevance. I think those later Swedish guys looked west – you know, those guys who came along in the '90s like Cheiron Studios, Denniz Pop, Max Martin – and they saw what was happening in the States, they saw what was successful and they came up with a formula – a strict formula – for success and Sweden became literally a pop factory. Again, I go back to one of my favourite business books, *Bounce* by Matthew Syed. He was the number-one male table tennis player in the UK and the Commonwealth at the same time as someone from the same tiny club in Reading was the women's number one. Was it a coincidence? No, it was the fact that here was a bunch of people who knew each other, trained together and drove each other on.

G: So why did it happen in Sweden and not, say, in Norway or Greece? How can a small country 'up there' on the map do all that, and that includes producing ABBA?

F: I don't know!

G: Which is the correct answer, maybe! Again. it's very easy to come up with glib answers – climate, social democracy, community, folk tradition, blah, blah, blah – but I think it just might be a classic accident of history.

F: It's a question, perhaps, of whether they were successful and incidentally Swedish, or Swedishly successful, so to speak. I think you're right. I don't think there was a particular aggregation of circumstances in Sweden that meant all this was destined to happen. I just don't believe that there were these magic beans in the ground that just had to be cultivated.

G: Looking at ABBA as that foursome who all brought their talents to the party – well, I don't think you can legislate for that. I don't think you can say "all the right conditions were in place in that location and at that time". It's more than that. That foursome were, during that crucial period when they were emerging, an astoundingly cohesive, perfectly balanced unit – certainly in terms of the impression they made on the world at large. Name me another group of that scale and stature who projected that sense of unity and who seemed to effortlessly dovetail the individuality of the members as effectively as ABBA did.

F: Yes, they're a kind of perfectly symmetrical foursome. But then you pick away at the veneer and you have to ask yourself, for instance, how content was Agnetha to sacrifice her own songwriting skills and opportunities for the sake of collective success? You say they appeared perfect to us but we know, from the eventual dissolution of the two relationships, that there were enormous tensions making themselves felt as well.

G: I guess achieving a perfect or at least a workable balance is all about what people are prepared to sacrifice and live with and how other priorities such as family commitments stack up. Can it all hold together or will the centrifugal forces win in the long term or even the short term? Well, ABBA made it work – even when, towards the end, to outside eyes it looked completely and utterly unworkable. And that's because the pieces seemed to fit. OK, Agnetha didn't much care for touring but Benny and Björn were more than compensated by the extra time they had to be writing the songs or holed up in the studio converting them to final product. All the various forces acting on them kept everything locked neatly in place for a good few years.

F: Absolutely. For that sweet spot of two or three years, in particular, they had that perfect equilibrium. It was idyllic. Or appeared idyllic, at any rate.

G: And it came at exactly the right time, in terms of their career trajectory. If that period of optimum equilibrium had dissipated earlier or not arrived till later, you don't get the same ABBA. The chance element again, perhaps. Although I guess we do have to touch on the fact that the success this enabled never really extended to the US in the same way as it did for other territories. Is THAT somewhere where the Swedish factor comes into play or is it simply all about the style of music, being too far from what was happening in America around soul, disco and the rest of it? Plus, famously, ABBA wouldn't tour there in the same relentless way that all the big British rock bands, for instance, needed to in order to make a massive and indelible impact. ABBA simply didn't want to do it the American way, in terms of performing as well as the music itself.

F: I can't disagree with any of that. I think probably the most telling factor was that perhaps – or so it seems to me – they were never really that intent or interested in conquering the States. I'm sure their record company and so forth were very keen on that rather large pot of gold at the end of the Atlantic rainbow but I don't think the States was where the band themselves really wanted to make their biggest splash. ABBA had a lot of success outside Europe in places like Australia and Japan, and then you get those TV shows and appearances in places like Germany, the UK, Poland – they seemed to be so in their element as fellow Europeans. And then you come to the US music market – and we shouldn't forget its complexities and idiosyncrasies, nor indeed the fact that there are PLENTY of people with Scandinavian heritage, especially in the north – and ABBA's music simply WASN'T right place, right time, they didn't invest in it enough, they kind of missed the boat and – as you say – they didn't back it up by getting on the bus.

G: Just rowing back to a previous point, are there any tracks lurking there, tucked away on ANY of the albums, that might have if not matched the success they DID achieve in the States with 'Dancing Queen' at least helped them to wow the States more comprehensively than they actually managed to? I'm struggling to think of any examples.

F: Well you can bet your bottom dollar there were far better paid and far more expert people than you or I going through exactly that process and weighing up what might really fly in that market as far as ABBA were concerned. So 'probably no' is my qualified answer.

G: I get exactly what you're saying. Record companies have always been full of people asking questions like "is this a hit?" and "can I hear a single?". And yet they still sometimes get it wrong because music and people's reaction to it isn't, at heart, a science. One day it may be, but it isn't yet and certainly it wasn't in the '70s. I know there's a lot of hindsight involved but, with the bands we love, we've all had that experience of listening to the radio and thinking "why the hell have they released THIS one?". It's all too easy to make a big blooper with singles choices. And having been a member of a couple of excellent ABBA internet forums in the past, I can confirm that there are few topics which command the interest of ABBA fandom more than 'the one that got away'!

F: But I'll bet not many of them argue with that so-called 'golden run' of singles from 'SOS' through to 'Take a Chance on Me'.

G: Absolutely. But it's what came afterwards that really fascinates me. You've got the decision not to release anything else from *The Album*, then 'Summer Night City' turns into a relatively unsuccessful stopgap single and then you have, arguably, one of the biggest decisions of their career in terms of singles releases. This is all tied in, of course, with that appearance on *The Mike Yarwood Christmas Show* in 1978 – which is one of those events where I can absolutely remember exactly how I felt at the time – and their presentation of 'If It Wasn't for the Nights' as, de facto, the next single, even though those words weren't actually uttered. Because there's real pressure in terms of making the right call. Back then, bands could be having hits one minute, then have a couple of relative flops and literally have broken up by the end of the year. Mott the Hoople did exactly that in 1974, for instance. Things could unravel very quickly.

F: Yeah, with ABBA, you've got the *Voulez-Vous* material coming down the pipeline and the right choices have got to be made.

G: Exactly. Obviously, someone went cold on 'If It Wasn't for the Nights' and they went with 'Chiquitita' instead. Personally, I think they made the right call in pulling 'Nights', even if a lot of ABBA fans really do see that track as the archetypal one that got away. But we find ABBA in a music environment that's moved on to late disco, post-punk, New Wave and the rest of it. As I say, some big calls needed to be made. You could make a reasonable case for pretty much anything from the new album being released as a single, and I know a lot of fans think 'Kisses of Fire' should have been released as well as 'Nights' and 'As Good as New', in particular. I find that sort of conundrum and the counterfactuals that go with it endlessly fascinating. Picking the right singles – and in the right order.

F: With *Voulez-Vous* I think they pretty much got it right. In the end, half the tracks saw some form of singles release, in the UK anyway. And I say all that fully taking into account the fact that, between *Ring Ring* and *The Visitors*, it's the only ABBA album not to spawn a UK number-one hit record. I think they should have released the ones they did and shouldn't have released the ones they didn't. I really don't see any howlers in there. I don't see anything overwhelmingly compelling among the other five songs that has me fulminating that they missed a slam-dunk.

G: But what about the double A-side thing with the title track and 'Angeleyes'? Would those have been better – DONE better – as standalone singles?

F: I just don't think 'Angeleyes' would have stood up as a standalone. More of an album track, for me. But just while you were talking there, I was thinking about the timings. They've got the big tour coming up towards the end of '79 so they need to keep in the public eye throughout the whole of the year running up to that. It's the one year where we see an almost continuous singles presence in the UK. Five big hit singles – they never did that before or since. It was the nearest they came to being a pop sausage machine.

G: I've got a major hang-up, though, regarding the title track. I love it more than most ABBA fans do. If it's not all-time ABBA top ten for me, it's very, very close. I just think that, from my perspective as a teenage record-buyer at the time, putting it out as a double A-side sent out the wrong signals. Almost as if they were saying they didn't think either individual track was quite good enough for a singles release.

F: Well, I'm with you. For me, 'Voulez-Vous' is a staple. It deserves its seat at the banquet every time. It's up there, whereas 'Angeleyes' is a bit middling.

G: As you know, I'm mildly obsessed with ABBA tribute groups and 'Voulez-Vous' is always one of the showstoppers. I don't know about at the *ABBA Voyage* thing which, at the present time, I haven't seen yet. But at tribute shows it forms part of a holy trinity with 'Gimme! Gimme! Gimme!' and 'Does Your Mother Know' which reliably whip the crowd into a state of near-hysteria. And what do those three tracks all have in common? They were all released in '79 – ABBA's relatively fallow year, in terms of UK chart positions. It's a bit like Queen with 'Don't Stop Me Now'. That's became a core Queen song, an iconic entry in the Queen catalogue, but it definitely wasn't viewed that way at the time. It was a nothing single. 1979 again, coincidentally.

F: Plus, of course, the ABBAtars are based on the band as they were in '79. It's become a bit of a defining year for them, which is ironic, really, given the absence of a UK number one. So what are you saying? What might have been done differently?

G: Well, with the benefit of revisionist hindsight, I wonder whether they shouldn't have just said, "you know what – January 1979 – New Year, new ABBA – bang! – 'Voulez-Vous' is the album's lead single – pick the bones out of that!". I know it was the Year of the Child and so on, but I can't help wondering if that might have been a real statement of intent for the year ahead.

F: Who knows what was going through the agonised minds of the record company execs back then, in terms of which songs, what order, what country? But it turned out all right in the end!

G: Yes, but at the time I really felt I'd been a bit of a jinx on ABBA so I'm particularly sensitive on this point! They'd not had a number one in the UK with me on board. In the end I had to wait for two and a half years to experience that! It took them until 'The Winner Takes It All' to break the Gazza curse!

F: And lo and behold, it was nothing to do with you, after all! Ha ha!

G: Well, in your teens, you think the world revolves around you. It's the lucky underpants syndrome.

F: Which brings us on to 1980 when ABBA are very much right at the top of the tree again. Two more UK number-one singles – thanks to your underpants – and the sublime *Super Trouper* album to back them up. Quite a year to be on board the ABBA Polar express.

G: Yes, indeed. That album's a classic for me. A feeling not shared as widely among the ABBA fandom as you'd have thought, in my experience. And then there's *The Visitors* and we both talk in this book about how sensational that album is and how it'll probably always be an underappreciated masterpiece. It all looked set fair. But then ABBA drop off a cliff, pretty much. It's like what I was saying about Mott the Hoople, it all unravels shockingly quickly from a commercial point of view. The guaranteed big hits are no longer guaranteed.

F: Well, yes. They suddenly struggle to scrape the UK Top 30. It wasn't even a sedate and graceful decline.

G: It's the big question – why did that happen? It's not like they'd lost the art of writing great music. Was it just a wheel-of-fashion, cycle-of-public-approval thing? Had people just had enough of them?

F: I think it's all of that. And it's also to do with the personal side of things. With regard to their relationships, the marital relationships, they'd been hanging on in terms of trying to keep it together – to keep SOMETHING together – in the public eye. That's got to be a factor in the disintegration of the band.

G: Oh, I agree, but I think no-one in the UK, say, thought "I'm not going into a record shop to buy 'Head Over Heels' because Benny and Frida aren't together anymore".

F: No, but it did erode that perfect image which was such a hallmark of their earlier peak career years. It had all got a bit tarnished and that can't have helped.

G: Plus of course, linked to that, they're writing more mature, more 'adult' music. But do you reckon that, if fracturing relationships hadn't been part of the picture at that point, they might have just taken a relative dip in fortunes in their stride – just like Elton, Queen and so on all experienced at some point – and kept going, doing an album practically every year, confident that sooner or later they'd hit the sweet spot again? Or, because they were still perceived by the public largely as a disposable pop act, would it simply not have been possible to restore their position in the public's affections in terms of record sales?

F: I reckon that, if they'd been able to get past not just personal differences as couples but also the different things they wanted out of life, music and being part of a band, they'd have gone on and we'd have seen them relaunch themselves in '84, say, as the next stage, the next manifestation of the ABBA evolution. And I think we'd have been just as wowed and just as amazed by how they'd evolved, just like how we were every time Bowie reinvented himself. He was still doing that sort of thing, that constant evolution, right up until just before he died when he released *Blackstar*. But the fact of the matter is that the relationships were dissolving and although, musically speaking, the guys were still married to each other, their aspirations were turning to other areas – bigger, more ambitious projects in new contexts like musical theatre. They'd outgrown ABBA. But I think you'd have found that if ABBA had gone on through the '80s and '90s, they'd have continued to confound us. In terms of what they would have LOOKED like – and let's go back to that elephant in the room, namely the difficulty, in our society, for a female artist to retain her appeal to a mass audience as she ages – well, that's a different issue altogether.

G: I suppose I'm wondering whether two different, separate things happened, but we want to try to link them into a coherent story. One is that, again from a UK perspective, the public want new faces, new sounds, something fresh, all of that. The other is that ABBA have pretty much outgrown ABBA, for all the various reasons and to various degrees depending on the individual member concerned. Maybe there's no connection at all between those two developments. ABBA were evolving and changing, coincidentally while the world was falling a little out of love with them, but not BECAUSE of it. And vice versa.

F: Yes, there's always that human impulse to make sense of stuff and weave threads of a story together even when they're pretty much separate. I don't know. That brings us on to the whole issue of their solo experiences. Maybe we should summarise those experiences in terms of before, during and after ABBA. When I say "after ABBA", I'm leaving the whole *Voyage* thing out of the equation for now, of course.

G: As you know, apart from *Chess*, I generally find the post-ABBA stuff really hard to listen to. And I say that as a MASSIVE fan of European pop and rock music down the decades and indeed Eurovision specifically. But you've had a minor religious experience with some of this material, haven't you?

F: I must say it's been an absolutely humungous learning experience for me over the course of working on this book. Let's face it, anyone reading this is probably very, very familiar with ABBA's output. But many of them will probably be much less familiar with the other part of the iceberg – their output as four individuals. I've had the enormous good fortune to spend an enormous amount of time going over that stuff. I think it's safe to say that I've now listened to every single song that Frida and Agnetha have recorded outside of ABBA, plus a good portion of the lads' pre-ABBA stuff, and most if not all of their post-ABBA stuff. I suppose two things really strike me. Firstly, how much of the girls' early stuff I really, really enjoyed and found extremely pleasing. There are some lovely, lovely songs, Swedish-language songs, which are right up there. Then you come to Frida's *Ensam* album and Agnetha's *Elva Kvinnor i ett Hus* album in the mid-'70s and it's just a delicious range of music. And Benny and Björn's work with The Hep Stars and The Hootenanny Singers too – it's so listenable! Then the second thing I wanted to say relates to the sheer volume of output from – and the prodigious ability of – Björn and Benny, through *Chess* to *Kristina från Duvemåla*.

G: So where would you rank Benny and Björn overall?

F: You definitely have to put them in the same category as the likes of Lennon and McCartney, the Gershwins, Rodgers and Hammerstein, Jagger and Richards, Elton John and Bernie Taupin. They should definitely be spoken of in the same breath as them.

G: Is there a prejudice, then, about pop – and what people would wrongly dismiss as pure pop music? It may be changing a bit now but B&B don't routinely get grouped with those titans of popular music.

F: I think so, yes. And I'm interested in the way they went back to the Swedish well and kind of gloried in their Swedishness and kind of wrote songs again about being Swedish. *Kristina* is never going to be a pop greatest hits package, but that's because Björn and Benny have a kind of creative intellectualism about them alongside that fundamental ability to compose lots and lots of songs of extremely high quality. And *Chess* of course just shows how they'd gorged themselves on musicals from the 1940s onwards until they really understood what made that genre tick. But it seems to me, when you think about the two lads, almost any genre they turn their hand to...

G: ...they master it! They've showed themselves to be masters of multiple arts. And I think that's a vastly underappreciated aspect of what their capability actually is. They're not properly valued for that evolution, for the way they negotiated that path and for the sheer willingness to take risks and stretch themselves. That's not always the case even for some of the great writers of musicals, for instance. But when it comes to Agnetha and Frida, well, they're coming at it from a very different angle. Their role in the band was different. But they're still faced with pretty much the same kinds of questions. What do we do now, given what we've achieved with ABBA? Do we even do ANYTHING? How does it all fit together? To what extent are they, in some respects, going through the motions? Is their heart really in it? Or are these unfair questions?

F: I really don't know. One of the key things, for me, is that, post-ABBA, Frida and Agnetha essentially drew on the skills of a vast number and huge range of songwriters. So that's a very different beast from building up that understanding, that rapport with a bespoke pair of songwriters you're working with, living with every single day. I can see why they went down that route, of course, but it does create its own problems when you're trying to forge a distinctive solo identity while still remaining rooted in the great things you've achieved in the past. It's not easy. But they clearly wanted to do it. They didn't need the money. So, on some level, they clearly enjoyed it and needed it. All four of them wanted to carry on working, wanted to explore new creative avenues.

G: Plus of course it's a natural human tendency to prove, on some level, that you don't need the others to be a success, that you can do it on your own terms, in your own way and showcasing your own skills above all else.

F: For me, what characterised Frida's and Agnetha's stuff in the '80s...well, put it this way: you could argue that the guys have always written timeless music. I know that sounds ridiculous because so much of ABBA's material has a big '70s imprint, but if it wasn't timeless I don't think the whole *Mamma Mia!* thing would be the phenomenon it's been. But the ladies' '80s output was really of its time and as a result it immediately dated. It's their really early stuff and the sporadic, much later stuff that's the really good stuff.

G: And looking at those immediate post-ABBA years, when ABBA weren't generally seen as particularly cool and their music was perhaps regarded by many as just outdated pop froth, you'd have to say it was pretty extraordinary that all that turned around so epically and utterly in the '90s and into the new millennium. With hindsight, it can seem that the whole *Mamma Mia!* phenomenon was somehow inevitable. But it really wasn't. The fact that someone thought it was worth investing colossal amounts of time, energy, emotion and money to get all of that on the road for a band that had been and still was, in many fashionable quarters, still seen as a bit naff…well, it really is easy to underestimate how remarkable that was. So what was it about that intervening period between 1983 and, say, the Erasure EP thing and the release of *ABBA Gold*, when ABBA and everything that went with them was in a kind of cryogenic suspension, that ultimately meant it would all pan out so well in the end?

F: I think it comes down to that superb body of work. Obviously, *ABBA Gold* and *More ABBA Gold* came along eventually and reminded the world of that basic, undeniable fact. So the previous decade when they were basically off the radar to all intents and purposes turned out to be the exception rather than the rule, perhaps. But along come those compilations and you were just reminded what a ridiculous amount of fantastic pop music they'd generated.

G: Can I pitch in with a slightly different take on it? A key reason why *ABBA Gold* flew and I mean REALLY flew – mountains, forests and streams… – is BECAUSE ABBA had been so underestimated and taken for granted, even during their heyday, let alone in the decade after the painful, piecemeal split. I'm loath to ascribe to society or the record-buying public a single mentality, a single motivation but I think we all – and I'm including most fans in that, notwithstanding the incredible level of business ABBA did when they were flourishing and all the fanaticism they generated –

simply failed to recognise and appreciate just how good they were. People knew they loved or liked the songs, but even people like me perhaps didn't fully understand just how rare a talent, how precious a gift this foursome had. I think it took the release of *ABBA Gold* for most people to recognise just how special they were and I even think, on a kind of subconscious level, there was a sort of guilt that ABBA's sheer brilliance had been grotesquely underestimated. So it was a bit like the return of the prodigal son, an outburst of affection and esteem and, for many people, a kind of Road to Damascus conversion, a great outpouring which has pretty much sustained ABBA ever since. As you know, I held out from buying *Gold* for decades. But when I DID finally take the plunge, well – sheesh…!

F: It's just an impossibly high sustained standard. I think you're right. I think that's all fair. The thing is, they were bloody good in a parochial Swedish environment. They were bloody good as sort-of glam rockers. They were bloody good as a mainstream pop act. They were bloody good at writing musicals. All that kind of stuff. But it took somebody to gather together just some of that brilliance – be it in the form of *Gold* or *Mamma Mia!* – to really deliver the incontrovertible evidence that these four people were worthy of a place at the very top table.

G: Yes, but just to emphasise again: I think it took the fact that most people had pretty much forgotten ABBA for them eventually to appreciate that ABBA were actually more, a lot more, than 'bloody good' and to absorb the fact that this kind of ability, this kind of chemistry really doesn't come along too often. The penny finally dropped that there was something genuinely magical about ABBA. Without that lull – and maybe if they hadn't gone out with a whimper rather than a roar in '82/'83, when in all honesty it all got a little bit embarrassing – maybe that whole renaissance, rediscovery, rehabilitation wouldn't have had the same impact. It was like the public were making up for lost time.

F: I think I'm Exhibit A in that respect. Or one of the Exhibit As, at least! Between '82 and '92 I completely moved away from ABBA. It wasn't until I bought *ABBA Gold* on cassette and stuck it on in the car and went off driving around the country with it playing as my soundtrack that the wheel came full circle again. There I was, boring people with my music because there was just nowhere to hide. It was hit upon hit, classic after classic. Compare it to when The Beatles had that *1* compilation released back in 2000. The thing is, The Beatles were NEVER underrated. Never, ever! So it didn't hit you like a sledgehammer in the way that *Gold* did. ABBA's brand of music was supposed to be the lowest common denominator. So it took *Gold* to remind us that we'd been lucky to be of an age to enjoy something really rare and special.

G: And then there's the whole *Mamma Mia!* thing that comes along and takes on a life of its own.

F: Well, this might be heresy but I think *Mamma Mia!* is actually a little bit of a red herring too. For me, the vital point is that the underlying music is so damn good that we can even tolerate film actors butchering those beloved, perfect songs.

G: Tweaked lyrics and all...

F: It's like rewriting the Bible!

G: Absolutely! But before we close out this jabber about ABBA, I guess we should bring things right up to date and discuss the recent comeback. Again, because it's happened – and it really DID happen and it's now an established part of the ABBA story – it's all too easy to undervalue just how extraordinary, how audacious it's all been. Just the fact that, after forty years, all four of them could simply care enough to do it. And that's a testament to each of them. It's not just a question of "we could do it, we might do it, we want to do it, it's a nice idea" but "we CAN do it, we WILL do it and we'll do it at such a high level that it'll have all the hallmarks of a proper, credible, decent, worthwhile ABBA album". We'd all be poorer if we didn't have the *Voyage* album in our collections. To come back with what's properly and definitively an ABBA album, with all the hallmarks that label implies, is a hell of an achievement. It's easy to underestimate how incredible that is.

F: And then of course they kind of top it all off by coming up with a completely new, completely different way of preserving themselves in a kind of visual formaldehyde which means they can perform their material theoretically forever. It wasn't a surprise to me that they could come back and write another album that's as good as it is. But the *Voyage* show... That's something else again! Actually, I still think they may have another album in them.

G: I kind of feel we haven't heard the last from them as well. I think a whole album would be highly unlikely but I find it hard to believe there's absolutely nothing left in terms of a special one-off track or whatever. I still feel the final full stop has yet to be added. Which leaves us with the question of what comes AFTER the full stop. Here we are, celebrating fifty years of ABBA fandom. Looking ahead to 2074, will people still be listening to them?

F: Well, we're still listening to high-quality music from the seventeenth, eighteenth, nineteenth centuries. So I think, yes, people will still be listening to something which is the absolute peak of its art form.

G: I completely agree with that and I'll tell you why. I'm very much encouraged by the attitude of younger people towards older music, especially compared with how I used to be. When I was in my teens, pop music from the '50s – even a lot of it from the '60s and certainly stuff from the '20s, '30s, '40s – seemed to have absolutely zero relevance to me. It seemed almost comical in its primitiveness. The idea that I might want to trawl back through it didn't even get to first base, let alone past it. But take both of my kids. Enabled by the internet, they're incredibly open to music of all sorts, all periods. They're not remotely as fashion-conscious, if you like. Younger people, I think, are used to different sorts of sounds coming at them all the time.

F: I think you're right. The accessibility of music platforms means they can dip in and listen to anything they like, anytime they like. So they're not as conscious of the passage of time or the place in time that a piece of music holds. It's not like when we'd hear a bit of music and go "oh I remember that, it was number one when I was in Ibiza in 1983". You can't say that sort of thing anymore in the same way. You really can't. And certainly young people can't because they only heard it a fortnight ago and they've been listening to it nonstop since and it kind of exists outside time.

G: The other thing I'd just like to add – and again it ties in with my obsession with ABBA tribute acts – is just how emotional it is for me to see genuinely young people in those audiences. And I mean teenagers. And they've gone as a group – not dragged along by older family members. And they're really, REALLY into this music. There'll be a gang of five or six teenage girls, say, and they clearly absolutely bloody love ABBA. They're so up for those songs! They know all the words. They're among the most vocal, animated people in the crowd. I find it so moving to think of that torch being passed down the decades, down the generations. Some of those guys, with a following wind and a functioning Health Service, will see-in the next century in their dotage. Now I don't know how they came to ABBA's music – maybe through the internet, or through parents, or because they got dragged along to see *Mamma Mia! Here We Go Again* – but the net result is amazing. Add to that the undeniable fact that the only thing I can confidently predict about the future is that it'll be even easier to find and surround yourself with ABBA's music. So I just don't see how ABBA aren't listened to, valued, loved in fifty years' time. It'd need much more of an explanation as to why it DIDN'T happen rather than why it WILL happen.

F: I agree. And that's a great way to close this ABBA Jabber chat. It's a measure of their status as a band that we still want to connect with them and with their music as closely as we possibly can. We can't see them 'live' anymore, but we can see a facsimile of them in the form of a tribute act or a 3D digitised version. It's a testament to their popularity and the underlying quality of their output that we still desperately want to be in their presence.

The Songs They're Singing: Part 3

Ring Ring (from *Ring Ring*)

F: Well, this is a jaunty lead-off track for the ABBA debut album, isn't it? Immediately gets you in the mood with some catchy riffs and a real bouncy feel to it. The ladies' voices sound so young, like girls' voices, which is practically what they are, I guess. Then the plaintive chorus kicks in, the second part of which is delightful – I'm guessing it's a semitone or two lower, without remotely knowing what that means... – before repeating the main chorus line again. I like the twangy lead guitar bits too, which sound halfway between honkytonk and country. As a non-musical personal myself (apart from the odd – very odd – bit of singing), lyrics are always important to me – although ironically I'm notoriously bad for mishearing and mislearning lyrics, sometimes finding out my error decades later.[13] So I like the concept and the sadness behind the unrequited phone call, while the lyrics are crisp and move along very nicely. 7/10

G: It's arguably the biggest counterfactual in the whole ABBA story: how would they have done if this song had qualified for Eurovision in 1973? Good as it is, I'm pretty sure it would never have nudged Anne-Marie David out of the top spot; it may even have struggled to have edged ahead of other stuff such as Sir Cliff's mighty 'Power to All Our Friends'. So everything happens for a reason, as the irritating and mistaken saying goes. On its own terms, though, 'Ring Ring' is a real winner. Great riff, plenty of energy, hooks-a-plenty, a piano part that rollicks along like Jerry Lee Lewis lite, plus of course that fusion of plaintive and uplifting that would become such a hallmark of some of ABBA's very best and most effective output. Not quite the smack in the face that 'Waterloo' gives you, more like a very assertive tap on the

---

[13] A misheard lyric example from 'Waterloo': I always thought it was "How does it feel when you won the war?" rather than "I was defeated, you won the war" – d'oh!

shoulder. But as a kind of mission statement – first track, first album – job done! 7/10

Rock Me (from *ABBA*)

F: This is one of the few songs that I've always struggled to appreciate, to explain to myself, to rationalise. When I'm writing about ABBA songs the words generally come pretty easy. Not with this one. It's a bit of a conundrum for me. It's corny, but it kinda works. It's clumsy, but it's kinda fun. It's got glam appeal, but it's a touch anodyne, lacking that politically incorrect undercurrent of sleaze that usually comes with the genre. It's enthusiastic and makes me feel good, but at the same time doesn't quite feel genuine enough, honest enough. It's not fraudulent, it's just not quite 'on it'. I do like bits of it though, like the "don't stop the rocking, don't stop the rocking", and Benny's piano keeps it moving along, while Björn does a decent job too, in the same way as your history teacher might have sung a bit of Slade… I'm not really a fan, but it's a good song, I guess. 6/10

G: Here we go again. Let's play another game of Inexplicable Soft Spot. I've already mentioned multiple times that the lesser-known songs which take up a good chunk of *ABBA: The Movie* are indelibly dowsed with fantastic connotations for me. But of course they wouldn't have SUCH great connotations if I didn't actually like them. 'Rock Me' has got natural 'live' number written right through it, but it more than holds its own on its parent album. The arresting drum-and-vocal-only intro gives your eardrums a pleasing kick and sets the scene for the track to take on more and more instrumental cargo as it ascends to cruising altitude. My highlight is Björn's satisfyingly growly, completely convincing lead vocal, which ensures this is comfortably among my favourite songs he grabs the main mike for. He sounds like a man on a rock mission on this jaunty, jerky track which is guaranteed to deliver a decent dose of feelgood vibes if you'll only lie back and let it. The backing vocals are a treat too. 7/10

Rock 'n' Roll Band (from *Ring Ring*)

F: (First time.) This is an up-tempo track to draw a curtain on the debut album. This rocky-ish number – if that's not too grey a made-up term – feels emblematic for the original *Ring Ring* as a whole: a country-rock feel, Björn doing the heavy lifting, the ladies as reliable as ever on backing vocals, and the insistent piano of Mr Andersson. Some quite rocky and accomplished guitar work on this one. I quite like the chorus but the only thing that rankles is due to my slight rhyming OCD: ABBA lyrics are usually exquisitely tight, but the pairing of 'dance' and 'band' doesn't quite do it for me. That said, I don't mind the rhyming of 'girl' and 'world', contrary old soul that I am. Not my cup of tea, but a decent song nonetheless. Good enough to close the album? Just about, à mon avis, mes amis. 7/10

G: This is just the sort of paint-by-numbers rock schlock that I've got a surprising and almost insatiable appetite for. I can imagine a song very like this turning up on a Wings album, for instance, or nestling there as a bonus track on a reissue of *Frampton Comes Alive*. It's the sort of chorus that floats my whole flotilla and it propels this track perilously close to my all-time ABBA top twenty. The bit about hiding behind the flowers is one of my favourite dumb lyrics ever, but Björn just sounds so *comfortable* singing this sort of unthreatening stuff. It's an archetypal early '70s light-rock album-closer with a fuzz-guitar sound that dates it very much to a precise moment in time. One-dimensional life-affirming hokum that I simply can't help absolutely adoring. 8/10

Santa Rosa (B-side of 'He Is Your Brother')

F: (First time.) A tough act to live up to the song on the reverse, 'Santa Rosa' reminds me a lot of 'Merry-Go-Round' (another *Ring Ring* B-side which finds itself on the Deluxe Edition of the album) and not just because it's got Mr U on lead vocals. I wonder how many Swedish bands could carry off early '70s Americana like this? You'd never know the origins of the band listening to the confident lyrics and their command of the 'folk pop' musical genre. The most ninja of ABBA fans will know that 'Santa Rosa' was performed before ABBA were called ABBA at the third World Popular Music Festival in Tokyo, not getting past the preliminary round. I found myself pa-pa-pa-ing along to the song, safe in the knowledge that I probably won't listen to it too many times again. (I would go on to prove myself wrong.) It's such early ABBA when they were experimenting with a bunch of different styles and really belongs better with their pre-ABBA heritage. Pleasant enough. 6/10

G: More cod-rock baloney by numbers. But so what? If the description 'harmless fun' sounds like a classic case of damning with faint praise, it's nevertheless entirely warranted. Not really an ABBA track, being Agnetha-and-Frida-free, but there's nothing especially wrong with it. It just sounds very, very generic, very, very derivative and very, VERY dated. But I do quite like the twangy piano. Basically a heavily diluted pre-tread of 'Rock 'n' Roll Band'. 4/10

She's My Kind of Girl (from *Ring Ring*)

F: (First time.) Wow, this one's different, sounds very old. This could be late '60s, early '60s, or even '50s, I feel. It's so gosh-darned wholesome, lyrically and musically. Everly Brothers, anyone? It starts with a couple of instruments I don't know, maybe something stringed accompanying a triangle I think, and it's sweet and delicate like one of those really light iced buns. I really like the low stacked chords Benny plays to underpin Björn's vocals, very clever. Irrepressibly positive and uplifting, and it sounds like the ladies got time off for good behaviour on this song too. It works though, I like it, including the bass line which is not too intrusive but noticeably catchy. This one makes you feel like everything's alright with the world and reminds me a little of 'California Dreaming', which is – Freddie pop quiz trivia time – my fave song of all time. 7/10

G: Not remotely my sort of song or sound. I used to find this one pretty much unlistenable. These days I can appreciate it just a little more as a kind of period piece – even though the period in question was a good few years before ABBA's. Here they ostensibly go full-on retro by evoking (though not in over-florid style) Woodstock-era flower-power and overtones of an early-autumn smooch behind a bike shed, if not quite a full-on summer of love. Or they would be going retro if this song didn't actually pre-date ABBA and fail to feature either hide or hair of Agnetha and Frida. As album-fillers go, however, it has a certain curiosity value as well as an undemanding sort of charm which make it impossible to be completely dismissive about it. 5/10

Should I Laugh or Cry (B-side of 'One of Us' and 'When All Is Said and Done')

F: 'Should I Laugh or Cry' is a rare lyrical effort for me as it suggests the emotion of disdain, stuff you don't hear very much in ABBA's output. Delivered by Frida, some of the lines she sings are dripping with scorn, making me feel that I wouldn't want to get on the wrong side of this lady. As always with ABBA songs, there are some nice touches, like the pappy bassline and Benny's keyboard fills. The chorus disappoints slightly; it feels too light after the darkness and negativity of the verses, almost like she's letting him off lightly, though the lyrics don't suggest that. Frida's vocal is excellent, as is Agnetha's backing work, yet the song doesn't quite build enough, doesn't quite get into the station marked 'Satisfaction'. So a slight miss for me, and probably not a surprise that it didn't make the final nine on *The Visitors*. 5/10

G: Nice intro with that slightly clucky riff and, strangely, I quite like the way the song never really goes anywhere. It just moseys around, never overreaching itself. Frida's slightly ethereal, at times almost ghostly vocal works very well and gives it a decent lift. It's all tidy and neat, but a big step down from almost everything that did actually make it onto *The Visitors*. Solid, fairly decent B-side material. 5/10

Sitting in the Palmtree (from *Waterloo*)

F: (First time.) A rather chilled calypso feel to this as it starts. It's got pleasant, unusual percussion that helps set the genre. ABBA doing that thing I like where the title of the song is the first lyric you hear. It moves along rather nicely but then kind of morphs into another song that I'm not sure about and doesn't seem to belong to the verse, which is a bit disappointing. Then the bridge comes in, which feels like a third piece that doesn't mesh with the other two in this higgledy-piggledy jigsaw of a song. Björn's voice is solid for this number, if unremarkable. I can get the idea of a bloke sitting in a palm tree with Jeanie on his mind, it kinda works for me, but the accompanying music is too much of a patchwork to get me comfortably from one end of it to the other. Don't actually like it much, on further reflection. 3/10

G: Four minutes that feel like fourteen. Hours. I've never been able to connect with this track at any point, in any way, on any level. At best, a disappointing B-side. It doesn't help that this song is so exposed on the *Waterloo* album. It's not just that it comes along second; it's also that it follows the near-faultless title track, magnifying the inadequacies tenfold. Its general pointlessness might not have been quite so glaringly evident if it had been politely hidden three-quarters of the way through the album. Hemmed in by its unconvincing reggae/calypso groove, the most I can say for this song is that it's chirpy. Which is just another way of saying harmless but really quite irritating. 3/10

Slipping Through My Fingers (from *The Visitors*)

F: Lurking towards the end of side two of *The Visitors*, this delicate little flower of a song with Agnetha in the lead vocal captures the parent's-eye view of the bitter-sweet rite of passage for the child as it builds its independence and starts to make its own way in the world. The lyrics can't be anything other than inspired by true experience; they're simply too good, too on the money. It doesn't quite tug on the heart strings as much as some of their other work, perhaps because I'm getting past this stage in my own parental journey, although the absence of college-bound kids of course resonates. Musically, it's very pleasant, perhaps a touch on the anodyne side, but as always it's so tightly put together that I find it hard to criticise. The lead guitar instrumental break, together with the synth violins, echoes the chorus perfectly. Well put together, without setting the world on fire, it's nonetheless definitely an extra string to the album's bow. 7/10

G: Some songs take you to the cleaners emotionally, leaving you drained and a bit disorientated but somehow left with a life-affirming reminder of what's really important to you. And then there's 'Slipping Through My Fingers', which not only takes your emotions to the cleaners but also empties all your pockets first and hangs you out to dry afterwards, before sending you spinning round the spiritual tumble-dryer just for good measure. The sentiments of this song used to cut right through me long before parenthood came a-calling. Its sense of something lost, opportunities missed and time squandered meant it simply couldn't avoid leaving me in a metaphorical crushed heap after I'd listened to it. To say it's the sound of ABBA ratcheting up the mature lyrical content doesn't go anywhere near far enough in conveying the soul-piercing depth of this extraordinary track. The vision and the composition – they're just incredible. And then there's Agnetha's vocal, living every moment with us and seeing right through us. Needless to say, becoming a dad only invited the song to slam down even harder on my emotional accelerator. A nailed-on eye-mister every single time and a quite awesome feat of songcraft. The last fifteen seconds – they're simply devastating. ABBA's finest ballad. It may even be ANYONE's finest ballad. 10/10

So Long (from *ABBA*)

F: What a gloriously bracing rock 'n' roll song this is, like driving fast with the roof down and letting the wind tousle your hair (I don't have any hair, I'm projecting here)! 'So Long' is irresistible, like a virus in a hadron collider. Who thought that parting could be the opposite of such sweet sorrow? This is a 'see ya later, loser' song with a finger-and-thumb 'L' shape on the forehead. Despite the lyrics I'd find it really hard not to be in a good mood after listening to this whirlwind of a close to the album. Somebody turn the clock back to 1975 and add me a few years so I can put on my dancing shoes and twirl some lady with a big skirt around the place. Wow, what a rush. You need a lie down after listening to this one, I can't imagine what it must be like performing it or seeing it performed. The energy! 8/10

G: Just a pale re-tread of 'Waterloo', predictably shunned by the record-buying public virtually everywhere in the world, apart from a few scanty European markets? So runs the conventional wisdom about this song. I take a deeply contrarian and still very unfashionable view. For me, it takes the Eurovision-winning template and cranks it up a couple more notches in terms of attitude and swagger. The guitar riff that's front and centre sends the track careering along like an out-of-control dodgem car, while Agnetha and Frida really commit to the vocal full-throttle, creating that exhilarating sense of being let off the leash. As ever, cracking hooks abound, drenching the verse, pre-chorus and chorus with a whole plague of earworms. The ascending, energising, straight-out-of-the-blocks intro is a beauty. At the other end of the song, the outro is on another plane altogether as Benny's piano-clatter paves the way for the brass to see out proceedings in blood-pumping triumph – and to close the album in a way that SCREAMS "Play me again! AND AGAIN!". The confidence now oozing from every musical pore of the band is simply palpable. Come on, people! What's the matter with you? Show this classic a bit more love! You really are missing out. 10/10

Soldiers (from *The Visitors*)

F: You're left in no doubt as to the military theme of this song as the marching band-like drum opens up 'Soldiers'. It reminds me of something Sting might have written in his post-Police, Cold-War-era career (around the time of 'Russians', for example) and 'Soldiers' fits into a similar '80s mindset. Appearing on the same album as the 'The Visitors' title track, it's another example of a willingness to grasp the more mature subjects occupying us all, delivered with the gift for poetry and musical craft that come along so rarely in popular music. For me it's also a song about bravery, about admitting that soldiers do the things that we can't do, are afraid to do. We might not approve of war, but we're thankful to those who step up to do the needful. And no ABBA song would be complete without the earworm twirly trills and elements of keyboard and guitar artistry that fit so well into the finished product. I'm between a seven and an eight out of ten on this one, rounding down by a scintilla. 7/10

G: Singing soldiers and dancing to buglers doesn't sound like especially fertile territory for a pop song (although decades later Coldplay would, of course, tackle this shibboleth in curious fashion by invoking Roman cavalry choirs, of all things, on 'Viva la Vida'). But ABBA were absolute masters of making you forget – and sometimes not even notice at all – just how outré some of their chosen subject-matter was. It's a tradition that went right back to Napoleon, David Livingstone and King Kong. And it's evident again here on this excellent track. That semi-martial drum pattern provides the spine for another totally convincing, moodily compelling slice of chilly brilliance from *The Visitors*. Sumptuous melodies and tasty lead-guitar work are complemented by superlative lead and backing vocals which project a strange sense of apprehension, anticipation and inspiration mixed up together. I still haven't got the foggiest idea what it's all got to do with soldiers. And I've yet to hear a bugle tune I can dance to. But, by God, I live in hope. 8/10

SOS (from *ABBA*)

F: Are there more recognisable introductory B. Andersson piano notes in all of ABBA's work? You'd better not listen to the first verse of Agnetha's plaintive desperation in a less than optimistic frame of mind or else it'll bring you to your knees. There's so much raw emotion in it. And then the piano takes over again, building progressively into the chorus. The song title is so simple, and figures so effortlessly in the chorus lyrics that I have to remind myself that these blokes are composing in a foreign language. It's simply not fair. Music takes us to other places and this one does it for me without even trying. Cue the thousand-yard stare, the pensive prestidigitation and the blunted sense of the passage of time, as the final few chords gently twist the knife. So beautiful it could make you weep. 9/10

G: Right from the get-go and those ringing, doleful, instantly recognisable descending piano notes, we've entered a brave new world where ABBA are suddenly the musical masters of all they survey. There's simply not a note out of place here, there's nothing that doesn't work beautifully, there's no idea that isn't both top-drawer creatively and delivered flawlessly. It's like a three-minute highlights reel brim-full of unforgettable vocal and musical moments. I especially love the raspy synth that sits behind the "when you're gone" bit – not to mention the iconic organ/keyboard run that sets the stage for the chorus and kind of seals the deal for ABBA's future. Alongside this masterpiece, songs like 'Hasta Mañana' and 'Honey, Honey' feel positively prehistoric – even though they were barely a year old when 'SOS' came out. This is the sound of a band evolving at lightning speed. And this is the song which announces the arrival of ABBA's golden age. Perhaps nigh-on half a century of hearing the track has dulled my enjoyment of it just a tad – it's strange how that happens to some songs but not to others – but the dazzling brilliance of 'SOS' is simply beyond question. 9/10

Summer Night City (standalone single)

F: As you know by now, I love an ABBA song that comes straight out with the chorus and title of the song. There's no time wasted after the high-pitched keyboard 'WOW!' noise kicks things off and we're straight into the riff that's the thread for this excellent good-time, summer-night song. ABBA conform to no-one and nothing and this is a classic example of leading with the chorus and following up with a gigantic three-part verse. This is another ABBA song where Björn's vocals work really well, and lyrically this is one of my favourite songs, encapsulated perhaps by the line "can't resist the strange attraction of that giant dynamo". Giant is the word for this song, and it rankles with me somewhat that it wasn't a more giant hit. It should be a huge summer party or festival anthem. Pass me a pint of Sangria and let's par-tay! Really rather good. 9/10

G: The best first second of any song, ever? It's got to be in the conversation. POW! What a (welcome) punch in the ear! And the next fifteen seconds are none too shabby either. They generate such a giddy feeling of excitement and anticipation. This is archetypal music for a Big Night Out. But then... Well... I've got a major issue with the ever-present, over-intrusive hi-hat on this track, tishing away like a disco metronome you simply couldn't disable even if you took a sledgehammer to it. And the more I try to ignore it, the more I can't ignore it. Overall, I'd rate the song as nearly-but-not-quite. In terms of melodies and memorable moments, it's lacking that indefinable 10% that would make it a drop-dead classic worthy of a seat at the top table of timeless ABBA megahits. Mixing up the vocals between Björn and the girls works really well, though, and I love the strings' interventions towards the end of the track, swooping down from on high like a weird bird of prey hoping to get stuck in a village hall during a '70s-themed disco. But even that can't completely drown out the bloody hi-hat, still tish-tishing away like it's going out of fashion, and the song finally fades away leaving you wondering whether you're suffering a mild dose of tinnitus. 7/10

Super Trouper (from *Super Trouper*)

F: When I first saved this song as I was writing, I saved it in block capitals by mistake, which is somehow so appropriate. "Super trouper, beams are going to blind me, but I won't feel blue...". I could write a chapter on this song. The unmistakeable ABBA trait of starting a song with the song title, and the album title no less, the gorgeous assonance and alliteration of the first line, the fab melody, and we're barely five seconds into the darn thing. Then Benny's simple yet sublime piano takes over and we're treated to a fascinating insight into what it's like to be on tour, the huge highs and the lonely lows of the adrenalin-driven existence that is performing. There's pathos also in the word 'trouper', with its positive entertainment vibe yet also its stoic, try-hard meaning too. And then there's the famous "su-pa-pa, trou-pa-pa" bit in the chorus. Too much philosophy and not enough critique of this song, except this: what a tune! 9/10

G: Ah, that famous intro... Just vocals... To start a song, to start a single, to open an album like that – that's seriously ballsy! It's so understated, yet so immediate. Wistful, but reassuring. So very ABBA – the masters of happy sadness and breezy vulnerability. And then the piano riff cuts in, with its expert blend of plaintive melancholy and instantly memorable melody. This is one of those ABBA songs that seem to operate in about four parallel universes at once, the gnawing world-weariness effortlessly co-existing with those famous, playful "su-pa-pa, trou-pa-pa" bits in the chorus. In four minutes, a track offering routine observations on the downside of being sensationally rich and successful leaves you with a hard-to-nail-down sense that it's actually put its hugely catchy finger on the double-edged meaning of life! I love that burbling, bubbling synth sitting just under the chorus, while the backing vocals are, as ever, a masterpiece of imagination and execution. So as this superb song washes over me, should I feel glad or sad? Both, obviously. But that predictable answer scarcely does justice to the range of sentiments set running whenever I listen to this perfectly formed yet slightly underappreciated gem. 9/10.

Suzy-Hang-Around (from *Waterloo*)

F: (First time.) And it wasn't my last time listening to it either. I'm a sucker for '60s American pop and this one for me is a round peg that fits fairly and squarely in that snug round hole. Benny is definitely channelling his inner Davy Jones on the lead vocal, and I don't mind it at all. I like the '60s guitar sound on this one and feel it works really well. Lyrically, it captures rather neatly the angst of being left out of playground bonds and the unvarnished binary nature of childhood friendships, something that you'll be able to relate to if you're young or have heard from your kids if you're not so young. I'm trying to find faults with the song or reasons why I shouldn't like it, but I'm not succeeding. It's well put together and while you might accuse it of being a bit twee or schmaltzy, it totally conveys the zeitgeist. 7/10

G: Hyphenated song titles. You don't get too many of those. If anything, most song titles have a dearth of requisite punctuation. So I'm immediately positively inclined towards 'Suzy-Hang-Around'. I like the keyboard sound it's built around and the chorus is sufficiently catchy for me to appreciate why they chose to close out the *Waterloo* album with it. I also quite like the outro. But, when it comes right down to it, the song's generally pretty lightweight stuff and it's hard to believe the next track that would appear on an ABBA album would be 'Mamma Mia' just a year later. That's an almost unimaginable leap in quality. But this song does get an extra mark for being Benny's only lead vocal, which kind of works in its once-in-a-blue-moon kind of way. 5/10

Take a Chance on Me (from *The Album*)

F: The staccato beat and the title of 'Take a Chance on Me' were inspired by the rhythm of Björn running round his opulent home on an island off the coast of Stockholm – or 'Stockers' for the initiated – according to the great man, and a pretty inspiring result too. 'Chance' chugs along like a steam engine, with the male backing vocals "take a chance, take a chance, take a, take a chance, chance" setting a tone that's hard to resist. Did you ever listen to one of those songs so good that you're not really conscious of it moving from verse, to chorus, to bridge, to verse? Well, this is one of those for me. I'm carried along like a youngster bobbling on the back of a cantering horse, and there's no getting off. It's another delightfully penned number containing everything on the spectrum, from the bass-y oom-pa-pas to the treble-y keyboard trills, and the stunning vocals in the middle. Impossible *not* to take a chance on this one, impossible. 9/10

G: The song that helped give jogging a good name. As their career gained traction, ABBA certainly mastered the art of opening their albums with an exceptional one-two punch. *The Album* is a great example, with this phenomenal song following in the mighty slipstream of 'Eagle' to keep proceedings firmly in the stratosphere. Like so many other ABBA classics, 'Take a Chance on Me' has become so much part of the furniture it's easy to forget just how brilliant it is. Let's start with the iconic intro. How original! How arresting! It ensures the song has a great big smile written right across its face from the very first second, and at no point does the life-affirming, blood-pumping euphoria slacken until the track fades away four minutes later. Agnetha and Frida's voices complement each other wondrously, with Agnetha arguably stealing the show here thanks to that hint of near-desperation at the heart of her contributions. And some of the keyboard flourishes are off the chart – top of the shop being that discordant bit at the end of the second chorus. Kraftwerk would have been high-fiving passers-by in the streets of Düsseldorf for weeks if they'd come up with that one. This really is the sound of ABBA at the top of their exceptional game and a fitting reminder of the heady phase in their career when everything they touched literally turned to gold and platinum. 9/10

Thank You for the Music (from *The Album*)

F: The first song in the mini-musical *The Girl with the Golden Hair*, 'Thank You for the Music' is a song I've slightly struggled with. With lyrics by Björn for his at-the-time adorable wife, and sung by her, it's a not-very-humble account of her abilities but it always makes me feel sorry for Frida having to play second fiddle, since they were a band with two lead singers, not one. Obviously the 'aren't I great?' bit is a very small part of the whole lyric, but still…it's OK, Frida, you may not have golden hair but your backing vocals are awesome. One of the great ABBA choruses too, with the lovely little keyboard fills as well to complement the whole aural aesthetic. The Doris Day mix of this song, included in the *Thank You for the Music* box set, gives it a '40s/'50s musical heyday twist that sounds very stripped down and intimate. 7/10

G: Over-exposed? Probably (and paradoxically, given that originally this wasn't a single). Over-sentimental and a bit obvious? Quite possibly. Slightly cheesy, even? Maybe. But this is still every inch a fabulous song. Agnetha's vocal expertly draws you into the character's world – as it was then and as it is now. The song's also got a phenomenal singalong chorus that feels like an old friend even the first few times you hear it. There's real art in that. And obviously the track fully embraces the world of musical theatre, as you'd expect from the opening song in a mini-musical like *The Girl with the Golden Hair*. If you can't compose a bit of high-class schmaltz for the stage, when can you? (Additional observation: the Doris Day mix is a fun curio, but it's no more than quirky B-side material.) 7/10

That's Me (from *Arrival*)

F: (First time.) Actually, this might possibly be my second listen. Anyway, I really like the way this builds up and rises into the first verse, and then it's an oh-so-jaunty number that makes me hark back to my youth and feel uplifted at the same time. I rather like this! It reminds me of *Voyage*'s 'Just a Notion' from the *Voulez-Vous* sessions (I sound very erudite there, and that's because Garry H told me) in that it's upbeat and suggests those exciting, nail-biting early stages of a relationship. The only thing that slightly jars for me is the line "I'm Carrie not-the-kind-of-girl-you'd-marry, that's me", which doesn't feel like it belongs in the melody at that point. Lots of fab piano and 'stringy' keyboards on this song which continue to build and carry you along. Agnetha and Frida execute this kind of song so well, the purity of their voices having an undercurrent of sexiness too. Nice. 7/10

G: No, I've never been mad about this one. It feels like a bit of a survival from old-style ABBA and lacks not just the multi-dimensional qualities of a lot of the material on *ABBA* and *Arrival* but also the drop-dead brilliant hooks that now seemed to be scattered through virtually every song they put their minds to. The harsh reality is that there was a time when I didn't care for this track one little bit. Unusually, I found Benny's descending synth riff really quite annoying, while the "I'm Carrie..." line was almost as bothersome. But in much the same way as with 'Fernando' and 'I Do, I Do, I Do, I Do, I Do', over the years we've kind of learned to live with each other in a spirit of peaceful co-existence, even though it's a track I let wash round me rather than over me whenever I hear it. 5/10

The Day Before You Came (standalone single)

F: A fairly slow number, and a quirky one. At least, it's always felt quirky to me, from the first bit of flute-y keyboard that opens the song. Released as the first single from the compilation album *The Singles: The First Ten Years* (and who thought we'd one day be talking about the first fifty years...?), it was tacked on to the original *The Visitors* album in later editions. I always like songs that tell a tale, and this one goes into the detail of 'a day in the life'. Lyrically, there's something undeniably sad and humdrum about this person's typical day, and musically it echoes this with quite a repetitive, downbeat feel to it. A pleasing and melodic enough song, and something new for fans when it anchored the release of the compilation album, but for me it's one that's never entered the pantheon of ABBA greatness, and let's face it there's not a whole heap of singles in that 'nay' pile. Dare I say it, a bit of a dirge? Well, it's out there now. 6/10

G: What a very clever song. What a very neat idea to go almost minimalist and let Agnetha's marvellous vocal and the smart lyric do almost all the work. So why don't I love this track more? More to the point, why don't I want to listen to it, basically, at ALL? I'm really not sure. If there's a mental picture that it conjures up for me, it's of lead-grey skies, squally rain and collars turned up against an icy wind. Maybe that's the video talking. Plus there's that (deliberate) monotony about proceedings, with that dominant little keyboard riff almost actively trying to make itself just a little bit irritating. As I mentioned, it's all extremely clever. But all I can say is that the song just leaves me feeling a bit down, a bit flat – and that's how it's always been. Maybe my subconscious associates it too closely with ABBA's gradual, before-our-very-eyes fragmentation and their surprisingly precipitous downward spiral in the singles charts. Whatever the case, to my ears 'The Day Before You Came' will always sound like the end of something, rather than the beginning of anything. Despite its overt intention, I get absolutely no whiff whatsoever of something good being just around the corner. Mind you, it's still completely ludicrous that it placed so low in the UK charts. On the upside, you could argue that this was a perfect swansong record. And it's truly fitting that Benny finds one last sublime keyboard motif as the curtain's coming down on this phase of ABBA's career: that lovely bit arriving just at the end of "watching something on TV". What a very brilliant chap he is. 6/10

The King Has Lost His Crown (from *Voulez-Vous*)

F: (First time.) Another 'spurned lover' theme to go along with 'Angeleyes' on the *Voulez-Vous* album, and a curate's egg for me, this one. Some bits of the vocal I like, others leave me a bit cold. Same with the instrumentation: a lot of stuff going on, with different elements that might all work well if they had more room but instead are left jostling for position like a meal you might hastily throw together with whatever's not gone out of date in the fridge. The chorus is pleasing enough and has the feel of a musical or movie number to it. It's the best bit of the song and, perhaps coming to the same conclusion themselves, the lads opt to stay with it for the final last third, thereby moving the song from the 'a touch ropey' shelf and depositing it in the 'not bad but not great either' pile. 6/10

G: I wish I loved this song. I really do. Benny clearly rates it and that's got to count for quite a lot. I've *tried* to love this song. I really have. But it's resisted all my attentions these last forty-odd years and I've run out of ideas as to what to do about it. I don't hate it – it just doesn't do much for me at all and simply makes up the numbers on the *Voulez-Vous* album. From that opening, shimmering faux harp intro I find everything – melodies, lyrics, arrangement – quite ordinary. Which is my way of saying I think it's a bit boring. Not bad. Just uninspired. I'm really surprised it ranks so highly in Benny's affections. 5/10

The Name of the Game (from *The Album*)

F: ABBA have written a lot of truly remarkable songs, a world-leading Premier League assembly. 'The Name of the Game' is at the very top of the second tier, almost at the top of the Championship and pushing for promotion to the top division. Except it doesn't quite get there, always running out of steam and losing in the play-offs, destined forever to be merely 'bloody good' rather than 'unbelievably bloody good'. It is, of course, a really good ballad, doing a really good job of conveying the heartache of unrequited love, desperately seeking the answer to 'what's going on here, with us?'. ABBA songs have so much going on in them, it's not fair to the others. This song's no different, as two different yet great verses lead into a great chorus and then the chorus takes on a new direction with the "tell me, please" section, before moving on to something different again with the "and you make me talk" part. Incredible. 8/10

G: One of ABBA's best intros paves the way for a remarkable five-minute mini-opera teeming with neat ideas and clever touches which enhance what is, underneath it all, probably a fairly straightforward song. Everything locks together like a millimetre-perfect piece of civil engineering and the level of precision on display is genuinely awesome. It's like the musical equivalent of the Øresund Bridge. You could maybe argue there's almost TOO much creativity here. I've always had a nagging feeling that this is one of those ABBA songs that might have been equally, if not more, stunning if it had been stripped right back to basics. But what do I know? It's great as it is and, like any fan, I'm probably just being greedy. 8/10

The Piper (from *Super Trouper*)

F: ABBA's ability to turn their hand to any style of music – I hesitate to use the word genre since the variety within their albums defies such clumsy categorisation – is evident in this jaunty jig of a song. It's got pipes in it, as you might expect, but also clever, slightly staccato lyrics in the chorus which reinforce the idea of stepping in time to the piper's calling. The pipe work is awesome too and sounds super-traditional but also has a ring of Jethro Tull about it, and as Garry will tell you those lads know their jester-ish instruments. It's really rather fetching stuff, nor should we be so surprised at their mature command of the music at this stage in their careers, since they set the bar so high in all they do. It sits well within the 'entertaining' theme of the *Super Trouper* album, a rock-solid album track. 7/10

G: So. Not satisfied with dissecting the thorny topic of Freudian psychoanalysis in 'Me and I', this album also dares to grapple with the subject of cultish messianism, while (just for good measure) also making a compelling case for the inclusion of more Latin in song lyrics... Meet 'The Piper', a highly entertaining cocktail of multiple styles and moods all wrapped up in three-and-a-half simultaneously breezy and portentous minutes. At times folky, or even folksy; at others, a little bit proggy. At times somewhat spiritual; at others, a tad demonic and mildly disturbing. In fact, at heart, it's all a bit *The Wicker Man*, but that's a massive plus in my book (speaking as someone totally traumatised by seeing that near-flawless movie for the first time the year before *Super Trouper* came out). It also worked perfectly as the B-side of the 'Super Trouper' single, walking that tricky tightrope between whetting my appetite for the album (which, as I've already mentioned, was firmly ensconced at the top of my 1980 Christmas list) and not wasting a song that might potentially serve as an A-side further down the line. An archetypal solid album track but with added interest lurking everywhere just below its deceptively simple surface. 7/10

The Visitors (from *The Visitors*)

F: First track on the eponymous album, this song is, simply put, the definitive album track. Rather like, in fact, if your memory serves you well, what I said about 'Eagle' on *The Album*. It's impossibly good, the sort of song where it would have been essentially unfair on the other songs of the time to release it as a single. You could say the same about Oasis's 'Champagne Supernova', and you'll doubtless have your own nominations too. 'The Visitors' is superbly powerful, atmospheric and scary. It could serve as the proxy response to any kind of unwanted visit, confrontation, attack or invasion. It's super-sinister and also a brilliantly crafted song that subverts the norms in typical ABBA form in terms of things like memorable keyboard melodies. Lyrically, it's as close to perfect as you'll ever get; the words are so, well, lyrical. It might not be on everyone's fave list, or get shortlisted for shows or musicals – at least not until (spoiler alert) the *ABBA Voyage* show – but it doesn't matter. It's just too darn good. 9.49/10 (to avoid rounding)

G: I'd never dreamed that ABBA had anything quite like this in their locker! Talk about widening their musical horizons! Dark, disturbing, slightly disorienting, with just a dash of proggy-ness and a masterful Cold War lyric – this was ABBA daring to veer further from the script than ever before and pulling it off with astounding brilliance. I'd obviously been waiting for these visitors but had never actually realised it! When I first put the album on, I played this track ten times or more on the spin. Tony, my college neighbour, knocked on the door just before dinnertime and, slightly quizzically, commented: "That song you keep playing sounds a bit like ABBA...". He was spot on! Because this song was ABBA taking yet another big, bold step in their evolution, refusing to retreat to the tried and tested, and still striking out to subdue new territory. Sensational synth and hi-hat touches are just two examples of the extraordinary musical platform constructed for that arresting, oblique verse melody (expertly delivered by Frida) and a logic-shredding chorus which somehow fuses panicky, paranoid numbness with instant singalongability. As for the lyrics... Line after line of perceptive, penetrating brilliance. I'm delighted this track wasn't released as a single. It probably would have bombed (by ABBA's standards) and, even now, I'd still be incandescent about it. As it is, I can just be left to savour this extraordinary creation – with my books, paintings and furniture for company, naturally – every single time I play it. 10/10

The Way Old Friends Do (from *Super Trouper*)

F: 'The Way Old Friends Do' is a thoughtful end to the original *Super Trouper* album, rather like what 'Ode to Freedom' does for *Voyage*. For those of us who never had the pleasure, this version gives a flavour of just how damn good they must have been 'live'. The voices are, well, spectacular, there's no other way to put it. It's a short, simple song that belies the effort that must have gone in to keep it that way. As Mark Twain said, "I didn't have time to write you a short letter, so I wrote you a long one". It's inspirational music and lyrics: whatever curve balls life throws at you, you can withstand them with the help of the people you've trusted for decades. This song led the encore during the 1979 tour, and you can see why, sending concert-goers home with a spring in their step and hope in their heart. Good, wholesome stuff, like a sticky toffee pudding with gooey custard after the main dish. 8/10

G: Well, better late than never. For forty years, I consistently dismissed and disregarded this song and, whenever it came on, hoped it would be over soon. It just felt like a groove-filler tacked on the end of the album, a slightly muddy modern 'Auld Lang Syne' that generally fell a bit short – and, to be more specific, a great deal short of the standard set by the rest of *Super Trouper*. Plus there was always the little matter of how well a lone 'live' track can genuinely bed down on a studio album. But now something's changed just a little. It's almost certainly something to do with the COVID-19 pandemic creating a sharpened sense of separation from friends, family and familiar haunts and activities, and of the void that can easily open up in our lives when we're denied many of the basics of contact and communication. Suffice to say, I think I *finally* 'get' this song and that, at last, it's speaking to me on some kind of level. It's never going to be a favourite of mine, but I see it now as a kind of counterweight or complement (not sure which…) to 'Happy New Year' and a decent fit for the album overall, if still a big step behind most of ABBA's other album-closers. Still, after so many years with my finger hovering over the 'eject' or 'skip' button, I'll definitely settle for that. 6/10

The Winner Takes It All (from *Super Trouper*)

F: From the moment Benny's piano starts 'The Winner Takes It All', you know you're in for a heart-wrencher, and it doesn't disappoint. You've got your winner, and your second place is simply first loser; the brutal, binary, black or white nature of it. It's never seemed truer than in love, and this song, told through various metaphors, conveys this so simply, so powerfully. Incredible vocal by Agnetha, peerless piano from Benny and one belter of a ballad, blimey. This is a surprisingly conventional ABBA song in terms of the way it's put together, but out of that simplicity comes something surreal. And if the song doesn't do it for you, you could always be transfixed by Agnetha's mouth and teeth on the official video, as well as the acting at the meal table when in reality their working relationships must have become strained to breaking point. Another almost perfect pop song. 9/10

G: Surely the ABBA track that's had the most words written and spoken about it, bar none. For me, this song has always been a curious one. Since its original chart run, I'm not sure I've ever dug it out for a standalone listen. All the hoo-ha and hoopla surrounding it probably hasn't helped. But the bottom line is that, generally speaking, I'm not much of a fan of slow songs. Yet when I actually hear 'The Winner Takes It All' (and even now to my slight surprise), I always thoroughly enjoy it. That's because it's not really a slow song at all. For all the pathos and the lushness, it's actually propelled forward by a decent driving beat. Apparently, its BPM (beats per minute) count is 127, several notches ahead of 'Gimme! Gimme! Gimme!', for instance, and almost identical to 'On and On and On', the 'fast' track that follows 'The Winner Takes It All' on *Super Trouper*. Indeed, on the album, it's perfectly placed, picking up the pace just a touch after the title track and conveying a sense of gathering momentum that sets up the rest of the album perfectly. For me, the tempo is key to the song's success, conveying a sense of Agnetha (and her amazing vocal) being borne along by Fate's tide, against her will, into a hollow-looking future. A fast-ish, heart-rending classic masquerading as a slow-ish, heart-rending classic – clever old ABBA! 8/10

Tiger (from *Arrival*)

F: Not my first time hearing this, but I can probably count them on the fingers of a three-fingered hand. This song, strangely you might think, reminds me of 'Waterloo'. It's got that relentless drive to it, it's really catchy, it's got that slightly adversarial theme that characterised the edginess of the '74 'vision winner and, yes, it feels Eurovisiony to me. Do you feel it too? The drums and piano keep the song in top gear and the vocals make me want to dig out a 'live' version of it from the Aussie tour, to see the kind of energy the ladies generated in the crowd. The change of pace after each chorus really works for me too, it gives you a chance to catch your breath before the chorus kicks in again and you get hauled back into the fast lane. I don't know how the ladies get to that note at the end but flippin' 'eck what a way to go. Breathless stuff, like being chased by, well, a tiger. 8/10

G: Now this really should be a stonewall ABBA classic. All the building blocks are there. Great verse, with its brooding air of nocturnal menace; decent chorus melody; exquisite bridge with its change of tempo and a slightly dreamlike feel. But somehow the song doesn't realise its full potential. The fact that the verse actually packs much more of a punch than the chorus is a big factor, hinting at the key problem overall – POWER, or rather a lack of it. I think I'd have thrown the kitchen sink at this track. I'd like the intro to offer much more of a calling card and I'd also like there to be much, MUCH more of a snarl to the chorus. Then the contrast with the bridge would be even more effective. Like I know what I'm talking about! But I do feel 'Tiger' could have been an unlikely rock classic had the brakes been taken off a bit more. Let the wild animal off the leash! Let the drums thud and the guitars wail! Great ending, though, with the screams of "TI-GERR!!!" encapsulating the sort of intensity I'd love to have been more in evidence from the very first note. 7/10

Tropical Loveland (from *ABBA*)

F: (First time.) I can see why they went with this song title and these lyrics, as it's got a seriously Caribbean feel to it, this one. I feel like I should be drinking a can of fizzy green pop in the early 1980s. The song has a very modern feel to it, in fact it doesn't sound out of place listening to it in the 2020s, perhaps because Caribbean music like reggae and its ilk has a timeless feel to it and doesn't seem to age. I swear, the more I listen to this, if I heard it on the radio this week I'd assume it's a current chart release. Light, airy and kept that way with some very nice work using those sticks with wooden balls on the end, he said authoritatively. That said, as I listen to it on a Saturday afternoon, earbuds in and fingers on the keyboard, it's a rather nice accompaniment, I'll be honest. Torn between a five and a six out of ten, so will round up as it's ABBA. 6/10

G: ABBA take the bold – potentially foolhardy – step of returning to the palm tree they absolutely insisted on sitting in on the *Waterloo* album, but with significantly more convincing results. I think that's largely because Frida achieves just the right feel here, with her ever so sultry, laid-back delivery conjuring visions of white beaches, cobalt-blue seas and shimmering azure skies. Nice backing vocals too. In fact, the only thing I really don't like about this song is its somewhat clunky title. Other than that, I've got no major issues with it and happily wallow in its languid optimism and gentle tropical breeziness. 6/10

Two for the Price of One (from *The Visitors*)

F: Björn takes the lead on this pre-dating-app story of getting two partners for the price of one – with a twist at the end of course – as advertised in the local paper's lonely hearts column. ABBA's lyrics are so good that they find it easy to do a story-telling song, and this one's no different in that sense. It's a gentle feel-good number that tips along, rewarding us with a double, repeated chorus, which is always a nice treat. The arrangement is firmly wedged in the '80s, with a nice bassline and percussion that doesn't intrude. There's also a nice jaunty instrumental finish to the song. In fact, 'nice' is the word that sums up the song really, in a way that nice can be a compliment but also tends to damn the recipient with faint praise. It's clever, is tightly put together and while not making many people's ABBA top twenty is pretty inoffensive fare. 7/10

G: Brace yourself. Time to reach for my contrarian hat again, I'm afraid. Rubbished by many, lampooned by many more, this song's always in the conversation when I'm refining my all-time ABBA top ten (if I'm waiting at a set of slow-to-change traffic lights, for instance). Right from that little three-note guitar figure at the start, I'm fully signed up all the way through to the dying moments when the track shifts to that offbeat but endearing brass-band-style, Floral Dance-y fadeout. And the silly narrative doesn't bother me one bit. In fact, it's a made-to-measure match for the melancholic mood of the music – with its oh-so-ABBA sense of hopeless yet hopeful vulnerability immaculately conveyed in Björn's trademark all-time-loser vocal. I love the verses, with their melodic twists and turns, and then – whap! There's that lovely light snap of the snare drum as it introduces then drives along a chorus which provides, with all its bubbling energy, the dictionary definition of underappreciated gem. Absolutely brilliant, with the brapping bass guitar another key component here. But what elevates the chorus to heavenly realms are those slightly pleading, slightly coquettish backing vocals from Agnetha and Frida. Initially, they lure you in by shadowing Björn. Then they slip into that astounding, faster-running counter-melody ("if you are dreaming...") – reaching its peak with that stupendous "weeeeeeeee may be...". It all adds up to a track that's Exhibit A in my open-and-shut case defending the proposition that ABBA did the best backing vocals of all time. The way the voices intertwine is a thing of almost architectural wonder – like a Brunel bridge or a Wren church. A chorus for the ages and a cracking little song. No, really. 9/10

Under Attack (standalone single)

F: 'Under Attack' was the second 'new' single on the compilation album *The Singles: The First Ten Years* and was later tacked onto the *The Visitors* Deluxe Version along with a couple of others. Conceived, in my view, in a similar vein to 'The Visitors', 'Under Attack' lacks the atmosphere of that album's title track and is arranged in a much more poppy way, with the synthesised voices and the 'thin', almost disembodied – that's the only way I can describe it – voice of Agnetha on the lead. Musically, the chorus is also too poppy for someone who's feeling under attack. I think they're going for abrupt, clipped and edgy but for me it comes across as jaunty, which surely isn't the intention. Benny leads the way on this one, with some strong keyboard work complementing the vocals and a nice bit of synthesised stuff here and there, but it's not enough to rescue the song, give it a clean, dress it up and put a label on it saying 'singles material'. 5/10

G: Little did we know, when this came out, that ABBA would return in triumph four decades later. Little did we know that, after forty years of hurt, they'd crash back into our lives as a working band with some brand new, world-class material that would amaze and astonish us. Back in 1982, however, we all kind of knew this was probably 'it'. And we knew 'it' was probably just as well. Because this song – not to diss its reasonable catchiness – really did sound like the work of a band not just struggling to keep up with trends and times, but not particularly wanting to either. In short, it's the sound of four people with other plans, many of them exciting and none of them particularly involving ABBA. Competent but fundamentally anonymous, this one. A bit of a whimper, not a roar. Set the alarm clock for 2021... 5/10

Voulez-Vous (from *Voulez-Vous*)

F: If there was ever a song to give the heterosexual male a spot of trouser trouble, then *Voulez-Vous* is that song. Have the ladies ever looked better? From the first bar you're immediately swung into the mood to have fun. The lyrics are a swirl of sensuality, experienced lovers who know what they want, and you have a few moments to decide if you're to be a part of it before you lose your chance. The chorus is epoch-defining: the mellifluous French tones, the "a-ha" backing vocals – the Norwegian lads knew what they were doing with their band name a few years later – and the pappy brass mixing superbly, before the keyboard takes hold of the central melody and spins us towards the second verse. There are some songs that you simply can't finish after three or three-and-a-half minutes and in the last ninety seconds you're treated to some deliciously subtle bass guitar to go with your "a-ha"s. There can be no better song to cook a meal or get ready to go out to, full stop. 9/10

G: This track's a monster, in the very best sense of the word. It's another one of those songs that I'm gobsmacked so many ABBA fans seem a bit 'meh' about. For me, it's their definitive disco statement and a supremely skilful one at that. On 'Dancing Queen', I feel like I'm observing and dissecting the action from somewhere near the bar area. Here I feel I'm trapped smack in the middle of the dancefloor, swallowed up by the disco explosion – and absolutely bloody loving it! A lot of acts tipped their hats to disco around this time, of course. But the real joy of this track is that it shows ABBA riding the wave but not getting submerged by it. All the ABBA hallmarks are here, but they're given a good disco dusting. Great intro riff, great bass guitar throughout (only sparingly – and therefore more effectively – resorting to disco-isms), hi-hat not too intrusive, neat brass fills in the chorus, plus that dreamy, semi-distant sax adding just the right amount of sultry sleaze to those few bars before the verse begins. And it's a track where Agnetha and Frida really hurl themselves into the seething fray. The way they use the pre-chorus to set up the chorus is quite superb. Plus those handclap effects help transport you to the heaving dancefloor (if you're not there already, of course). And let's not forget the welcome return of the "a-ha!" and its knowing nod to 'Knowing Me, Knowing You'. ABBA: masters of the Euro-disco scene! 9/10

Watch Out (from *Waterloo*)

F: (First time.) A rocky departure for ABBA, and I don't mean that in the pejorative sense, more their choice of musical genre. I don't mind it either on first hearing. I knew after the first few bars that it would be Björn leading the vocals. The ladies' vocals are more strident than usual too, but I like them, they sound pretty darn good to me. Gorgeously glam, this one, I'm warming to it instantly. It makes me think of Alvin Stardust's 'My Coo Ca Choo', except it's got a lot more going on and the band clearly know their way around their instruments. Great bass line too on 'Watch Out', really gets you in the mood. I'm willing to bet that the louder you play this the better it sounds, and is the lead guitar the inspiration for Lenny Kravitz's 'Are You Gonna Go My Way'? An ever so slightly teensy weensy question mark over Björn's vocal, but ABBA can do rock, no question. 8/10

G: A song that's the dictionary definition of flattery to deceive. Ushered in by a very nifty guitar riff, the intro lures you into thinking there could be something quite meaty and substantial at the end of it. But the verse is no more than reasonable, the chorus is pretty slight and the early promise largely evaporates into the ether. To be honest, this track sounds like a bunch of glam rock clichés thrown randomly into a pot and the net result isn't exactly a banquet – more of a fairly decent packed lunch. But at least there's a spark and some intent here, qualities absent from a lot of the rest of the material on the *Waterloo* album. Some Cozy Powell drumming could really have elevated it, though. And I've awarded this song an extra point for some stonking bass guitar. Oh and top marks to Björn for vocal effort! 6/10

Waterloo (from *Waterloo*)

F: Of course, a seminal song which opens the eponymous album. Where to start with this? It should really have its own chapter. A song which grabs you by the hair, pulls you up to standing and makes you move, from the very first chord. Irresistibly catchy as well. Then there are the insistent vocals and the piano chords that sound like Benny's playing them with his feet not his hands, since he gets so much damn energy into them. The lyrics wrap themselves around the theme so cleverly, so effortlessly – well, there are far too many adverbs in this paragraph, a sure sign I'm reviewing from the heart and not the head. The bridge, the sax so complementary yet noticeable too. I think that might be the fastest a 2:49 song has ever passed, it's gone so quickly. I'm going to stop now, this is getting ridiculous. No song is perfect, but this one's bloody close, a hair's breadth from it. 9.49/10 (to avoid rounding)

G: Put aside the Eurovision connotations and this really is the archetypal don't-bother-ringing-the-doorbell-just-kick-the-door-down album-opener. Yes, I've heard it thousands of times over the last fifty years. Do I really need to hear it another thousand times? Yes, I rather think I do. The thing is, it's so familiar, such a milestone in pop music history that it's all too easy to forget to listen to it properly when you hear it. But when I do take the trouble, rather than just letting the song wash over me, it's nigh-on impossible not to get carried away on the riptide. The whole thing's borne along at dizzying pace not just by hook upon hook but also by any number of perfectly judged musical embellishments, from the sassy sax breaks to the rising-staircase bassline behind the chorus, while the piano clangs away merrily with keyboard-battering abandon from start to finish. It's easy to forget, too, what a satisfyingly odd title it is for a song that delivers such a powerful sonic punch. This song really was quite a calling card. 9/10

What About Livingstone (from *Waterloo*)

F: (First time.) Not content with addressing one historical figure in the title track of the *Waterloo* album, our Swedish friends switch continents and go exploring the Nile, arguing that David

Livingstone's journey of discovery was just as big as discovering the Moon. It trots along nicely too, bumping us up and down like we're on the back of a show pony, with some nice guitar work answering the vocals. It sounds quite stripped down too, with the vocals, the piano and the bass guitar chugging along rather enjoyably. Just as the lads can turn quite easily to a variety of genres, sometimes in the space of one album, so too are the ladies perfectly adept at whatever style of music they take on. It's no surprise how good their voices are of course, but they're so strong and true in 'What About Livingstone'. I liked it despite not thinking I would. 7/10

G: What, indeed. Here, ABBA plough the ultra-light, ultra-anodyne, middle-of-the-road furrow that drags down so much of the *Waterloo* album. Inoffensive it may be, but there's really nothing here at all to get your teeth into. It's one of those songs that seems to be trying ever so hard to convey an indispensable life-message. But I've really got no idea at all what it's supposed to be. 3/10

When All Is Said and Done (from *The Visitors*)

F: There's one word which comes to mind when I hear this song. Well two words actually: weepingly beautiful. There's something of the underdog about it for me. For a start Frida's singing the lead, and Frida could only sing the lead on this one. She's also the one who perhaps subconsciously gets labelled 'number two female' in the band, while Her Royal Blondness seems to get the lion's share of the attention. The vocal line "birds of passage you and me, we fly instinctively" is the best-sung line on the entire album. And then Frida has the ability to make you shudder slightly at the line further into the song "slightly worn but dignified and not too old for sex". It's the brazenness of the sex reference but also the typically ABBA-ish sadness of ageing and ageing relationships that underpins a lot of their later work. I always root for the underdog, me, and 'When All Is Said and Done' is an ABBA underdog song which belies its true beauty. 8/10

G: A song that looks (sort of) positively towards the future while (sort of) looking back fondly on the past. A bit of a complex one, this. That's before we even get to the issue of explicit reference to the potentially iffy topic of slightly older people having sex. But it's to ABBA's huge credit – and particularly Frida's, delivering a career-defining tour de force here – that they pull it off (so to speak) with such great aplomb. That distinctive rhythm with its driving, offbeaty feel provides an ideal foundation, nicely underscoring the lyrics' focus on pushing forward determinedly but into something of a head wind. Agnetha's backing vocals are also worth a big shout-out, perfectly complementing the mood of the track, while brilliance continues to fall out of Benny's keyboards on demand. You can sum it all up by saying that this song crams half a lifetime's experience into three short minutes. Another track that wouldn't have suffered if it had been a minute longer. 8/10

When I Kissed the Teacher (from *Arrival*)

F: I'm not particularly familiar with this one; it's probably had all-time single figure airings for me, so it's nice to hear it again. Lovely acoustic guitar to start this, and peerless vocals from the ladies, natch. ABBA are perhaps the only group that could have the title of the song feature in both the verse and the chorus and it not feel at all lazy, or overdone, or laborious, such is their musical artistry. And is that a bridge coming in after the first chorus? It's a touch screechy for me. Well, perhaps it's not a bridge, since it appears at the end of the second chorus too. The lead vocals feel like they're overpowering the rest of the band on this one, it seems a bit top-heavy. The ABBA hallmark backing vocals, on the other hand – clever, varied, turning the song almost into a dialogue as with many other songs – elevate this one above a fifty percent score. 6/10

G: Another one of those songs I tend to enjoy a lot when I'm listening to it but don't especially look forward to listening to. Not really sure why, because it's a great album-opener and cleverly keeps the gunpowder of 'Dancing Queen' dry for three minutes, building the sense of anticipation to something approaching fever pitch. As a standalone, too, it makes for a pretty good romp, although it's one of the vanishingly few ABBA tracks where I'm not terribly keen on some of the backing vocals. I find them a tad intrusive and distracting during the chorus. On the plus side, the low-key intro is inspired. But I've also been known to have the odd nasty flashback to the song's butchering in *Mamma Mia: Here We Go Again*. 7/10

When You Danced with Me (from *Voyage*)

F: While being famously trend-free, ABBA nevertheless felt the Celtic calling alongside the likes of Ed Sheeran and others with this amiable, upbeat jig that emphasises music's easy ability to take us back to an earlier time in our lives. I really like the way the ladies duet in sync throughout the song, and there are the familiar touches of mellifluous melody to complement the vocals. There's a positive quality to the song that belies the slightly less positive lyrics, and the line "there's a darkness deep inside your eyes" jars for me because it's sung at such a fast tempo. Despite that, 'When You Danced with Me' is easily good enough musically to get you dancing with me, and vice versa. Can you imagine how enjoyable it would be to swing your partner in a full hall with a massed pipe band blasting this one out? Released in late 2021 when we were starting to see light and social life at the end of the pandemic tunnel, this number reminded us what we'd been missing. 7/10

G: It's so important to back up a great album-opener with a really solid second track and this song does the job very well, picking up the tempo after the emotional wringer of 'I Still Have Faith in You' and infusing *Voyage* with an early injection of a feelgood factor. Plenty to enjoy here, though if I were being super-critical I'd argue that the Celtic musical flavour doesn't really need to be backed up with quite such overtly Celtic-themed lyrics. I think I'd prefer some less geographically specific, more universal words to avoid the feeling that the song's overegging it. But just as those thoughts cross my mind, the excellent synth riff kicks in again and such minor criticisms largely melt away. 7/10

Why Did It Have to Be Me? (from *Arrival*)

F: Not my first time hearing this, but I've only maybe heard it a couple of times before. The introduction reminds me of 'Just a

Notion' from *Voyage* in the way it chugs into action. This is one of those songs where you get to hear both sides of a relationship, and it's always fascinating to me how the two parties play off each other. Björn always does these numbers really well. There's also a smell of 'Rock Me' coming from 'Why Did It Have to Be Me?', especially in the middle of the number. It's got such a cheeky – as well as tongue-in-cheek – quality to it, you can't help but tap along, particularly when the saxophone picks you up and propels you along in its wake. The ladies' vocals are so strong on this song, I can picture them recording and performing it with huge smiles on their faces and a twinkle in the eye. Benny's just the right side of honkytonk on this one. Fun, fanciful frippery; I like it quite a lot. 7/10

G: I'll readily admit to being easily seduced by a bit of swagger and strut. Combine these two essential elements with a dual to-and-fro lead vocal where Björn and Frida dovetail superbly and you've got a thoroughly engaging track that never fights shy of flaunting its sassy simplicity. Another one of those songs which sounds like it was written in a tea break and would have been completely ruined if it had taken any longer and if the writers had gone through an entire packet of biscuits while composing it. Perfect neither-one-thing-nor-the-other tempo, a great Fats Domino undercurrent and that lovely tenor sax adding just the right amount of muscle to proceedings – enormous fun all round and an inevitable addition to a 'live' setlist. 8/10

You Owe Me One (B-side of 'Under Attack')

F: (First time.) Another of those songs that didn't get into the first team for the original *The Visitors* release but made the lower reaches of the squad for the expanded Deluxe Edition. Gotta make a move to a town that's right for me! No, wait, it's not 'Funky Town' by Lipps Inc. I'm sure every single ABBA song is in someone's top ten, but this isn't floating my boat I'm afraid. It's not a bad song, it's just that I don't like it much since there's nothing that really resonates with me. It almost sounds a bit amateurish, and I'm glad I'm at least six city blocks from any ABBA fan reading this. Best thing about this song? The backing vocals and harmonies are great. Nonetheless, it must have been a slightly WTF moment for most people who bought the single and flipped over after 'Under Attack'. You owe us one too, folks, methinks... 4/10

G: Can't stand the intro. It's as if someone set out to rework the famous riff from Lipps Inc's 'Funky Town' but surgically remove all the snap and sass from it. Overall, the song sounds like a jumble of off-cut ideas that needed a good home but didn't really find one. The verses don't bring very much to the party but, to be fair, the chorus isn't too bad. But the whole arrangement and slightly odd instrumentation take us to Tinny City, making everything sound amazingly lightweight. This is the sound of a band going through the motions of searching for a new direction. As it turned out, they'd find it – but not for another forty long years. 4/10

Masters of These Scenes: Part 2

As we've already mentioned multiple times, ABBA's visual impact has always played a crucial role in their phenomenal appeal and their ability to attract and retain interest. In many ways, with ABBA, what you see is almost as important as what you hear in terms of what you get. And a pivotal part in securing them the levels of near-continuous global exposure essential to cementing a position at the apex of Planet Pop was played by promotional films and videos for individual songs. Arguably, these were every bit as important as the songs themselves in establishing and securing the band's reputation and in creating an indelible imprint on people's minds.[14]

Original Official Song Videos:

Ring Ring

F: (First time.[15]) At first glance it's a functional glam-pop video from the early days of the art form, the band plus backing musicians in a pretty static on-screen set-up. Ah, but then again it's so damn wholesome, so '70s! The girls look like a truckload of butter wouldn't melt in their mouths. Even Björn looks like you could bring him home to mother and she wouldn't be put off by the merest hint of eye shadow. Going back to mouths, not sure when this official video was recorded, but Agnetha's teeth are definitely post-straightening, so mebbe 1974? I feel sorry for the drummer, who seems to be completely blocked out by Agnetha for the whole video. The guitarist in green, however, is in full view, and I'm assuming the other two backing lads felt the same way –

---

[14] We're focusing on the original videos here, not on the brand new set of lyric videos that's been released over the last couple of years.
[15] As with the song reviews, I'm seeing a lot of these videos for the very first time.

he's grinning like a Cheshire cat, and who wouldn't in the presence of such majestic beauty. Lucky ducks. Pleasant enough. 5/10

G: I'm not completely sure what steals more of the show here: Björn's big cape or Benny's big blue feather. Of course, it's not really a video at all, in the sense of what we'd soon come to expect from the term. But it's bright, it's confident, it's fun and the sax layered over the top gives the track an extra bit of fizz. Plus you get an early glimpse of those trademark sideways camera shots that ABBA would soon become renowned (notorious?) for. Not sure Frida and Agnetha miming the dialling of a telephone adds a lot to the spectacle, but otherwise they're completely in command of the screen – despite Björn's earnest attempts to grab a great big, bubbly slice of the attention. 6/10

Waterloo

F: (First time.) Another routine mid-'70s pop promo, nothing too adventurous here, but still lots to enjoy, such as Björn's ridiculous glam platform shoes as he stomps away, and Frida's single hoop earring – a-ha, me hearties! The opening, with the rapid zoom-in of the Napoleon bust that my Dad might have sculpted (pottery and sculpture were not his strong suit, it has to be said), interspersed with a similar treatment for each of the band members, is a crude but effective way of setting both the subject and the tone of the song. It is a bit weird, though, watching these videos from the 1970s and seeing the ladies in their prime. Their figures are not the super-toned versions you get in bands these days, as image has taken on a life of its own. They look both beautiful and natural, of an era when having fun performing wasn't perceived as nerdy, innocent and a bit passé. Fun fact: as I've mentioned earlier, I never knew the lyric was "I was defeated, you won the war..." Thanks to this video I now know it after five hundred listens. Nice. 6/10

G: The crunch of the opening and the shot of the bust of Napoleon-gone-glam set out the stall from the very first moment. Strangely, from there on in, everything's toned down considerably compared with the 'Ring Ring' video. No extraneous band members, a bit more sartorial reserve (notwithstanding Agnetha's iconic blue outfit), a bit less movement from Agnetha and Frida.

Basically, they let the song itself do all the heavy lifting and don't take any chances whatsoever. Everything's a tad more stilted, as if they're determined not to frighten any horses, with only Frida's widening of the eyes conveying a welcome sense of spontaneity. A solid, risk-averse video – and who can blame them at this point in their career? 5/10

I Do, I Do, I Do, I Do, I Do

F: (First time.) This has got the early ABBA feel about it: looking young, the pre-symmetrical ABBA logo, and Frida's curly hairdo. And what's not to like? I'm loving Frida's halo on this one. Video-wise, it's all pretty basic fare, a bit of camera trickery as music videos continued to find their way. It wouldn't surprise me if the lads could play the sax as well. On a sidenote, I must educate my laptop; it keeps autocorrecting Frida to Friday. Sacrilege! 5/10

G: Arguably, ABBA's first proper stab at an actual video. Not a song I especially warm to and the video doesn't really do anything to stick our relationship on the defrost setting. All very safe and I'm not quite sure whether having Frida and Agnetha not looking into the camera when they're doing most of the singing works or doesn't work. The Benny and Björn double-sax shots add a much-needed dose of fun, but not so much fun that it isn't a bit of an achievement to make it all the way through to the end of this promo. 3/10

SOS

F: (First time.) This strikes me as their first semi-decent video production. There are a few mirror-y and spinning kaleidoscope-y special effects going on and there's been a bit more attention and a few more Swedish Kronor lavished on this production. Not sure about the view of them from above. I can see Agnetha's not-so-blonde roots, which has weirded me out slightly since I assumed that she was as natural a blond Scandinavian as it was possible to be. Ho hum. Many ABBA songs have that sense of underlying melancholy and the sadness of separation, and this is the first video where that longingness for connection comes through; Agnetha conveys it particularly well. If she wasn't so keen on staying in, she might have made a pretty good film actor I would say, with almost no evidence to back up that statement. Good vid, though. 7/10

G: Now we've stepped up a few levels! That initial shot of the hazy, reflected piano keyboard, as if you're looking at it through tear-filled eyes, really is the perfect set-up. Then they hit you with the cutaway to outdoors with its chilly winter feel, bare trees and hard rocks all reinforcing the song's morosely brutal majesty. The kaleidoscope effects provide a wholly appropriate sense of disorientation and then you get all four members looking up as if they're waiting to be plucked off the harsh terrain by a rescue helicopter. Absolutely everything's really well-judged and coherent, enhancing the song's message very effectively. Even Björn manages to suppress a smile (just about). And the helicopter would have to wait just a little while longer, of course. 9/10

Mamma Mia

F: Ah, this video, a top five — by which I mean a fave five — ABBA video for me, coming in at number three, as we'll see later in the book. It's archetypal, almost stereotypical ABBA. The up-close piano hammers and the white outfits. But really it's all about the famous lip close-ups in profile and face-on. Despite the effect I remember this video having on me when I was a young thing, there's also an innocent, almost amateurish quality about it. Björn is clearly having so much fun, even though he's miming the life out of his guitar. Looking at the video now, I think it's the lack of make-up on the girl's faces and necks that shows up the era this video comes from. Loads and loads to enjoy, especially the choreography which also looks a little dated but which certainly felt state-of-the-art back then. Joyous, wholesome loveliness. 9/10

G: Back to the 'white room' videos and this really does feel like a bit of a retrograde step after the cleverness of 'SOS'. To put a positive spin on it, the band are perhaps saying "this is us — no frills, no bells, no whistles". But apart from the sideways camera shots, this is about as unambitious as a promo film could get. Fortunately, it's ABBA and it's definitely worth watching them being ABBA. Plus there's nothing to get in the way of the song. I suppose you could even say it's the video's very simplicity that makes it iconic and, without doubt, it does stick in the memory. Maybe keeping it simple really can be the best policy. Well, it can be when you're ABBA and all you've got to do in a video is just be ABBA. 6/10

Bang-A-Boomerang

F: (First time.) They're clearly having so much fun in this one. Are they in Stockholm? It's probably why they look so relaxed since they're homebirds, and also in a phase of their lives when both couples had a deep love for each other, and the strain of upper stardom hadn't yet extracted its inevitable toll. At this point they would already have been massive stars in Sweden for some time, so how they managed to make the parts of this video when they're strolling around the city is pretty impressive. That said, the quick intersplicing of cartoonish, batman-like onomatopoeias, face shots and waterside band shots makes my head hurt a bit. A touch too much going on for me to process, so I'm going for a lie down. Jaunty video. 4/10

G: There's absolutely nothing wrong with a cheap outdoor video shoot and this pulls that trick off pretty well. The happy-go-lucky, off-the-cuff treatment suits the song perfectly, while the tactical sprinkling of comic book BANGs and POWs makes quite a nice point of difference. The walking down the pavement sections neatly add to the whole home-video feel and I'd be absolutely amazed if this one didn't come in well within budget and enable them to afford some chips on the way home. Never underestimate the importance of keeping the accountants happy. 6/10

Fernando

F: (First time.) Frida has ditched her curly locks for the iconic, straight, dark brown and super-shiny version which would become the most legacy-inspiring form of her. It's a nice enough, cheesy gather-by-the-fire band video, with more of the face profile and full-on close-ups that worked so well in 'Mamma Mia'. They also pay homage to the Mexican vibe with the dresses and neckerchiefs in a nod to Mariachi groups the world over. Odd things stay with me, though, and I found myself wondering how they managed to get the fire to rage so high while also so contained that it doesn't melt them to a crisp. The ladies do a great job of conveying the sense of camaraderie engendered by the song in their close-ups, so all in all it just about holds up as a video of what was a blockbuster of a tune for them. Bravo! 6/10

G: Things get a lot more cinematic here and I have to say, although this has never floated my boat as a song, Frida is pitch-perfect in terms of how she sells it. She absolutely nails the cocktail of emotions that underpin the story and its message, expertly dovetailing the right amount of wistfulness, a touch of melancholy and quite a decent dollop of steely determination. Agnetha, on the other hand, looks just a little too happy too often for my personal taste. Overall, though, it's a pretty well-judged video and the campfire cosiness just about stays on the right side of rather annoying. 6/10

Dancing Queen

F: I accidentally watched an amateurish and bitty 'montage' video of 'Dancing Queen' the first time I reviewed it, scoring it a miserable 2/10. The official version is altogether better; much, much better. Iconic, in point of fact. (As a sidenote, it now comes with some handy lyric footnotes, again reminding me of several wrongly learnt lyrics. For example, I always thought they were singing "where they play the rock music", when in fact it's "where they play the right music". In my defence, they then go on to sing "with a bit of rock music", and I can't hear the difference.) 'DQ' shows a band in the disco milieu when the genre was at its height, and boy do they own the genre in this video. It's from a period in the band's development when the ladies both sported straight hair. It was the best look for them: as joint lead vocalists, with the symmetry-and-hair-colour-asymmetry thing that they've made their own. Heck, the guys look good in this video too. Showing the band in concert in an intimate space, close to an audience peppered with seventeen-year-old dancing queens, creates the best kind of disco nightclub atmosphere for the exuberance and coming-of-age, anything-is-possible rush you get when you listen and dance to the 'right music' – how the lyric all makes sense now! The video comes at a time when producer-directors were starting to experiment with frequent cutaway shots to keep you watching. At the end we're treated to slomo footage of the ladies rocking out, and it still works really, really well. With my uber-critical hat on, watching over four-and-a-half decades later, some of the video work and the transitions look a little clumsy. That said, they don't detract from the overall feeling that you were – and still are, today – watching a magical moment in time. Magnificent! 9/10

G: Right from the shot of Benny's opening sweep down the keyboard, this video takes the feelgood factor and multiplies it by seventeen. It's delightful to see ABBA drenched in confidence and so in love with what they do. But much of the charm of this video, paradoxically, comes from its low-budget feel, whether it's the jackets unsuitable for disco-dancing worn by some of the disco-dancers, or the entire school hall/wedding reception feel of the scene. Agnetha and Frida move brilliantly, the word 'joyous' is redefined and the overall result really is the mid-'70s on a stick. 9/10

Money, Money, Money

F: A big video, this one, with more money being thrown at the subject of money. The acting is better, the lighting is really good and the production values are superior. I especially like the touch where they lead with the Swedish money first, when the band was global at this stage and could have sold out with some silver dollars on there. They save it until later in the video to do that...that said, it seems a bit weird to feature a coin with a king on it, one of whose names was Adolf; just saying. A top five ABBA video for me, coming in at number four. Even though this is Frida's song, there's the ultimate close-up of Agnetha's mouth while she's singing the chorus. The camera's practically inside her chops for goodness' sake. Nowhere to hide there. Especially in another close-up where Frida's supposed to say "my life would never be the same" and mimes "my like would never be the same". No-one would have caught it in the analogue-video days, but it's a different story on digital. Epic. 9/10

G: No sane person would deny that stylish fedoras and '70s-style kung-fu pyjamas make for a powerful sartorial statement, even when they're not being worn at exactly the same time. This is just a perfect little video, bringing out the character of the song but without weighing everything down with too much detail and a load of unnecessary narrative. Everything complements and accentuates the music, but there's still plenty going on and lots of variety of scene to ensure momentum is never lost. Just a great, professional video in the very best sense of the word. 9/10

Knowing Me, Knowing You

F: Another very well-known video, and of course another real take-it-to-the-bank song for them. On the churlish side you'd say that it's a little too hackneyed a video, a little too cliched, to score particularly highly. I don't have an encyclopaedic knowledge of '70s music videos, but maybe ABBA set the tone, established the mark with these huggy close-ups. One thing's for sure, back then the lives of famous people were not so well documented and accessible, and I remember thinking it was just a sad song, rather than one that could easily have been inspired by real-life events. Frida's face, being a few years older than Agnetha's, looks more mature on this video, but is also starting to show the first signs of tiredness in the profile and full-face close-ups that have become the ABBA hallmark. Tough to watch as a fan if you're in break-up mode as well, I imagine. 5/10

G: The definitive ABBA video, I reckon. I think it's the snow, Frida's furry hood and those footstep traces in the white stuff that seal the deal. Plus the way they glide around the studio from one position to the next and we get all those camera angles, profile shots and the rest of it – like ABBA are engaged in some weird kind of three-dimensional chess-ballet. It's all played to emotional perfection by Frida and Agnetha, with Björn and Benny providing the perfect deadpan foil. (But does Benny have to suppress just the hint of a smile at one point? I'd almost like to think he got the giggles during the filming – we all know that nothing brings out the urge to laugh more than the need to keep a completely straight face.) I still might have been inclined to give the dustsheet-style curtains an iron, though. 10/10

That's Me

F: (First time.) Weird, this one, it's a real hotch-potch of a video. The hugs are from 'Knowing Me, Knowing You' and other bits from 'Money, Money, Money' are in this one too. It looks like just the ladies have done new work for the filming of this vid. It feels a bit shoestring, a bit slapdash to me, like they only had a few metres of video tape left and had to nail it in one take. There's yet another profile and full-face close-up at one stage, but at this point you feel like saying "enough, already" as the Americans might put it. Always good to get close-ups of the ladies, but that's about it.
2/10

G: It feels somewhat churlish to judge this as a video when it's essentially just a very basic promo film, with its almost camcorder-style close-ups fleshed out with a few clips from the 'Money, Money, Money' and 'Knowing Me, Knowing You' videos. Agnetha and Frida sell it as well as they possibly can in the circumstances, and you just hope that Benny and Björn were making the most of their day off to pen another classic or nine. It's not totally unenjoyable but it's unlikely to win over too many new fans to a song which, personally, I can very much take or leave.
3/10

When I Kissed the Teacher

F: (First time.) The definition of cheese: there's the dairy version, of course, and for non-dairy it's a case of 'q.v.' the 'When I Kissed the Teacher' video by ABBA. It's cheese on wheels. Were they touring the US when they made this video, with all the US sports teams' shirts? Or trying to appeal to the US perhaps? Anyway, it might have caused palpitations across the global population of school-age boys, but for me it's so incredibly cloying that you almost have to watch it through your fingers. Anyway, how come Frida always has to play second fiddle in the 'sexy' songs? That's not right. She looks pretty miffed at having to play along. It's also interesting (to me at least) that towards the end of the video the map of Europe on the wall doesn't appear to be out of date, geopolitically speaking, since Agnetha's head is blocking Germany,

Eastern Europe and the Balkans. She fails to do as good a job at the beginning though. Treacle. 3/10

G: Again, simple as simple can be and scarcely a budget-buster. Only the teacher who's apparently teleported in from the 1830s adds any hint of the unexpected. Nor am I keen on the US high-school stylings delivered by the wardrobe department. Overall, however, our favourite foursome carry off this bit of minor hokum with extreme ease. I actually think Frida's acting abilities are somewhat underrated and this video provides not a bad example. In her supporting role here she does a great job of portraying a slightly bored, too-cool-for-school teenager, without going too far and risking upstaging Agnetha, but adding just a hint of depth to what are otherwise very much one- or at best two-dimensional proceedings. 5/10

The Name of the Game

F: A simple, nicely shot video where the sepia tones in the introduction give way to full colour, before returning again briefly. It shows the fab four in a natural, relaxed setting and looks like it was very easy for them to make, almost like they were on a Swedish coffee break fika thingy and the cameras just kept rolling. There's a lot more going on here though, with the cutaways to a guitar being strummed or a piano being played, Plus Frida in the bushes with a 'come hither' look (which appears to work since a bit later on she's smooching bigtime with Benny), the whirling around on the playground roundabout, and the straightforward metaphor of the ludo game. A busy video, then, in contrast to a lot of early ABBA efforts, but it all works pretty well and fits together handsomely. 8/10

G: As with the 'Knowing Me, Knowing You' video, ABBA set out their stall towards the 'serious artists' end of the musical spectrum. It's all mature, reserved and understated, and the obvious metaphor of love as a game is brought out without being done to death. The switches between sepia and colour work quite nicely and the trips to the garden and the children's playground break things up too. But while it's all a pleasant enough watch, it's all a bit anodyne and I'm left feeling that the song's lyrical content – with its neat take on the complex cocktail of emotions typifying the early stages of a love affair – deserves something a little braver in terms of video treatment. 5/10

Take a Chance on Me

F: Quite sweet this one, another well-known video, and nearly a top five ABBA video for me. It's an upbeat, first-flush-of-a-relationship number and the ladies sell it very well, at their flirtatious, sexy as all-get-up best, winking away at us as if their lives depended on it. I like the minimalist white backdrop and floor, with the ladies circling the guys but really working the camera too. It's infectious fun in the winter woollies, with not a trace of melancholia in the air. Frida has that frizzy hair thing going on, the first sign in my view that her hair peaked with the lovely straight version in earlier videos. I like Benny rushing off to take a chance on Frida towards the end, you have to believe he was going a little off script there, and who cares if he does, the spontaneity suits the song's mood perfectly. Not sure about Frida's boots, but we'll let it go. 8/10

G: Those opening shots with the quartered screen have a very decent claim to being the most memorable, most instantly recognisable from any ABBA video. And this definitely feels more like a proper video, rather than just a simple promotional film – albeit by the still fairly modest standards of 1978. Looking at it through a 2020s prism, there are a fair few cringey or slightly suggestive moments but it's all so fun and life-affirming that it almost dares you not to utterly buy into it. It's also ripe for parody, as Erasure were to demonstrate. For me personally, this was very much where I clambered on board the ABBA Express, so this video gets an extra point for that reason alone. 8/10

Eagle

F: (First time.) Well this is different, for ABBA anyway. It reminds me of that phase of *Top of the Pops* where one of the technical team had discovered the nuclear splurgy effect and decided it was here to stay. There's a Warhol-like neon quality to the video which puts it in the same period and I'm not sure I'm a fan. It's all a bit psychedelic for me, even down to the animal prints on the ladies' outfits, a riot of colour which doesn't convey strongly enough the sweeping majesty and freedom of the eponymous bird. I guess it's difficult for such a visual band to carry off the metaphor of the eagle without showing themselves most of the time, which is why perhaps they went for an almost abstract rendering of the winged colossus. Not a bad video, then, but not a great one either. An easing-off of the glitter ball and strobe lights might be in order. Wacky. 6/10.

G: For the first time, ABBA get a bit cinematic and a little artsy, all of which neatly disguises the fact that this is actually just a pretty basic promotional film. Bearing in mind that the ideas are all quite small, it's amazing that the final result ends up feeling fairly big and expansive. It's aided immeasurably by Agnetha and Frida selling it for all they're worth and the credit is largely theirs, I think, that I don't reach the end of the video feeling that either I or the song itself have been sold particularly short. 6/10

Thank You for the Music

F: (First time.) "You do the melodies, I do the lyrics, so I'm giving my baby this one to sing, alright?" So it is with 'Thank You for the Music'. Taken from a 'live' performance, Frida is notable for her absence off camera for all the Agnetha preamble and then she walks to the front of the stage and sits down for the rest of the performance, presumably either to give the floor to first fiddle, or to change it up a bit, or to commune with the audience a bit more. Whatever the real reason for the stage direction, it looks a bit odd to me. And are those the animal print outfits from the 'Eagle' video too? I think they are. Agnetha's a rabbit and Frida's a...badger? Not sure what's going on there. It's not a favourite song of mine, but it's one they've been asked to perform many times over the years and so it must be a huge fan favourite. The video, therefore, is not a worthy companion to complete the sensory package and drags it down. The lighting's not great either. No thanks. 4/10

G: There's such a warmth and confidence about this one – arguably, indeed, an almost over-polished professionalism – that there's simply no room for any doubt that ABBA are at the phenomenal peak of their powers. You almost *want* to see the odd rough edge somewhere, the odd imperfection in sound or look, just to remind you that ABBA aren't simply a figment of your imagination. How easy (and lucrative) it would have been for ABBA to settle into this kind of MOR space (I nearly said 'rut' there) and milk the market with 'Thank You for the Music' re-treads for the next three to five years, and to keep portraying the same visual squeaky-cleanness that we see here. Massive credit, then, that they didn't fall into that fur-lined trap but instead kept pushing themselves and kept on growing. 4/10

One Man, One Woman

F: (First time) This 'performance' video opens with a close-up of Björn on the guitar, moving to Benny in his winter cardigan at the piano, before moving on to Frida in the lead, a bit outshone by the studio stage-light version of a starlight filter. At first I felt the lighting on this video was a bit dark. As the song draws you in, however, so does the acting performance of Frida, whose range of facial emotions needed for this song is not far short of magical. Towards the end, as she sings "you smile and I realise", all you can see is her eyes sparkling with a feeling that's totally believable. (Isn't it amazing too how the simple act of looking happy or sad, in the right performer, can be *heard* in their voice?) Visually, it's an OK video. The half-and-half swapping faces of the folks probably felt quite avant-garde back then but look a bit clumsy now. Benny's possibly going for the moody look, but it comes across as 'don't-really-want-to-do-this'. That said, a pretty assured, heart-warming visual experience. 7/10

G: Dead simple again, but extremely assured and quite effective. Benny never really commits when he mimes backing vocals and this video is no exception, but Frida really does provide the safest possible pair of hands in terms of delivering the song's emotional trajectory in a highly capable way. The mildly 'trick' face-merging photography gets a little over-used, but overall this is a video that definitely doesn't detract from a very fine song, even if it doesn't add an awful lot to it either. 6/10

Summer Night City

F: (First time.) On first glance it's aged really well. Most of the video is night-time and so we see the car lights rather than the dated cars themselves. Also, the band head shots are framed in a rainbow-like hue of nightclub lights, which give the video a Pride-ish 'right on' stamp of approval. The song itself is about Stockholm. I wonder if it was filmed there? It must have been, I guess. The guys are having too much fun. They seem to be at their most relaxed when they don't have to travel to make their videos, and to be at their happiest when they're showcasing their home city. The video closes with a somewhat jumpy panorama of the Stockholm skyline, at dawn (presumably) after a night on the tiles and all is quiet in the capital. A capital which looks like it's got a lot of quite impressive but almost uniformly light-brown architecture. A decent ad for Stockholm nightlife, then, but not necessarily from a daytime tourist's point of view. Given what giant names of Swedish pop penmanship were to stand on the shoulders of B&B in the '90s and noughties, a night of music in this city is on the Fredster's bucket list at any rate. Groovy. 8/10

G: The first and quite possibly only video where ABBA seem a bit (by their standards) naughty and really quite dangerous. Pretty much every hint of squeaky-cleanness has been kicked into touch and they drag us along for a Big Night Out which we're almost certainly going to bitterly regret in the morning. For the first time, Agnetha and Frida come across as slightly frightening and certainly, in the eyes of my sixteen-year-old self at the time of release, alluring and intimidating in pretty much equal measure. The video has excellent pace to it and conveys a genuine sense of excitement, even though Benny looks like he's more than ready to hit the hay. But Agnetha and Frida still clearly have plenty more miles in the tank and we'll all find ourselves crashed out on the hard shoulder or slumped in the bushes when dawn finally breaks. 8/10

Chiquitita

F: When I think about 'Chiquitita' the song, I don't think about Agnetha and Björn's daughter, I think of a warm Latin American country, since the name sounds Latin American to me. Surprising then that it's a Christmas-type video for a song that's not about Christmas. Mind you, there are a good few songs that became Christmas smashes and were swiftly recast in a Christmas light to cash in. Still, with Björn's ski jacket and Benny's warm top, the lads look ready for anything. At one stage Frida does a very deft job of removing hair which is persistently blowing into her face, and that's not easy when you're in front of a giant bloody snowman, you're singing about the sun "shining above you" in the near total darkness, and with the odd punter walking in the background like a yeti. Pleasing enough though, all the same. 7/10

G: After the excesses of 'Summer Night City', ABBA play it ultra-safe again. There's nothing wrong with it – it's just very static and a trifle dull, that's all. It's not a video you need to see in order to help you appreciate the song, or to enable you to appreciate it more. Five minutes where not an awful lot happens, and it's a bit long for everything to be rooted to one spot. And pretty unambitious for a video promoting a lead single from a new album. I do think the snowman needs a hat too. 3/10

Does Your Mother Know

F: (First time.) I tried to sing this in a singing lesson the other day, and made a right bags of it. It's harder than it sounds! It's another jaunty performance video, featuring loads of kids in the audience which, with the hindsight that the woke 2020s bring to the video and its lyrics, is a bit odd. Under other circumstances this wouldn't raise an eyebrow, just another concert for some schoolkids. But these days, the lyrics suggest otherwise. That said, one of the comments on YouTube suggested, "A song about refusing advances from a minor while still acknowledging that their feelings are valid, and encouraging them to calm down and think about it instead? Amazing". Hmm, not quite vindicated though. But a harmless enough video, with the bandmates singing to themselves. No, she probably doesn't know that they're out. 5/10

G: Returning to a similar dancefloor set-up to the one 'Dancing Queen' pulled off so successfully probably seemed like a safe bet, but it somehow falls a bit short here. It's fine as far as it goes, but it doesn't really go very far. There's not very much of interest in terms of camera shots and angles, which makes it hard to squeeze much extra energy out of the song and I do get the feeling that I'm observing the action from the outside rather than immersed in the middle of it. Two very unambitious videos in a row for the first two singles off the *Voulez-Vous* album is a bit disappointing after the oomph of the 'Summer Night City' offering. 4/10

Voulez-Vous

F: Discotastic, spandextastic, it's pop perfection and the video, another performance-based one, does a really good job of conveying the energy, joy and anticipation of going out, dancing and meeting people. And that's hard to do when the viewer's watching it on a laptop screen with average audio quality! Seeing this song performed 'live' must have been a feast for the eyes, and a performance-based video is a good call. It wouldn't have the verve otherwise. This is one of those performances where the ladies sing the lead together and we get to judge them not just on vocal merit but performance merit too. They're both consummate artists of course, but I get the impression Frida's having more fun and is more comfortable with the spotlight than Agnetha. It's all pretty well done, with a quite strong strobe-ish feel towards the end, reflecting the vibe and the time. 7/10

G: Back to the dancefloor for what is, in many ways, a re-tread of the 'Does Your Mother Know' video, but this one makes the grade much more convincingly. 'Voulez-Vous' is a vastly better song than 'Does Your Mother Know', so that obviously helps. But quite apart from that, sights are set slightly higher right across the board, there's much more spectacle and the whole video feels like much more of an *event*. A few strobes thrown in add to the energy and urgency and you're left with the impression that this disco-dancing nonsense is actually quite a serious business. There's just a whiff of the vamp about Agnetha and Frida, and Agnetha's swishy hair routine sticks in the memory. A very decent, if fairly obvious, attempt at a disco video. 7/10

Gimme! Gimme! Gimme! (A Man After Midnight)

F: This video is done in the style of immortalising the recording session for the actual song, which has been done to death in later years but was probably pretty darn innovative back in the day. The whole extended band is in the studio and it's somehow got a real party vibe to it. Let's also be honest here: the ladies have never looked hotter. And this is 1979, the year they've chosen for the ABBAtars, and quite right too. Let's also face facts: if you'd written this, you'd know it was going to be an absolute smash and you'd be having a total hoot making the video too. It's total bank, baby. A few shots of some knowledgeable tweaks on the mixing desk, the girls looking pretty pleased with themselves, feeling that this could go on forever if the lads carry on writing this kind of stuff, and that's a wrap. Just outside the Fredster's top five ABBA videos, but sumptuously good all the same. Studio joy. 8/10

G: It's always interesting to see bands at work (or pretending to be at work) in the studio but I'm not sure it's right for a song like this. Obviously, we haven't yet reached music videos' 1980s heyday, so it would perhaps be a little bit hopeful to wish for too much by the way of narrative content (even though ABBA manage a bit of that in 'Money, Money, Money', for example). But having the whole thing constrained within the confines of the studio militates against the song's let-me-out-let-me-at-'em message. It's all a bit claustrophobic and Agnetha's headphones are *massively* annoying. 5/10

I Have a Dream

F: The 'official' video on the ABBA YouTube channel is this 'live' one from ABBA in concert in 1979. As you might expect, the band are at the peak of their powers and they sound incredible. There's the verse and chorus featuring the kids on stage, which is all very cutesy and wholesome. There's not much to add; any video from that concert tour is going to be a winner and have you pining for a chance to see them 'live', as they were back then. 6/10

G: Not a genuine video or promo, obviously, just a concert film and I suppose that, if you're going to let a kids' chorus accompany you on a record, you might just as well let them on stage with you for a quick warble as well. It's all very professional, unthreatening and harmless, and it's kind of tolerable if it catches you when you're in a slightly soppy (sorry, I mean reflective) mood. 4/10

The Winner Takes It All

F: Well, this is a bit of a heart-wrencher, isn't it? A top five ABBA video for me, despite the hairstyles, blue eye shadow and the clothes. It almost falls out simply because the subject matter is so damn sad. It's really well judged, well delivered, well directed and well edited. It opens (and closes) with a series of stills of the band either in concert, the studio or other places in happier times, before Agnetha starts to layer on the misery, surrounded by the other three appearing to have fun despite her. Can you imagine what this was like for them to make, with all of their own stuff they were going through? Sheesh, what a downer. Good video, though. 8/10

G: The video machine really cranks up a gear in terms of scale, ambition and that somewhat intangible quality called artiness. Like the song itself, the video really goes for the emotional jugular, which is something that ABBA only very, very rarely steeled themselves to do in their little films. This is Agnetha's defining video performance, of course, and quite possibly her career-defining performance, period. That shot with her head slumped against the partition in the café, in particular, says it all in terms of the sheer realism of what she was portraying and the reality of the situation she found herself in. Everything here is beautifully shot and perfectly delivered – this being one of the best-known, dare I say most iconic videos of the early 1980s for a very good reason. There. I never mentioned eye shadow. 9/10

Super Trouper

F: This is another top five ABBA video for yours truly. I've always loved the circus, so this one's a smash for me, coming in at number two. It's got all the elements: the band in white, lots going on, multi-coloured lights, the moving spotlight, big budgets and production quality. It's a veritable carnival on the small screen. If you can excuse Frida's jumper, then you can see how effortlessly they manage the transition from before the show to during the show, how performing in front of someone makes all the difference. Maybe I'm projecting here too, but they also seem to convey the irony of being a trouper both in the sense of the performing team and someone who gets on with things and makes the effort for everyone else. Yes, it's one of those videos where sight and sound go together, and the visual side reinforces for you just how good the song itself is, and you can't say that about that many ABBA videos. Super stuff! 9/10

G: This is an unusual video for ABBA in that it's jam-crammed with moments that insist on popping back into your brain long after you've finished watching it. That iconic shot of the spotlight being swung round to fire straight down the camera lens right at the beginning really does set the tone. We also get Agnetha's arm extension and finger pointing heavenwards, those close-ups of Benny and Björn doing their "su-pa-pa"s (with Benny opening his mouth to mime wider than on almost any other ABBA video, for some reason) and of course Frida's great big chunky jumper – all of these scattered liberally around and held together by the glue provided by the circus acts. The extra layer of brilliance here is, I think, the fact that there's something indefinably melancholic about a circus. So it reinforces the song's bitter-sweet theme absolutely beautifully. I love the pulsing coloured lights too, although I don't need the stop-shots of our favourite foursome near the end. But overall I'd argue that this is one of ABBA's very few videos which authentically adds an extra dimension to the song it promotes. 9/10

Happy New Year

F: (First time.) It's in a similar style to 'Super Trouper', and in fact is a kind of sister video to it, since the video shows Agnetha and Björn with their party clothes on from the night before. Everyone does a Christmas song, but not many do a New Year's song, and they seem to get the morning-after mood just right on the video, with the house showing the after-effects of the previous night's frivolities. The video includes a mix of posed stuff and party stuff from the filming of the 'Super Trouper' video – two for the price of one, if you pardon the in-joke. The recent fad of ABBA producing lyric videos reminds me how I never really cottoned on to what they were singing about some of the time. (Decades of misunderstanding and misconceptions.) The 'Happy New Year' video closes with Agnetha getting off the couch and joining Björn, with their backs to us and looking out of the window. A penny for their thoughts as they contemplate the dawn of a new year. Some like January, some don't, but regardless the video nails the feeling that all good things come to an end. 8/10

G: It's amazing what balloons can do. It's also amazing that, in ABBA's estimable hands, a balloon can represent not just joy and fun but sadness and melancholy too. Come to think of it, that really is all you need to know about ABBA and their consummate ability to lock into and unpick different emotions with almost surgical skill: yes, this is the band that can make even a brightly coloured balloon seem unhappy. Making the most of the footage from the 'Super Trouper' shoot, this is actually quite an effective video. In fact, it's so clever that even the back of Björn's head as he's staring out of the window manages to nail the mood. I can't think of too many other videos by any act where you could make a similar observation. 7/10

One of Us

F: Boy, what a downer. A desperately depressing song, and the video's not much better either. Everyone looks so done with it all and going through the motions. The video starts with Agnetha looking out of the window, a bit like 'Happy New Year' ended, surrounded by unpacked boxes in an interestingly shaped but ultimately dingy room. Moving house to a place on your own – unless you're leaving something worse behind – has to be right up there with pulling teeth for any even moderately social animal. I wish I could unpack and decorate that quickly, but I digress. And what about my lovely Frida? What was she thinking with that hair colour and styling? "So over this", probably. And the nod to 'Bohemian Rhapsody' stuff with the floating heads thing is awful, no other way of putting it. Pass me a Valium, this one's a 2/10 on the enjoyment front, but if they wanted us to feel sad, then it's comfortably a 9/10.

G: Nice touch to start the video with Agnetha staring out of the window with her back to camera, picking up where 'Happy New Year' left off. But that's the high point as everything gets (deliberately, of course) very mundane indeed. Not only that but everything starts feeling very *awkward* indeed as shots of the four members in various stages of offpissment take over the screen. I feel I'm intruding just by watching the bloomin' thing. The song itself feels invasive enough, but then the video adds another dimension to the same sort of uncomfortable feeling you get when you're at a dinner party and the hosts have just had a blazing row. Should I make my excuses and leave? Yes, I rather think I should. 3/10

Head Over Heels

F: I have to say I don't mind this video, showing Frida running around the place all frocked up, slipping on the ice, pairing up with Björn for a change, and trying on a dozen or more outfits. She must have had a lot of fun making it, but it must have given the insurance company a conniption, watching her run in the snow, jaywalking, bumping into fellow 'pretend' pedestrians and the like. We need to talk about the haircut and that gold lamé jacket, though. What in the actual was the designer thinking? Agnetha's not much better in that black onesie, with the lads dressed like they're in the book room at home. The video does a decent job of telling the lyrics' story, but at the end of it all it's a song that doesn't quite hit the heights, and a video that does the same. Decent concept, well enough executed, without really lodging in our long-term memory. A sort of an Airbnb video... 5/10

G: A quirky favourite since the very first time I saw it on *Top of the Pops*. Frida tripping down and up the steps accompanied by the pizzicato 'strings' is one of those scenes indelibly imprinted on my memory that pops into my head from time to time, in supermarkets, in the street or just in my garage when I'm looking for my cordless rivet gun. Again, there's snow. But above all it's the shots of Frida fighting her way downtown that add such a fin de siècle, end-of-an-era poignancy – a kind of yep-it's-nearly-over-for-ABBA feel. This happy-sad video never fails to leave me with a strange sense of upbeat melancholy – a perfect fit for virtually ABBA's entire musical output over those first ten years. 9/10

When All Is Said and Done

F: (First time.) I'm not a huge fan of the soft focus. The scenery looks good enough and Frida's pensive yet majestic profile is always one to cherish, but even that can't bypass the thought process that the guys are pretty much signing off. A lot of the later videos have the main actors looking contemplative and treating us to their thousand-yard stare. They're still deploying the feature which freezes the soulful backward glance and which first found its place when the real-life relationships' rockiness started, but now you're left wanting something different, something new. The combination of the outside looking-back shots and the inside concert shots doesn't really work for me, like a patchwork quilt you stitched together yourself in Year 5. A video that's not too far up the pecking order. 4/10

G: I think this one works OK, actually. There's not all that much to it and the 'looking reflectively out to sea' and 'looking back over your shoulder' motifs are a tad overused. But the video catches the mood of the song pretty well and without the dreadful awkwardness that drags down proceedings on 'One of Us'. It's all fairly tactfully, delicately and maturely handled and, bearing in mind we're dealing with two couples who have gone their separate ways but still need to meet regularly at work, that's probably just about as much as you can hope for. Frida really does have an extraordinary gift for conveying exactly the right blend of emotions when she looks down the camera lens at you, and that skill is once again very much in evidence here. 6/10

The Day Before You Came

F: I'm guessing this is another video filmed in Stockholm, or Stockers as we ABBAites like to say, with our faux knowledge and 'been there, pretend we've done that' smugness. I don't understand this video, I never have. What's going on? Is it some kind of time slice thing to mess with our heads? All that running up and down platforms. Anyway, who cares when Agnetha is giving us that come hither, shy-not-shy look? Who wouldn't walk over hot coals for that? It's well filmed, big budget stuff too – how would they have done that shot of the train on the viaduct in the pre-drone era? Must have cost a fortune, unless it's library footage. All the same, there are some classic ABBA tropes here, the moments of intimacy juxtaposed with large dollops of loneliness and isolation. Then, two-thirds of the way through this (quite long for an ABBA video) tale of two lovers, the other band members appear, all looking moody in an empty theatre. Like I said, what's going on? 4/10

G: Just before it's almost too late – with the global music industry now really getting to grips with what the phrase 'music video' will come to mean in the context of the early 1980s – ABBA give us a proper music video. With a proper story and everything. And a mildly saucy bit (well, by ABBA's standards at least). I always get Interrailing flashbacks when I watch this one, which is very much a positive, although I must admit the number of occasions when a woman of Agnetha's calibre gave me the smouldering eye on an early morning platform – or indeed in a second-class train compartment – was vanishingly small. The award for best viaduct in a pop music video 1982 also goes to ABBA. Actually, I'm quite relieved when we ditch a lot of the trendy video-y nonsense about halfway through and Agnetha actually starts singing, in a vaguely Garbo-esque manner, while Björn, Frida and Benny strike appropriate moody poses, before the lights go out and the single spotlight picks out Agnetha. In fact, that super-classy minute or so is a decent candidate for my favourite section of any ABBA video. Then we're back to the arty stuff and a reprise of those Interrailing memories. But it was nice while it lasted. 8/10

Under Attack

F: (First time.) Dark clothes, industrial scene In a poorly lit split-level warehouse with pallets and machinery, lots of choreographed walking around, red lights flashing danger, danger! Hmm, '80s video, anyone? It seems too harsh an environment and too edgy a treatment for such a light and airy song, especially with such a poppy, '70s throwback chorus. There are many more rocky ABBA tracks than this and yet still they'd not be right for this video, which suggests how wrong the execution is. It's a meh video for me; they seem to be trying a bit too hard to be cool. ABBA are not cool, ABBA are above cool, so this is a trap they should avoid. At the end of the video, as they emerge 'into the light' of the up-rolling door, one thing can't escape my attention: weird how they're almost exactly the same height. Like AC/DC, only taller! C plus, could do better, otherwise known as 3/10.

G: We're still in proper '80s video territory, although I can't watch this one without (somewhat uncharitably) hearing in my head the old *Not the Nine O'Clock News* spoof 'Nice Video – Shame About the Song'. Not that there's huge amounts going on here, in among the wooden pallets, but the band do a decent enough job aided by a smoke (or is it a dry ice?) machine and a flashing red light. I'd love to know what Agnetha was looking for in among those pallets. Maybe she'd had a mail order left unfulfilled and had gone to the distribution centre in person to sort out the guys down there. And, of course, that final scene where they walk out into the bright daylight into the oncoming traffic felt very poignant indeed back then – with only a screech of brakes missing in terms of underlining the tragic fact that ABBA's career had clearly come to an emergency stop or (perhaps more accurately) been brought to an unflattering halt by life's version of a police 'stinger' device. 4/10

I Still Have Faith in You

F: Call me a hopeless old romantic, but who doesn't love a happy ending, even if you have to wait half a lifetime for it? The formula used to be ABBA = great songs, but not great videos. At least not until this one. It's my favourite ABBA video, my number one, which is probably why the 'hopeless old romantic' moniker sticks. We start with memories of their heyday, some from film, some from video and some probably never-seen-before stills. It captures the melancholy of nostalgia so perfectly, the fleeting wistfulness of time gone by. It's really well done. Generally, only the BBC is this good at montages set to music. And then they go from the wings in 1979 and emerge on stage in 2021 as a digital version of 1979, brilliantly introducing the ABBAtars and teasing the phenomenon that is the *Voyage* money-making machine, since no-one would have yet had the pleasure of enjoying the show when the video came out. The video closes with the almost timeless ABBA logo in golden globes, harking back to their real-life concert days. Awesome stuff. 10/10

G: It's all in here, isn't it? All of it. Their careers. Our lives. A photo album of memories – memories of how our wellbeing seemed (and indeed actually was) somehow connected with and invested in theirs. At no point since this video was released have I been anywhere near able to keep tears from welling up as I watch it. There are just so many moments, too many triggers, to keep emotions fully in check. It makes for an intense, almost spiritual – OK, I'll confess, almost religious – experience. And that feeling is absolutely cemented by the way everything builds to the moment of resurrection and the ABBAtars appear, in all their pristine, slightly idealised, other-worldly glory. And somehow we feel reanimated too. It's actually all too much. 10/10

Little Things

F: This is a very well-made video, but it's not in my *favourite* five. I don't particularly like it. It's simply a better standard of video, a modern standard, and when you spend the money and do it properly you get a better end product. Like 'I Still Have Faith in You', this video tees up the *Voyage* arena show to smash it four hundred yards down the fairway. The idea is tenuous enough, that the youth of today only really get interested in ABBA when they hear about the ABBAtar technology and why they can use it to imagine how they can put on their own show, but it works well. There's a nod to Christmas and wintertime too, in the outside shots of the entrance to the school building, which makes sense given the lyrical subject matter. But mainly it's all about the kids taking charge and owning their creativity. The Christmas No.1 song that never was. 6/10.

G: Like the song itself, we'll file this video under 'O' for Opportunity Missed, shall we? I get what they were trying to do (I think) and, in a way, you've got to admire the decision not to do the obvious. But there are times when the obvious is, obviously, the right thing to do anyway. Having said all that, once you get over the shock that this isn't at all what you expected to see, it's quite a well-executed piece. You'd have to be the very worst kind of curmudgeon to claim that the children do anything less than a brilliant job with their roles. The little clips of ABBA, past and present, are tantalising in the extreme and (just because it's Christmas) you really are desperate for them (or at least Benny and Björn) to walk into the school hall to surprise/shock the children right at the very end. That would have provided a real sense of resolution and transformed the feel of the whole video. Obvious, surely? As I say, opportunity missed. 5/10

Our Winners Take It All: Roll of Honour

OK – no hiding place! It's time for the impossible job! Time to stand up, be counted and come up with definitive lists that distil everything we've said into tablets – or maybe tABBAlets – of stone. Which we'll no doubt have completely changed our minds about by the time you get to read this...

Favourite Studio Albums

Garry:

1. The Visitors

2. Super Trouper

3. ABBA[16]

4. The Album

5. Voulez-Vous

6. Arrival

7. Voyage

8. Ring Ring

9. Waterloo

Freddie:

1. Super Trouper

2. The Album

---

[16] If you're 'Eagle'-eyed, you'll notice that I actually gave *The Album* a higher star rating than *ABBA*. I'd concede that it's a better album – but I prefer to listen to *ABBA*, hence my decision to place it higher than *The Album* here. Go figure.

3. The Visitors

4. Arrival

5. Voulez-Vous

6. ABBA

7. Voyage

8. Waterloo

9. Ring Ring

Favourite Tracks

Garry:

1. The Visitors

2. Eagle

3. Knowing Me, Knowing You

4. Hey, Hey Helen

5. So Long

6. Lovelight

7. Slipping Through My Fingers

8. Me and I

9. I Still Have Faith in You

10. Head Over Heels

Freddie:

1. Waterloo

2. Gimme! Gimme! Gimme! (A Man After Midnight)

3. The Visitors

4. Dancing Queen

5. Lay All Your Love on Me

6. Take a Chance on Me

7. Does Your Mother Know

8. Eagle

9. Super Trouper

10. Mamma Mia

Least Favourite Tracks

Garry:

1. Hasta Mañana

2. I Am Just a Girl

3. King Kong Song

4. Sitting in the Palmtree

5. Put on Your White Sombrero

Freddie:

1. Intermezzo No.1

2. Happy Hawaii

3=. I Saw It in the Mirror

3=. Sitting in the Palmtree

3=. I've Been Waiting for You

Favourite Studio Album Covers

Garry:

1. The Visitors

2. Arrival

3. Super Trouper

4. ABBA

5. Voulez-Vous

6. The Album

7. Voyage

8. Waterloo

9. Ring Ring

Freddie:

1. ABBA

2. The Album

3. Super Trouper

4. Voyage

5. Voulez-Vous

6. Arrival

7. The Visitors

8. Waterloo

9. Ring Ring

Favourite Official Videos

Garry:

1. I Still Have Faith in You

2. Knowing Me, Knowing You

3. Dancing Queen

4. Head Over Heels

5. Money, Money, Money

Freddie:

1. I Still Have Faith in You

2. Super Trouper

3. Dancing Queen

4. Mamma Mia

5. Money, Money, Money

Favourite TV Performances/Appearances

Garry:

1. Ein Kessel Buntes (1974)

ABBA mime on this show in the former East Germany. But I just love the hyper-relaxed, let-your-hair-down, end-of-term disco feel of this little-known performance of 'So Long'. It's also a bit of a curio because Benny's on guitar, while Björn gives it very large indeed as he assumes his best-ever 'axe hero' persona.

2. The Mike Yarwood Christmas Show (1978)

ABBA do comedy! Actually, they do it quite well – and even when they don't, they do it with an endearing charm. And how they shone and glittered like a collective Christmas bauble in the musical numbers on this BBC festive fixture that habitually drew in twenty million-plus viewers in the UK. OK, I'd have chosen different songs for them to perform but in terms of the look and the aura, this is pretty much acme ABBA.

3. Starparade (1977)

ABBA mime to 'Eagle' on this West German show and you get the full six minutes of the song's sumptuousness – none of that two-and-a-half or three-minute TV edit nonsense. Frida, in particular, really shines here, what with all those wistful gazes heavenwards. And you can't beat the old four-way split-screen trick. That was just *made* for ABBA.

4. Seaside Special (1975)

ABBA appear here on the BBC on a show (as the title irresistibly implies) broadcast in high summer, with a freshly recorded backing track to comply with music union rules. From a UK perspective, as I said earlier, the performance of 'SOS' here arguably represented the turning-point in their fortunes as they sought to escape the tag of one-hit Eurovision wonders. Within two months they were back in the UK Top 10 for the first time since 'Waterloo'.

5. Blue Peter (1978)

I've a soft spot for this interview broadcast on the legendary BBC kids' show, for a number of reasons. Firstly, this is how ABBA were at EXACTLY the time I was converted to the cause (February 1978). Irritatingly, I wouldn't have had any interest at all in watching it – but just two weeks later I most definitely would have… Plus you've got to laugh at Lesley Judd's pronunciation of "Ber-giorn…" and you've got to love that old warhorse of a phrase "hit parade". Interesting that Ber-giorn cites 1971 as the year when the group began.

Freddie:

1. Eurovision Song Contest (1974)

Here we are, where it all started. Not where it all started for the band members of course, who had many years of music and a couple years of proto-ABBA under their belts at this point, but for 95% of the general public this was the springboard to end all springboards. The Waterloo ESC 1974 TV performance is so seminal – sorry, another overused word, but what the heck, we're in eulogy top gear here – that it not only features in tribute band shows but can even (spoiler alert) hold its own perfectly well among the pyrotechnics and 'digitechnics' of the *Voyage* show at the ABBA Arena. I'm not sure which version I enjoy more, the ESC in-show performance or the winner's encore. The former is super tight and in the latter the release and perhaps the recognition that it all changes from here is palpable.

2. ABBA in Poland (1976)

I've already gushed about this fascinating glimpse into the lives of the band. The reason why I like it is that it feels like the living, breathing manifestation of 'Super Trouper': the yin and yang of life on the stage and everything apart from the stage; the epic highs of performing to thousands of admiring fans and the humdrum, why-are-we-doing-this tedium of travel, media, set-up, tear-down, travel. Sure, they're well recompensed for the sacrifices they and their young families make, but they more than pay us back in performances like these.

3. Ein Kessel Buntes (1974)

Die ABBA aus Schweden! Ace stuff this, I love a bit of cultural insight along with the band strutting its superlative stuff. This one's clearly done on a budget. I'm not sure about the spelling of Frida's name on her card, and there's no piano for Benny's comfy armchair, so he's miming away like a good thing. It looks such a formal audience, so I can't imagine what it must have been like in East Germany back then. It must have been like stepping back in time. You have to admire the bands that played behind the Iron Curtain for their free-spiritedness, but they must also have thought, "I wonder what it's like to go there?". I don't think I've ever seen Benny with a guitar before, and Björn's not even bothering with the pretence of a microphone on 'Honey, Honey'. 'So Long' sounds great, as it always seems to when it breaks the shackles of the recording studio. This must have been quite racy and risqué for this audience. The performance is topped and tailed with 'Waterloo', the German version going down sehr gut. I hadn't heard a German or other language version of songs like 'Waterloo' and 'Ring Ring' until the delights of Spotify and the Deluxe Versions of the albums.

4. Blue Peter (1978)

A crowd favourite this one. Garry has also shared his pseudo-phonetic spelling for the idiosyncratic pronunciation of Mr Ulvaeus' first name. I hear it more as Bajorn, myself. Again, so much useful information about the group: for instance, they mention they have a clothes designer while they plug *The Movie*. They're regular folk, or so they seem, preferring family time when they're relaxing, staying home a lot. What's not to like about them and this super little vignette?

5. The Dick Cavett Show (1981)

I've only watched this full recording all the way through once. The bits I go back to are the interview bits rather than the performances. As a fan I often wonder, "what are they really like, in real life?", and with an interview you tend to get a bit closer to this than when they're in performance mode. Dick is, of course, a master interviewer, the old-school US equivalent of the UK's Michael Parkinson, and he expertly draws out the kind of content that other interviewers can't get near. The performance element is so important too, if just for the reason that five songs get their only 'live' airing.

Favourite Non-ABBA Tracks by ABBA Members

Garry:

1. **The Deal (No Deal)** *(from the Benny Andersson/Björn Ulvaeus/Tim Rice musical Chess)*

This marvellously meaty chunk from late on in the musical has always been my *Chess* highlight, despite a lot of very stiff competition. *Chess* is actually my all-time favourite musical, so that's quite the accolade. As for 'The Deal (No Deal)', it's as aggressive a piece of music as Benny and Björn ever gave us, providing the perfect frame for pivotal exchanges that push the story towards its conclusion, and both devastatingly and cleverly tying together reprises of melodies from earlier in the show. Above all, it reinforces my deeply held conviction that ABBA really could have been a rock band if they'd wanted to – and that, unquestionably, I'd have been a massive fan.

2. **I Know There's Something Going On** *(from Frida's album Something's Going On)*

Even though this 'only' comes in at number two, I can't overemphasise that this is, to my ears, absolutely perfect. Phil Collins contributes wonderful drumming and production, the arrangement is pure genius and the core Russ Ballard song itself is a drop-dead instant classic, while Frida's delivery makes it one of the highlights of her career, inside or outside ABBA. You could say that this track set the bar at an impossible height for Frida and Agnetha's solo careers. And you'd be one hundred percent right. For my money, this can stand toe-to-toe with ABBA's very finest stuff and totally overwhelms everything that came from the foursome after the band's 'split', with the notable exception of *Chess*. Oh and the full-length album version of the song is even better, what with that "I know there's something..." bit towards the end. Flawless!

3. **Guld och Gröna Ängar** *(from Frida's album Ensam)*

In all too many hands, cover versions can feel pretty lazy – the easy option to fill up the grooves on an album. But Frida can rarely be accused of that. And here she starts with a great song – 10cc's superb 'Wall Street Shuffle' – and puts her calling card all over it. Her voice blends so well with the fuzzed guitar. It's great to hear her express herself on this slightly edgier kind of material. Plus, of course, she switches tone from section to section with all the consummate skill we expect from her. And a definite thumbs-up for the instrumentation – and the instrumental outro in particular – which is fabulous.

4. SOS *(from Agnetha's album Elva Kvinnor i Ett Hus)*

Yeah, yeah. I'm cheating a bit. Or am I? I'm not sure that I don't actually prefer this Swedish version just a little to the outstanding English alternative. Let me go a little further than that. I definitely *do* slightly prefer this version to the English alternative. I think it's something to do with the very slightly different enunciation of the title (to my ears, anyway) as well as the cadence of the Swedish language here. It gives everything a bit more bite, a little more incisiveness as well as making the song sound a touch more plaintive (as if that were possible!). In fact, the whole thing has slightly more urgency and desperation about it, which really suits the theme – and which I absolutely love.

5. One Night in Bangkok *(from the Benny Andersson/Björn Ulvaeus/Tim Rice musical Chess)*

This is one of those songs that (a bit like Billy Joel's 'We Didn't Start the Fire') simply demanded that I learn the words off by heart pretty damn quickly. From the pulsing orchestral opening, reminiscent of Holst's 'Mars', with the manic Jethro Tull-esque flutes rasping over the top of the cacophony, I just know I'm going to be on home ground here. Then the main event kicks in, held together by a remorseless, plodding beat that's right in my rhythmic sweet spot... Murray Head's slightly detached yet slightly snarly delivery, meanwhile, extracts the maximum value out of the genius lyrics, which have Tim Rice's DNA all over them (not forgetting Björn's contribution, of course). Plus of course there's the music, which is trademark Benny with an effortless '80s edge. It's all rather brilliant!

6. Nånting är på Väg *(from the Björn Ulvaeus/Benny Andersson album Lycka)*

I'm not massive on the *Lycka* album overall. But with its slightly hard edge and its insistent riff, I can't help liking this one more than perhaps I ought to. And Björn's voice sits perfectly with this type of material. All very throwaway and somehow skeletal, but none the worse – in fact, possibly slightly better – for that.

7. **The Arbiter** *(from the Benny Andersson/Björn Ulvaeus/Tim Rice musical Chess)*

I simply can't leave this one out. And while I'd concede that the album version isn't quite the tour de force of the 'live' version I witnessed multiple times in the West End in 1986/7, this song has such great connotations for me and files itself so readily under 'Instant Nostalgia' that it easily warrants such a high placing. To this day, it still gives me the proverbial chills at any time of the year.

8. **Threnody** *(from Frida's album Something's Going On)*

What a gorgeous, Mike Oldfield-y opening! And then that flirtation with folk-rock territory as the verse builds and the sort-of chorus arrives – this is a classy song all right! As the B-side of 'I Know There's Something Going On', it lured me into thinking the whole album would turn out to be a bit better than it actually was, although I must emphasise that I do find it pretty enjoyable. Frida deals with this track with all the ease and grace you'd expect from her.

9. **When You Walk in the Room** *(from Agnetha's album My Colouring Book)*

I'll readily concede that I'm not a colossal fan of Agnetha's post-ABBA solo output. For me, it generally falls short. At its best, it's a case of reasonably nearly but not quite. A lot of it doesn't quite feel like her, if you know what I mean. I used to own *Wrap Your Arms Around Me* and *My Colouring Book* but neither made an irresistible case to be retained when confronted with the realities of the dreaded decluttering and the thinning out of record/CD collections. The '80s stuff, in particular, veers towards the generic and strikes me as pretty inessential, to be honest. Moving on to *My Colouring Book*, 'When You Walk in the Room' is an enjoyable cover that plays to Agnetha's strengths. It probably helps that I'm not especially bowled over by The Searchers' original; perfectly pleasant, no more than that. It can be a real problem, when listening to a cover version, if an absolutely blow-you-away version of the song has already been done. So Agnetha isn't venturing on any sacred ground here as far as I'm concerned and produces something really quite nice. If that sounds like damning with faint praise, that's because that's precisely what it is. And that, in turn, is a fair reflection of my arm's length relationship with most of ABBA's non-ABBA work.

10. Ghost Town *(Andersson/Ulvaeus song from Gemini's album Geminism)*

You'll not be too surprised to hear that the Gemini stuff doesn't do a massive amount for me either. But I do enjoy the chorus here and I tend to be a bit of a sucker for a story song. The bubbling keyboard track, in particular, gives the intro and chorus some excellent, driving momentum. I get a slight wisp of Kate Bush in odd places too, for some obscure reason, and that's another substantial plus point. One of those tracks that needs a few listens to grab you, even if at no point does it really do so by the scruff of your neck.

Freddie:

1. Älska mig Alltid *(from Frida's album Djupa Andetag)*

I recently spent a glorious Saturday gorging on Frida's entire catalogue. I know, it should have been a Frida-y. In my head it was… In 1996, she recorded her Swedish language album *Djupa Andetag* which addresses matters close to the heart of the organisation Det Naturliga Steget-Artister för Miljön (The Natural Step-Artists for The Environment), to which she was closely aligned. 'Älska mig Alltid' is the first track and it's a beautiful, evocative and atmospheric ballad. It easily passes the test of you being able to hum the chorus after hearing it the first time. Frida's voice is in the foreground, as honeyed as always, and lovely strings, piano and percussion create the perfect natural landscape for her. There's a slightly incongruous and squeaky distorted-effect guitar solo two-thirds of the way through, but it's not long before the soothing vocals come back and mop my fevered brow, telling me it's going to be OK, entreating me to love her always. Can you imagine someone singing this to you, and you alone? Intoxicating.

2. Du Måste Finnas *(from the Benny Andersson/Björn Ulvaeus musical Kristina från Duvemåla)*

I hadn't known of this musical existence's until I started the research for this book and attempted to listen to every single syllable written and/or recorded by the FABB Four in their various guises. It's based on four novels about a Swedish family emigrating to the US in the nineteenth century. It premiered in Swedish in 1995 and was later adapted into English, and perhaps most famously performed in New York's Carnegie Hall in 2009. The phrase 'tour de force' is perhaps overused, but entirely justified in this case. The lads' mastery of different musical genres and their output puts them on a par with the great double-act singer-songwriters of the last one hundred years or so: the Gershwins, Rodgers & Hammerstein, Gilbert & Sullivan, Taupin & John, Lennon & McCartney, Jagger & Richards. They're that good. Returning to KfD, the best song of the thirty-nine is the thirty-fourth, 'Du Måste Finnas', where the lead character Kristina questions her religious conviction after her miscarriage. It's best experienced in Swedish, although the English version 'You Have to Be There' is pretty excellent too and has been covered a couple of times by the odd pop and reality TV star. OK, so enough context already, what's the song like? Moving, sweeping, majestic, fabulous; that's all really. If you've never heard it, do so as soon as you can. It's got everything.

3. Hey Gamle Man *(from the Björn Ulvaeus/Benny Andersson album Lycka)*

If you want the dictionary definition of 'schlager' music, there should be a single entry thus: q.v. 'Hej Gamle Man' ('Hey Old Man'). When I very first heard it, I felt it was a bit disjointed, the verse and chorus not seeming to belong together. But it's also on the Deluxe Edition of *Ring Ring*, and with frequent replayings has grown to be a firm favourite of mine. It's so gentle, so easy-going, so, well, schlager. It's clearly the inspiration for 'Hey Grand Ol' Man', Björn's seventieth birthday gift to his old man-friend Thomas Ledin, done in a country-music style. Incidentally, with apologies to the ABBA ninjas among you for whom this is common knowledge, Thomas and Björn are sewn together pretty tightly, since the former was a backing vocalist and active force on the ABBA '79 tour, performing his own song as well, and is also married to Stig Anderson's daughter. Thomas sang 'Just Nu' for the Eurovision Song Contest's 1980 show, which – fun fact – is one of Garry's and his daughter's all-time favourite ESC tracks, which in a nice way brings us full circle.

4. Man Vill Ju Leva Lite Dessemellan *(from Frida's album Ensam)*

This is one of those cover versions that's better than the original. The original being 'Chi Salta il Fosso' ('Who Takes the Plunge'), performed by Loretta Goggi and written by Vittorio Tariciotti, Marcello Marrocchi and Franca Evangelisti. The original Italian performance on YouTube is cringeworthy, the young woman performing in quite a sexualised way to creepy, fawning older men and a TV audience. Frida's version (meaning 'You Want to Live a Little in the Meantime') has Swedish lyrics by Stig Anderson and is produced by Benny and Björn. It was Frida's second Svensktoppen number one in late 1972, so it's no surprise that it finds itself nestling near the end of the Deluxe Edition of *Ring Ring*. I love it! It keeps getting better the more you listen. It's so light and clean with the gentle bass and Benny's harpsichord-sounding keyboard, leading into a chorus that's sooooo flippin' catchy. This is a bold closing statement, I know, but I don't think Frida's voice is better anywhere else than on this song.

5. Här Är Mitt Liv *(Agnetha-penned B-side of Melodifestivalen entry)*

On ABBA's 1979 world tour, Agnetha performed her song (with the help of her hubby's English lyrics) 'I'm Still Alive'. I've chosen the Swedish version ('Here Is My Life'), which was the support act to 'Men Natten Är Vår' ('But the Night Is Ours'), her entry into Sweden's 1981 Melodifestivalen competition and produced using the sizeable skills of the ABBA support musicians. The voice on the two songs, however, is not Agnetha's. It belongs to Kicki Moberg. 'Här Är Mitt Liv' is a rather delightful and sweeping ballad, starting gently with the strings, piano and vocal, before building into the chorus. There's no bridge as such and a sweet guitar solo closes the song. Imagine this being played 'live' and loud, the audience with their hands in the air, swaying to the rhythm and singing along. Emotional, isn't it? The Eurovision hit that never was.

6. En Ledig Dag *(from the album Frida 1967-1972)*

Easy Listening anyone? There's a very nice '60s vibe on 'En Ledig Dag' ('A Day Off'), and you're reading the words of a guy who loves a lot of the '60s pop thing and whose All Time Favourite Song Ever – you may recall – is 'California Dreamin'' by The Mamas and the Papas. This one easily captures the lightness of heart we feel when we get one of those days off from smelly work. Frida, of course, had been singing for a good few years at this point, especially as the front person with a big band or orchestra behind her, so it's no surprise she has such control over the vocal. The light percussion and the range of her voice – from the low and soulful to the unusually high falsetto – complement each other beautifully. I can imagine the young folk up and down Sweden were swinging away joyfully in the dance halls to this one when it came out. Turn the clock back fifty-plus years and the sound up, and escape your troubles with 'En Ledig Dag'.

7. One Night in Bangkok *(from the Benny Andersson/Björn Ulvaeus/Tim Rice musical Chess)*

I'm not a huge fan of *Chess*. This is in stark contrast to Mr H, who views it as the best musical in the history of musicals and who on a whim could probably fill his entire non-ABBA top ten with *Chess* pieces. It never quite did it for me. What I do like about the creative process is how Tim Rice, lyricist almost without peer, took the music from the lads and some sample lyrics-for-guidance from the Björnmeister which were so good that he, Sir Tim, left some of them in. Which ones he left in is the tantalisingly unanswered question, apart, apparently, from "one night in Bangkok leaves a hard man humble"; so partly answered, then. Anyway, 'One Night in Bangkok' was the one song that broke through onto my mainstream radar and attracted me from the get-go. The three-minute-fifteen-second version follows the superb 'Bangkok' preamble, which – it won't surprise you to know – I hadn't heard until recently. I'm partial to rap but I don't normally like the commentary style on songs, yet it works so well here as the counterpoint to the chorus. Yes, the lyrics are clever and immaculate, but so is the jangly keyboard, the chompy bass, the wompy drums and the backing vocals which push you forward relentlessly towards the city of sin. Fantastic!

8. Slowly *(Benny Andersson/Björn Ulvaeus song from Gemini's album Gemini)*

What do you do when you've written *Chess* and are twiddling your thumbs waiting for the West End musical to kick off? Well, if you're the lads you pen some songs for the Swedish brother-sister Glenmark combo called Gemini. In truth these differing projects were probably running in parallel, and a lot of the Gemini stuff sounds quite *Chess*-y – not cheesy, at least not very cheesy – to me. Perhaps it's *Chess* B-side stuff. There are a couple of gems in there too, particularly 'Slowly'. The first time I listened to it, I wasn't crazy about it, though I did acknowledge the quality and approach of the lyrics. For me it had a real mid-'80s middle-of-the-road American feel about it. The second time I heard it, I felt it was a winner, and that was before I read that it had in fact previously been recorded by one Anni-Frid Lyngstad. The sibling vocals work really well together, as you might expect: harmonious, yet insistent and despairing too, fitting the subject matter perfectly. There's the trademark 'double B' hooks in there, and the guitar and drums give it loads of attack and drive. It's a big arrangement, with big production values, and I like it bigtime.

9. It's Nice to Be Back *(from the album The Hep Stars)*

You have to look quite hard to find this gem. Originally the B-side of 'Malaika' from 1967, this song is one of the bonus tracks published in 1996, now collectively part of the *The Hep Stars* album on Spotify. Benny Andersson penned this, and while 'Sunny Girl' from the same era was apparently the song which convinced Benny he had the songwriting smarts to succeed, it's 'It's Nice to Be Back' that does it for me. I liked it from the first time hearing it, finding it super-uplifting. It's classic '60s feelgood fun, with punchy keyboard chords, sweet strings and a chorus so catchy it'll have you whistling along in no time. Lyrically too you can feel yourself settling into the comfy, well-worn armchair of your hometown after some time away. I'm a sucker for the simplicity and unsullied joy of '60s pop, so for me this one's a winner. I really wanted to include Frida's cover of this song as a separate entry, but I felt it was a tad over-indulgent; 'Min Egen Stad' ('My Own Town'), featuring three and possibly four members of ABBA, depending on which Wikipedia article you trust, reached number one on the Svensktoppen chart.

10. I Should Have Followed You Home *(duet between Agnetha and Gary Barlow from Agnetha's album A)*

Where the '80s Agnetha albums are a bit meh, and *My Colouring Book* from 2004 is nice, *A* is on another level in my view. To be expected when you have the Cheiron Studios' Jörgen Elofsson by your side, from the same hit factory that has Denniz Pop and Max Martin. All in all the *A* album is a great listen, and it was a tough call between 'When You Really Loved Someone', 'Dance Your Pain Away' and the one I've chosen. And what's not to like about another regal collaborator from pop's firmament in Take That's Gary Barlow? Performing on stage in November 2013 for the first time in a quarter of a century, Agnetha joined Mr B on the BBC to promote the song. It's a lovely song. While it might not hit the heady heights of a classic, with a bit of a weak bridge if you were being harsh, it nevertheless possesses a Eurovistastic chorus. They didn't record it together, but you'd never know; there's a definite chemistry in their voices and the level of emotion is just right to convey the wistfulness following a missed opportunity.

Epilogue: Only One of Us

Freddie here. In the first half of 2023, buoyed up by five decades of ABBA fandom, the last two years of research and writing, and slightly more free time than my co-writer Mr Holland, I took on a personal pilgrimage to two places of almost compulsory interest to the dedicated and upwardly mobile ABBA fan: *ABBA Voyage* at the ABBA Arena in London; and the ABBA Museum in Stockholm, Sweden. This rambling and unabashedly gushing epilogue is, admittedly, a bit of a 'Holmen Homily', but also contains some observations and insights into experiences that are as close as we'll ever get to seeing the band properly 'live' in the twenty-first century.

*   *   *   *   *

Spoiler alert: *ABBA Voyage* (the show, following the year after the album) is a pretty recent thing – at least compared to the bulk of the band's output – and as such many of you reading this may not yet have got round to getting to the Olympic Park in London. Be warned that I've tried to keep the following as unspecific as I can, but there are inevitably some semi-spoilers in it... If you haven't yet booked tickets, you must. It's a game-changer, in the broadest and most expansive sense of the term.

Speaking of overused phrases that have lost their original value because of said overuse, I'll add to that list the following: the anticipation was palpable; it was surreal; I experienced something spiritual, almost religious. When it comes to *ABBA Voyage*, all of these phrases re-acquire their original authenticity and power. Believe the hype. The show is unbefrickinlievable.

As I write this section, I've just returned from the hallowed temple. Everything is fresh in my mind. As much of it as I could manage is crammed onto my retina and seared into my brain. I must go again. I will go again.[17]

I'm not going to tell you what happens in the show. I'm going to share a few comments. First, you might remember that earlier in the book I talk about the announcement of the show, how what they were planning to do with the 3D holograms breaks the mould and casts a template for all other performers with ageing bodies and a stellar back catalogue to re-fill their coffers from the comfort of their couch (after a ton of work with nifty cameras and even niftier software). Here's the thing: the set list can't contain all the songs that you'd want to put in, so by the time you read this they may have adjusted it and effectively changed the show, and we'll all have to go and see *ABBA Voyage* 2. And 3, 4 and so on; this thing could run and run. What a concept. What a business model.

But to do this it has to be bloody good, and bloody convincing. And it is. The ABBAtars are jaw-dropping (sorry, another overworked but literally appropriate term) in their visual presentation. It's almost visceral. Their figures are perfect, you couldn't improve upon them. The faces are pretty good too, but not perfect. In fact there are times and angles when I think that Björn doesn't actually look like Björn, but that's a contentious quibble. The mouths – the most expressive element of the vocal delivery, spoken or sung, are not quite expressive enough, and are not really forming the words well enough. But they'll get better when the technology improves. In five years' time the faces and the mouths will probably be perfect too.

The band – I counted ten of them, but being short of stature and wedged in the mosh pit, I mean the dance floor, I couldn't always see them too well – are very, very good, and as you can imagine the collective sound of 'live' band and original, enhanced vocals is amazing.

---

[17] In fact, I did go again, in August 2023. It would have been rude not to. As amazing as the last time.

The visual accompaniment to the ABBAtars, by which I mean the animations, lights and other stage props, is nothing short of spectacular, and what a spectacle it is. Stunning, moving, all-encompassing, wherever you are in the arena. I'll just say that the visual transition from 'Lay All Your Love on Me' to 'Summer Night City' in the version of the show that I saw was out-of-this-world good.

Yes, there are horrendous, heinous song omissions, but you can't do everything. You gotta leave people wanting more, and perhaps they'll do this with a version 2 set list, a 'v3' and so on. All the way to the bank. After some very crude calculations, based on one matinee, I think the lads are probably grossing £1M each per week. They deserve every penny.

This show gets the Freddie 9.5/10. I never score 10/10, you should know that by now. If I was to criticise ever so slightly, I'd say that the show sags a smidge during back-to-back songs from the *Voyage* album, but they're relatively slow numbers, and you can safely argue that you need a change of pace to keep the punters on their toes.

Value for money? You betcha. The tickets are reasonable (I paid £72 – about €85 or AU$140 – for a dance floor ticket, booked around three months in advance; there are ticket-plus-hotel deals that you might need minor surgery for before shelling out the cash) and this 3,000-people venue feels more intimate than its capacity suggests. I was expecting to be fleeced in the shop, but merchandise is your typical tour pricing (quality t-shirts for £35, expansive programmes for £15); nothing more, nothing less. Throw in two drinks for £15, £50 on souvenirs, £50 on travel and you're looking at a day trip for the ages for under £200/€250/AU$400).

Man, you gotta get on this carousel.

And when you do go, pretty much any seat has a belting view. The best spot on the dance floor is actually in the middle. To be closer to the 'live' band, head to the left side, where you'll get to appreciate their artistry and still have your eyes popping out at the rest of the show.

Parting thought: after the show the guy I went with was singing one of the songs as 'Chicken Tikka'. Never heard that before, it tickled me a touch.

ABBA Voyage set list – February 2023:

1. The Visitors

2. Hole in Your Soul

3. SOS

4. Knowing Me, Knowing You

5. Chiquitita

6. Fernando

7. Mamma Mia

8. Does Your Mother Know

9. Eagle

10. Lay All Your Love on Me

11. Summer Night City

12. Gimme! Gimme! Gimme! (A Man After Midnight)

13. Voulez-Vous

14. When All Is Said and Done

15. Don't Shut Me Down

16. I Still Have Faith in You

17. Waterloo

18. Thank You for the Music

19. Dancing Queen

20. The Winner Takes It All

(The set list is also on Spotify: https://open.spotify.com/playlist/4Kfm7coqTd3ECCBEIcKoDs)

* * * * *

Where to begin the last part of the pilgrimage? At the beginning, I guess. One man, three days, one mission: to immerse himself in the city that defined, and is to a large degree defined by, ABBA. My first trip to Sweden, and not a moment too soon. With only a few days at my disposal, I initially resolved that the time would be best served by nominal tourist exposure, unless it coincided with maximum ABBA absorption.

At last the experience would become real, following in the footsteps of my fab four and getting as close to the scenes of the action as would be allowed under normal behaviours. The culmination of half a century of following at a distance was to indulge finally in some serious fandom proximity. With most of the background research done the summer before, until my first attempt to get there had been cruelly dashed by an epic lack of forward planning on the part of the aviation industry, it was a simple case of revising for the real thing.

Or was it? I had the ABBA Museum booked for the final morning of my trip, but beyond that there was nothing set in stone, or even scribbled in HB pencil. I figured I wouldn't have time for other distraction-attractions, like the Stieg-Larsen-Millennium tour, some Swedish table tennis – a sport at which they excel – or a 'manufactured pop' pilgrimage to Cheiron studios made famous by Denniz Pop and Max Martin among others, but sitting on the flight to Stockholm Arlanda airport I didn't have a firm plan of where to go or what to do. Too many choices! I'd waited all this time and I was now at risk of bottling it and wandering aimlessly around the 'Summer Night City'.

Day 1: Arriving at Arlanda airport I went to the spotless Arlanda Express train station and had my first experience of 'Swedish Cool' with the fabulous swirling wooden benches on the platform. Not that comfy but they looked great and I guess you're never waiting on them for long. I applied sun cream in anticipation of the summer heatwave and emerged from Stockholm central station at lunchtime into a fifteen-minute downpour. The best laid plans of man...actually I've already told you I didn't have a plan. I'll be honest, I was soon seduced by the city. I dumped my bag at the hotel, wandered down to the sea at Nybroplan and took the boat a few stops to Nacka Strand, where I did the 'Fika' thing, which is coffee and pastry, Swedish-style.

Back at the hotel, I thought I'd ask the advice of the receptionist, who must surely get this kind of question too many times to count. What should I see that's ABBA-related, but not the Museum which I've already booked? Apparently he didn't get the question too often, as I got nothing back but general city-touristic advice. Being in my bubble I'd overlooked the fact that there's way more to this city of two million-plus people than ABBA. I found a delightful Swedish restaurant called Nomad, with a small, reasonably priced menu, a good deal of charm and a lot of 'snaps' (sic). Full of meatballs, mashed potatoes, lingonberries and too much snaps, I repaired to my bed in preparation for the first of two full days of walking and experiencing. (Pro tip: I stayed at the Best Western hotel on Drottninggatan in Norrmalm. It was clean, affordable – a little over £100/€115/AU$200 per night – and very well placed for pretty much everything.)

Day 2: A lie-in, a superb breakfast, then a dash down to the Gamla Stan to do a free 10am tour of the Old Town in simply glorious weather. (Pro tip: these free walking tours of major cities are a great way to acquaint yourself with their high spots, at the small cost of a tip to the invariably friendly and encyclopaedic guide.) Where's the ABBA connection so far, I hear you mutter. Well, the tour also took in a passing nod to Benny and Frida's apartment on Baggensgatan where they lived in 1974. It's amazing how they're now part of a historical tour that represents the last eight centuries.

Stockholm seemed already to be embracing Sweden's hosting of Eurovision in 2024, as at the end of the Old Town walk I caught a bit of the Royal Guards Ceremony at the Royal Palace. As I was approaching it, the band played was playing 'Tattoo' by Loreen, 2023's Swedish winner, which the crowd loved. Outside the palace was a fascinating exhibition of photographs depicting the fifty-year reign of Carl XVI Gustav (only there from June to September 2023, before doing a tour of the country). There's a picture of his 1975 wedding, but in a serious error of judgement in my humble opinion there's no picture of ABBA premiering 'Dancing Queen' for the about-to-be-Queen Silvia at the pre-wedding gala in Norrmalm's Kungliga Operan.

After heading back to the hotel to re-charge body and mobile phone, I took a walk out to Sankt Eriksbron (Saint Erik's Bridge) to see the building that used to house Polar Music Studios, home to the last three ABBA albums before the band's forty-year sabbatical. It was hard to get the vibe and imagine the music while I was there, if I'm honest. There was no commemorative plaque that you might see in other countries like the UK. After dinner at another Swedish restaurant called Akkurat in Södermalm I got back to the hotel to find that there was an English-speaking, Swedish-subtitled documentary on ABBA from 2022 that I hadn't seen. It can't have been a coincidence, the broadcasters must have known I was there.

Day 3: The warm-up was over. This was ABBA Day. ABBA Museum Day. I followed up another lovely breakfast by trying to get the inside track from the hotel receptionist on where and when Eurovision 2024 was likely to be (no-one knew when I was there in June 2023 but everyone was guessing like mad and the hotels were already expensively full in Gothenburg, Malmö and the capital around the usual suspect dates). Superb weather again. I walked to Djurgården and got to the ABBA Museum way too early, so I had plenty of time to walk around the lush park neighbourhood (containing a fun park and more museums than you can count on two hands). I went to Skansen (an outdoor park) to see if this was the one month of the year when Julius Kronberg's studio, scene for the *The Visitors* album cover, was open. They didn't seem to know, but thought I could book my own visit where they would open it just for me, at a cost of 2,000 Swedish Kronor… I graciously declined.

I also took a look at the Pop House Hotel, next door to the Museum. It's now called the Backstage Hotel but apparently still has the ABBA-themed rooms in it. Before going into the Museum I got my photo taken in the put-your-face-in-the-hole-where-the ABBA-band-member-of-your-choice's-face-is thing by the entrance. (Pro tip: put your face all the way in, especially if you have a tiny head like me). I was Björn, in case you were wondering.

I spent about three-and-a-half hours in the museum, which opened in 2013 by the way. Two in the Museum, half an hour in the shop and an hour in the bar. I could easily have spent three times as long in the Museum. It's great value, as I find all super-popular attractions to be. I paid SEK310 (roughly £22/€26/AU$43) for a ticket with an audio guide which you can use on your smartphone or a device they provide. There's loads of content: visual, audio, interactive and even participative, all of it very authoritative, entertaining and excellent. The spaces between the exhibits and the pods are quite narrow, and the Museum is pretty well organised. It was very busy when I was there (11am-to-11:30am entry) and you do sometimes hear music from one themed area encroaching into the next. This is a very minor complaint, however.

In case you've not been to the Museum, I don't want to give too much detail away; there should be a bit of mystery left after all. The Museum covers everything, from the pre-ABBA musical experiences of each band member, to the ABBA pre-*Voyage*, to the post-ABBA projects of each band member. There are loads upon loads of artefacts to bring each period to life. The first thing you see, however, on a different floor, is a space dedicated to updating fans on – and promoting with plenty of visual spoilers – the post-2013 incarnation of ABBA, namely the *Voyage* album and show.

Why did I only spend two hours in the Museum? It's a fair question, and I'll do my best to answer it. It felt like a microcosm of my whole ABBA experience, the synopsis of fifty years of fandom and the culmination of two years of research and writing for this book, all rolled into a rollercoaster lasting a hundred and twenty minutes. There's a psychological condition where you're so looking forward to something and then it happens so fast and you can't remember much about it. It's full-on sensory overload, or something similar I guess. It happened to me, so I took loads of photos and videos, destroying my phone battery in the process. It was too much to take in for this fan, I was full and had to move on. I will go again.

I had a beer in the café after a fair-to-moderate amount of expenditure in the shop, which was very reasonably priced with everything from fridge magnets up to replica Japan Tour jackets. A thought occurred to me as I pondered the merchandise for both the Museum and the show: what is this strange fascination we have – and which they project – with images of the band members from the past, their best visual selves from the late 1970s, frozen in time and remarketed, perhaps for ever? I'm not sure I've an answer.

I then spent another two hours walking around Kungliga Djurgården Park looking for the famous bench used for the *ABBA Greatest Hits* album cover. This is a big park, with a hundred-plus benches. After asking about five park staff, none of whom knew what I was talking about (that should have been a warning sign, admittedly) and who all looked at me like the slightly off-kilter individual I am, I found a fan page saying it was fifty metres from a restaurant called Ulla Winbladh. I eventually found the restaurant and was met with similar looks of befuddlement from their staff. I combed every square metre within a hundred metre radius, finding nothing that resembled the bench, in the right terrain, and with a tree behind it that I estimated to be twice as wide in the trunk as when they took the original shot nearly fifty years ago. Talk about a cold case, and another case of 'so near, yet so far' for this intrepid and mediocre sleuth. I walked back into the city centre, blessed with beautiful passers-by and beautiful weather.

Last on the list for my Stockholm-ABBA tour was a walk to the Metronome Studios at Karlbergsvägen 57 in Vasastan. Still an active studio called Atlantis, it's where the group recorded their earlier albums, from *Ring Ring* to *The Album*. As with Polar Studios, I struggled to register any resonance with this nondescript building. I did feel like a proper fan, though. It was me alone, the solitary admirer, at these ABBA haunts, with the exception of the Museum, which was super-busy.

There are other ABBA-related Stockholm places you can visit that didn't make it onto Freddie's packed itinerary. For research, I recommend you check out:

- https://www.cntraveller.com/gallery/abba-guide-to-sweden
- https://orbzii.com/guides-tips/ABBA-guide-to-Stockholm/
- https://abbaofficial.wordpress.com/tag/abba-the-museum/ (a *lot* of Museum spoilers in this last one)

All the places I visited you can walk to, if you like a good walk, but I thoroughly recommend the boats from Nybroplan.

Reflecting on this wondrous three days in the architecturally, naturally and culturally overflowing capital, I found myself drawn to Swedes, who seemed very cool, in what is a very cool city. I didn't really experience the 'Summer Night City', more the summer evening city, but the weather was very warm, which helped the allure of the place immeasurably. It gives me a barely needed excuse to head back with my party hat on. I ended my last night slightly disappointed that I didn't bump into anyone famous. I guess they're all in their weekend houses dotted around the islands of the archipelago, something else which will have to be savoured another time.

A parting thought: I think I understand why all four members of ABBA, like so many people, have a desire to move on after big creative projects, and keep moving. I'm spent after my own project; it's been close to all-consuming. I hope it's consumed you to a small degree too.

About the Authors

Freddie Holmen

If the world's entire musical output was one giant left-to-right quality continuum, with ABBA way down the right-hand side, you'd find Freddie Holmen just to the left of the left edge. Unable to read or write music and barely capable of holding a tune, Freddie has occasionally lent his inconsiderable talent to Garry Holland on assorted mini-projects over the last four decades, contributing so little to the musical partnership that it would be a gross mis-service to use the word 'collaboration'. Not particularly well educated across the universe of musical genres, but nevertheless keen on ABBA, Eurovision and most mainstream fare, Freddie spent a good part of the 2020 pandemic lockdown absorbing over a hundred top ten song-lists created especially for him by the worryingly indulgent and generous Mr Holland. Freddie divides his time between Ireland and England, and between wishful thinking, wondering what might have been and imagining what it would be like to be Swedish. This is Freddie Holmen's first co-written book, but it's not his first book, in part because Freddie Holmen isn't his real name. He could tell you his real name, but suspects you wouldn't be interested.

Garry Holland

Garry Holland loves music. If only it loved him back! In particular, he loves Eurovision and he also quite enjoys writing. So the idea of writing about Eurovision really was a no-brainer. To that end, before turning his hand to a co-written book about ABBA, he knocked out a Eurovision trilogy whose sole common denominator was having the word 'Eurovision' in the title. First came *Big Dreams, Bum Notes: How Music Led Me to Eurovision Oblivion* – a 'confession' about his own feeble music-making missteps down the decades, and specifically his pitiful, Freddie-bolstered efforts to enter iffy songs into the Contest. Then came *Eurovision: A*

Funny Kind of Euphoria – a 'fan's-eye view' of Eurovision, its hypnotic appeal, enduring charm and endless oddities. Finally emerged *A Man Called Eurovision* – a slightly surreal comedy-thriller based around the dog-eat-dog world of that inimitable annual musical fixture. Modest sales failed to stop Garry developing a kind-of parallel career as a radio pundit on all matters Eurovision, appearing on BBC Radio 2, a plethora of local BBC stations and the odd community station willing to give him airtime to articulate his highly unscientific views in a highly artistic way. Garry still harbours a dream – but that's strictly a personal matter between him, his conscience and his inexhaustible capacity for self-delusion.

Acknowledgements

Freddie Holmen

As someone who generally starts any book in the order (i) front cover (ii) back cover and (iii) acknowledgements, before diving in, I'd like to thank Garry Holland for sticking with me on this project and for allowing me to insert this paragraph. Humblest gratitude also goes to my extended family for humouring me in my late middle age.

Garry Holland

I don't really do acknowledgements, as I know the reader couldn't be less interested and anyone who needs to be thanked (i) already has been and/or (ii) knows who they are anyway. By the way, I'm donating my royalties from sales of this book to Cats Protection: www.cats.org.uk – a fabulous charity that does outstanding work.

Book cover: Sophie Pelham Design.

Printed in Great Britain
by Amazon